Saving for Retirement

without Living Like a Pauper

or Winning the Lottery

FINANCIAL TIMES

In an increasingly competitive world, it is quality
of thinking that gives an edge—an idea that opens new
doors, a technique that solves a problem, or an insight
that simply helps make sense of it all.

We work with leading authors in the various arenas
of business and finance to bring cutting-edge thinking
and best-learning practices to a global market.

It is our goal to create world-class print publications
and electronic products that give readers
knowledge and understanding that can then be
applied, whether studying or at work.

To find out more about our business
products, you can visit us at www.ftpress.com.

Saving for Retirement without Living Like a Pauper or Winning the Lottery

Gail MarksJarvis

An Imprint of PEARSON EDUCATION

Upper Saddle River, NJ • New York • London
San Francisco • Toronto • Sydney • Tokyo • Singapore
Hong Kong • Cape Town • Madrid • Paris • Milan
Munich • Amsterdam

Vice President, Publisher: Tim Moore
Executive Editor: Jim Boyd
Editorial Assistant: Pamela Boland
Development Editor: Russ Hall
Associate Editor-in-Chief and Director of Marketing: Amy Neidlinger
Publicist: Amy Fandrei
Marketing Coordinator: Megan Colvin
Cover Designer: 4 Eyes Design
Managing Editor: Gina Kanouse
Project Editor: Betsy Harris
Copy Editor: Cheri Clark
Indexer: Susan Loper
Proofreader: Karen A. Gill
Senior Compositor: Gloria Schurick
Manufacturing Buyer: Dan Uhrig

© 2007 by Pearson Education, Inc.
Publishing as Wharton School Publishing
Upper Saddle River, New Jersey 07458

FT Press offers excellent discounts on this book when ordered in quantity for bulk purchases or special sales. For more information, please contact U.S. Corporate and Government Sales, 1-800-382-3419, corpsales@pearsontechgroup.com. For sales outside the U.S., please contact International Sales at international@pearsoned.com.

Company and product names mentioned herein are the trademarks or registered trademarks of their respective owners.

Disclaimer Required by IRS Circular 230

Unless otherwise expressly approved in advance by the undersigned, any discussion of federal tax matters herein is not intended and cannot be used 1) to avoid penalties under the Federal tax laws, or 2) to promote, market or recommend to another party any transaction or tax-related matter addressed.

Printed in the United States of America

First Printing March 2007

ISBN 0-13-227190-7

Pearson Education LTD.
Pearson Education Australia PTY, Limited.
Pearson Education Singapore, Pte. Ltd.
Pearson Education North Asia, Ltd.
Pearson Education Canada, Ltd.
Pearson Educatión de Mexico, S.A. de C.V.
Pearson Education—Japan
Pearson Education Malaysia, Pte. Ltd.

Library of Congress Cataloging-in-Publication Data

MarksJarvis, Gail.

Saving for retirement without living like a pauper or winning the lottery / Gail MarksJarvis.

p. cm.

ISBN 0-13-227190-7 (pbk. : alk. paper)   1.   Retirement income—United States—Planning. 2. 401(k) plans. 3.   Individual retirement accounts—United States. 4.   Saving and investment—United States. 5.   Finance, Personal—United States.   I. Title. II. Title: Retirement planning made easy.

HD7125.M323 2007

332.024'0145—dc22

2006028626

Contents

Acknowledgments

Over the past decade, thousands of readers have called me or sent e-mails asking questions about the financial issues they struggle to solve. They have pulled me deeply into their lives, sharing their hopes and sometimes tears about their futures and the role of money in life's challenges. I have been struck by the common questions and misconceptions that arise as people try to do what's *right* with their money. And I thank my readers for providing this insight. Their frustrations—both in interpreting financial advice and in using it—have had a major impact on how I have written my columns and this book.

I am grateful to the many sources of information that have been available constantly to me during 20 years as a financial journalist, especially The Leuthold Group, Ibbotson Associates, Morningstar, Lipper, and the Employee Benefits Research Institute. Their research has enhanced my columns and also this book. I also want to thank the CFA Institute for facilitating some of my travels through modern portfolio theory and introducing me to provocative thinkers ranging from John Neff and John Bogle to Robert Arnott.

I must also thank money managers, financial planners, and certified public accountants who have spent hours with me explaining how they make decisions for clients. Because they have helped me understand both the science and art behind their work, it is possible for me to give you the principles you need to help yourself. Special thanks are due to Gary Greenberg, Paul Lewis, Marc Hadley, Matthew Hanson, and Beverly DeVeny, for reviewing calculations and assumptions in my manuscript. Gary Greenberg, in particular, must receive extraordinary thanks that go way beyond special ones. He has been a friend and mentor for more than a decade—critiquing my columns and going over a draft of my manuscript from cover to cover.

As I look back at a decade of personal finance writing, I must thank my former Managing Editor Chris Worthington for nudging me to start my first personal finance column in the *St. Paul Pioneer Press*, editor Sue Campbell for embracing the column and encouraging me to write a book, plus *Chicago Tribune* Associate Managing Editor for Business Jim Kirk and *Tribune Your Money* editor Andrew Countryman, for their continuous support.

I also feel great appreciation for the team at Pearson FT Press, who enthusiastically welcomed the idea of helping everyday Americans handle their money and who piloted this book to publication. My thanks go to Executive Editor Jim Boyd, Development Editor Russ Hall, and Project Editor Betsy Harris, who was flexible with my last-minute thoughts.

Finally, my family has been extraordinary. I must thank my brother-in-law and statistician Tom Jarvis for checking calculations, but—most of all—for touting the power of compounding as a 20-year-old, while most of his generation was "living for today." No thanks are enough for my husband Jim and daughters Lauren and Rebecca. Besides editing, Jim helped move a dozen boxes of my research from city to city while I moved to Chicago in the midst of writing. Lauren and Rebecca floated ideas for the book by their friends. And all three of them cheered me on and graciously gave me space as I committed more hours to this book than any of us had anticipated.

About the Author

Gail MarksJarvis is one of the nation's most respected personal finance columnists. Her *Chicago Tribune* columns reach millions of readers in leading metropolitan newspapers throughout the U.S. She has been named "Best Financial Columnist" by Northwestern University Medill School of Journalism.

MarksJarvis provides financial advice weekly on CLTV and is heard on Chicago's WGN radio. She has provided financial news and commentary on public television, NPR, and NBC, CBS, and ABC affiliates. Formerly a reporter for public radio's "Marketplace" program, *USA Today*, and the *St. Paul Pioneer Press*, she currently serves on the board of directors of the Society of American Business Editors and Writers.

Reach her at www.gailmarksjarvis.com.

Introduction

It was a brilliant college professor, at wits' end about investing, who first planted the seed for this book seven years ago.

Despite his accomplishments in the social sciences at St. Thomas University in St. Paul, Minnesota, he called me at my newspaper office one day because he didn't have a clue about how to invest his money. He was in his 40s, had been saving for retirement for years, and did not like the look of his future.

"There will be no golden years for me," he said.

This man had diplomas on his office wall and accolades for research in his field. But like the great majority of Americans, he felt like a dunce when it came to his money.

Every time he read a headline about the unstable future of Social Security and Medicare, he imagined himself eating cat food in retirement. He had just read an article that said people would need $1 million to provide $40,000 a year for living expenses after they retire.

"Getting there is hopeless!" he said.

Actually, he wasn't in the bad shape he imagined. He had amassed almost $200,000 the hard way—socking away large amounts from his paycheck into a savings account. It was a flawed approach. He was earning virtually no interest. If he kept that up, I told him, he would never get anywhere.

Fortunately, he had options, and they wouldn't be difficult. They are the same options available to everyone. If he just invested money in a smart mixture of mutual funds in an IRA investment account, fed his retirement plan at work on payday, and kept stashing money regularly into the appropriate stock and bond mutual funds, there was still time to transform his lethargic, go-nowhere savings into the $1 million he wanted. He could actually save less than he had been saving and still make it to $1 million by investing with a little finesse.

Over the years, as a personal finance columnist, I have received calls from thousands of people asking for help with investing. They are surprisingly alike. They are rich and poor, young and old, highly educated and less educated. Yet they are all wresting with the same basic confusion as the professor.

Overwhelmed with the responsibilities of building careers, putting food on the table, or taking kids to music lessons and soccer practices, they have little time or money to devote to investing.

And they feel inept. They put money into a savings account, and it never amounts to anything. They put money in a mutual fund, and it evaporates through some mysterious process known as the stock market. They try to listen to financial experts talk, but they hear a language that seems to come from a foreign country. They consider investing, and they get those school-day pangs of math phobia.

So they procrastinate and ruminate or defer to friends, spouses, or even incompetent financial advisers who know little more than they do.

When they call me for help, they think they are unique. Whether millionaires checking on the stocks their brokers picked or 21-year-olds trying to make sense of their first 401(k) at work, they are sheepish. They confess their ignorance to me and think they should know more than they do about investing in general or some aspect of it.

They think somehow—maybe through osmosis—they are supposed to know how to handle their money. In fact, the majority of Americans do not.

In a 2004 Harris Poll of Americans, 76 percent said they didn't think people could handle private investing accounts if the federal government offered them for Social Security money.

It doesn't have to be this way. The concepts involved in investing for retirement are not difficult. But the insider language of the financial services industry has made it that way. And neither schools nor employers have done much to help Americans understand the very few basics they need and can handle.

So people feel paralyzed. Stock market news sounds like chatter. People let valuable years pass by without starting to save in 401(k) plans or IRAs.

Others invest but commit the same mistakes repeatedly—choosing mutual funds that were wrong for them or letting the stock market wipe out a chunk of savings they worked so hard to build in the first place.

If people get beyond the mystery language the financial world tosses at them, the concepts are simple. The average person can make them work with less time than they devote to planning an annual vacation.

And for those nervous about math, relax. You need nothing more than fourth-grade arithmetic. In fact, with the free Internet calculators that I will help you find and use, you don't even need to do any math.

I hate gimmicky books. And this is not one.

I'm not going to promise to make you a millionaire. But I am going to assure you that if you start investing as little as $20 a week early in life, use a few basic investing concepts, and follow the steps I lay out in this book, an ordinary American can accumulate $1 million for retirement without living like a pauper or winning the lottery. If you missed out early in life, knowing just a few techniques that financial planners use will help you catch up.

All the conversations I have had with people like you tell me that when you finish this book, you want to be smart, right, and fast about using simple ways to invest money.

This book is designed to give you exactly that. I've listened to the investing messes people get themselves into and the confusion that thwarts their good intentions, and I've written this book to spare you the grief and give you easy strategies that work.

Too many books, articles, and workplace 401(k) instructions start you in the middle of the investing process. So you never get it, no matter how hard you try.

It's comparable to telling people not to get hit by cars when crossing a street but failing to tell them that a red light means "stop" and a green light means "go."

Somewhere along the way, someone taught you to recognize the lights. So you know how to take care of yourself in traffic.

Now you are going to know how to take care of yourself as an investor, too.

Whether you are 15 and trying to figure out where to invest summer job money or 55 and coming up short for retirement, this book will help you. In easy language, I'm going to tell you what financial planners know so that you can think like they do instead of feeling like a foolish outcast from a complex secret society. But I'm not going to bog you down with theory and rules. I'm just going to explain the gibberish and tell you how to apply it so that you can make wise, fast investing decisions yourself.

This is not complicated. You will find it reassuring. You will carry solid investing concepts in your brain from now on so that they become common sense—like stopping at red lights and driving through green ones, with barely a second thought.

How to Use This Book

Here's how to navigate through this book.

I've organized this book in the way people seem to think—step-by-step through the investing process, with everything explained simply. I start with your basic questions about how much money you will need by the time you retire, and why: Is it $50,000 or $1 million? Without that information, you can delude yourself or worry needlessly. I don't want you to do either. I want you to have the facts so that you can take control.

Chapter 2 should be eye-opening for you as you contemplate your future and how to get there through investing. If you are in your 20s, you can move through Chapter 2 quickly to get a flavor for where investing is supposed to carry you. Whatever you do, don't skip the section on compounding. It's vital. It tells you how to apply magic to your money so that nickels and dimes turn into hundreds and thousands.

If you are older, you might wish you'd known how to harness that magical power earlier, but go for it now while you can still turn hundreds into thousands. Also, if you are approaching 35 or are older, spend some time in Chapter 2, and run the easy calculators I suggest so that in ten minutes you will know whether you are headed to the retirement you want or need to invest smarter.

In Chapters 3 and 4, I start giving you the investing strategies you need to begin making a major difference with your money. I don't want you to suffer like the professor—pulling painful amounts of money out of your paycheck and getting nowhere.

If you've wondered what to do about a 401(k) or 403(b) at work, I will answer every question you've ever had so that you harness the power of these money-making gizmos and transform pocket change into thousands. I do the same with IRAs, another tremendous money-grower.

If you've maxed all of these out, I'll tell you what to do next. And if you only have a little money and are trying to figure out whether you should fund college for the kids or your retirement fund first, advice is on the way.

Then it's on to the stock market, because you must invest in stocks and know how to do it right. If you've never invested a cent, I think you will find it fascinating to understand how stocks move up and down and why and what mutual fund managers do to try to make your money grow. If you've been investing for a while and mutual funds seem to act in mysterious ways— eating your money instead of growing it—we'll put an end to that.

If you look at mutual fund names and see wacky words, I will decipher the code in Chapters 8 and 9 so that you know what to pick and why. You can read over Chapter 9 quickly at first but then come back to it time and time again, whenever you have a mutual fund choice to make for a 401(k) or another retirement fund. For IRAs, some specific fund names in Chapters 9 and 13 will help.

Ultimately, I'll teach you to mix and match the right funds so that they do no harm and give your money a good jolt. Chapters 10 and 11 will keep you from running in front of oncoming traffic. Chapter 11 is like a paint-by-number chapter for mutual funds, or a cookbook with easy-to-follow recipes. They will help keep you from using too much of one ingredient and not enough of another.

When you arrive at Chapters 13 and 14, you will be ready to take some shortcuts with your money. You might wonder why I didn't start there. It's because people destroy thousands of dollars by using shortcuts in the wrong way because they didn't understand the stock market or mutual funds at the outset. With shortcuts, you can make money easily, but only if you don't commit the mistakes the earlier chapters help you avoid.

This book is all about making money and keeping the money you make. So learn the logic and basics of investing first, and then head to the shortcuts if you'd like.

Finally, I will help you find advice that's reliable if you think you need it. Some people go to advisers as a first step—an easy way out. That would be fine if all financial consultants were capable and interested in people like you. Unfortunately, too many aren't. They can't put food on their own tables if they spend time telling you how to invest a couple of thousand dollars in a retirement fund at work.

So get informed about both investing and picking qualified advisers. Then if you seek help, you will be the type of client that good financial planners say they like best: informed, smart, not a coward, and not a daredevil.

Jump right in—no more thrashing about in the dark; no more second-guessing. You are about to become a competent, confident investor.

1

START INVESTING EARLY, OR START NOW

What a confusing mess.

Whether you are 25 or 45, you are probably getting this message from political feuds over Social Security, from chatter at work, or from conversations with friends or relatives: You need to figure out how to save more and invest right for retirement so you don't end up living a dreary life in a broken-down hovel when you are 70.

Yet, responding is daunting.

You probably have a job that takes too much of your time, family and friends vying for your attention, a need to have a little fun and more sleep, loans to pay, and a paycheck that is already stretched to the limit.

In short, you are like most Americans: stressed out about time and money.

So maybe you look for a quick fix: Perhaps you turn to a friend, a coworker, a neighbor, or a spouse thinking that person must understand the mystery behind the befuddling process of investing better than you. Maybe you defer to that person—sticking your money where he or she says to put it, or second-guessing yourself.

But you could end up like Lorraine, the 72-year-old woman who called me for a way out of her job at a Minneapolis dry cleaner a few years ago. Despite failing health, she couldn't quit because she had turned to a coworker for advice on her $120,000 in savings. She did exactly what he suggested, and put the full $120,000 into a mutual fund that had made him a lot of money. Unfortunately, he—like most Americans—knew little about investing. The mutual fund he recommended turned out to be a disaster. Lorraine lost all but $55,000 in a few months, and if she responded to her achy back and knees and retired at that point, she wouldn't have enough to cover rent, food, and medicine each month. She could count on less than $1,000 a month in Social Security and not even $400 a month from her savings.

At 72, Lorraine's mistake was a devastating one—one that would keep her toiling at the dry-cleaning business for years longer. But people of all ages commit similar errors when they follow their friends and coworkers, or—even worse—procrastinate.

If you have been procrastinating, you are the norm, not the exception. Over the years, I have heard from thousands of people like you.

You may be afraid of making a mistake with your money, and you probably promise yourself that when you have more time or more money you will figure out the 401(k) retirement plan at work, or all the TV blather and hype about IRAs, mutual funds, and the stock market.

But if you follow the usual pattern, the extra money never materializes. If you are like today's average college graduate, you start life sickened when you think about the $20,000 in college loans hanging over your future. You are figuring out a job, or hoping to find the right one. You tell yourself there is plenty of time for retirement saving later—time to make sense of the confusing 401(k) plan at work will come another day.

Then come car payments. And time passes. There's still no money left just before payday, and you are so busy you can hardly think. Next your first home and mortgage payments arrive, and maybe kids. You are buying Adidas and PlayStations, helping with homework, rushing from work to parent-teacher conferences at school. And the kids' college years get closer and closer with nothing stashed away to pay for any of it.

That's why you need to start saving small amounts for retirement now and, if you've already begun, to invest smarter now so that each penny counts. What you do matters. And saving early matters greatly. It saves you from the heavy lifting you will need to do if you wait. Here's the illustration often tossed about in training seminars for financial planners:

Imagine two twins—both 18. One twin decides at 18 to start stashing money away. So she opens a Roth IRA—a magical moneymaking tool I explain in Chapters 3 ("Savings on Steroids: Use a 401(k) and an IRA") and 4 ("An IRA—Every American's Treasure Trove").

She puts $2,000 into that Roth IRA retirement savings account at 18, invests it in the stock market, and adds another $2,000 again each year when she's 19, 20, and 21. But, then, after age 21, she never puts any new money into that account. As the years go by, her money grows 11 percent a year, on average, through the good graces of the stock market. And when she is 65 and retires, she has $1,031,700.

Now consider her sister, who decides at age 18 that there is plenty of time left to save. She waits until she is age 30. Then she invests $2,000 in the same mutual fund her sister has been using for years. And then every single year until the day she retires, she diligently invests another $2,000.

Despite that determination, she never catches up to her sister. The twin, who simply waited until she was 30, ends up with only $843,900—about $187,800 less than the sister who became an investor at 18. And to amass that smaller amount, the 30-year-old put aside a total of $72,000 of her own money, or $2,000 year after year. Contrast that to the sister who started at 18. She only took $8,000 out of her pocket during four years and ended up with over $1 million.

Let's look at this another way: Assume you would like $1 million when you retire at age 65. If you start investing at age 18, you will only have to put about $20 a week into a mutual fund to get there if you earn 10 percent a year on average on your money. In other words, you would invest roughly $1,000 a year, and earn approximately what the stock market has provided investors historically.

But if you wait until you are age 25 to start, you'll need to invest about $39 a week—or roughly $2,000 a year—to get to $1 million. If you are 35 when you start, you will have to devote about $105 a week, or approximately $5,500 a year. And if you are 45 and haven't saved a dime, you will have to stash away close to $300 a week—or over $15,600 a year—to get to the same point at retirement that the 18-year-old does by investing only $20 a week. You can try this yourself on Internet calculators like "What Will It Take to Become a Millionaire" at www.choosetosave.org. (Keep in mind as you use various calculators that each rounds numbers and makes assumptions about timing. So outcomes will vary somewhat. Seek a ballpark idea, rather than expecting a precise number.)

The moral of this story: Start investing early, because your early savings magically transform nickels and dimes into thousands of dollars. Although you might think you are making a sacrifice to save when you are young, you are actually making life easier on yourself later.

On the other hand, if those early days have already passed you by, don't think it's futile. Starting now still puts you way ahead of where you would be if you waited 10 years, or even a few more months. If you are 40, and start investing $50 a week sensibly now, you still could have about $300,000 when you retire.

Is that a lot or a little? I'll help you put that into perspective in the next chapter.

The key is to start now, because today's money will get you much further than next month's.

Feeling Incompetent

Let me assure you, if you feel unsure of your capability to invest wisely, you are not alone. In a Harris poll of people who were investing in stocks, bonds, and mutual funds in 2002, only 2 percent said they felt like they knew everything they needed to know to make their investment decisions. And 82 percent wished their financial advisers would do more to educate them so that they could make better investments.

If you were investing in a 401(k) or IRA at the beginning of 2000, you are probably still wondering where half of your hard-earned money went, what you did wrong, and how to fix it so that it never happens again. Or maybe you aren't wondering—but just hoping. The bruising blows of the stock market crash probably eroded what little confidence you had.

This book will remove the confusion and help you put your good intentions into action that works. Saving merely $20 to $50 a week now could rather easily set you up for a $1 million retirement if you start when you're young, understand the simple lessons I will provide on the stock market and mutual funds, and use retirement accounts that give your money the best boost possible.

I'm not going to thrust theory and tips at you and send you away to struggle with this later. I'm going to tell you where to go to get the best investment deals and how to buy what you need to buy. I'm going to provide models you can easily copy. There's no "just trust me" to this book. You will know why you are doing what I'm telling you to do. That will give you the confidence to proceed through life—even during times when the stock market seems scary.

Everyone who has graduated from high school has the innate ability to grasp and do what I will suggest.

Shared Ignorance

If Lorraine's story didn't make you cautious about trusting another person with your money, maybe this one will show you that you are part of a large club of people—all in the dark about handling their money.

A couple years ago, I got a call from a 25-year-old who had just graduated from business school. He wanted to know the names of good index mutual funds and where to find them. In Chapter 13, "Index Funds: Get What You Pay For," I'll tell you more about these funds because they are an excellent, and easy, investment choice. But for now, I just want you to focus on this 25-year-old business school graduate.

He'd learned in business school that an index fund was a smart way to invest. But that was it. He still had no idea how to put the concept to work. So he called me for advice.

"Where do I find the best index fund, and how much money do I need to get started?" he asked me.

I ran his question in my column, along with tips for him, and it caused quite a stir among my readers. Because his question was so elementary, some of my readers were sure that either the question was a phony or the young man had attended a rotten university.

Neither was true. And I tell you the story now, as I told it then, for one reason: A person can be educated in business, run a business, be brilliant in math, and read the business pages in newspapers and still lack practical tools for investing—for example, where to find a good mutual fund.

So before turning your investing decisions over to a friend or spouse, think twice about your own capabilities. As a columnist, I hear continually from perfectly capable people with valid questions. Still, they believe they are unusually ignorant. They almost always start their calls to me with a confession: "I don't know what I'm doing." Many assume they are lacking some innate ability. But it just isn't true. It's primarily the language of the financial world that makes people feel incompetent—that, and the fact that the stock market appears to work in mysterious ways.

Yet you should know that few people have an edge over you. You would be stunned by the number of multimillionaires who successfully run businesses and ask me to review their investments because they aren't sure whether their broker has led them astray.

Keep this in mind: The person you think is so advanced compared to you might simply appear more confident or more educated. He or she might simply be more willing to jump into the task of investing money. But you can do it, too—and maybe better than a financial adviser—if you merely follow the steps I will lay out for you.

If you learned addition, subtraction, multiplication, and division in grade school, you have more math than you will probably need. And the Internet calculators I suggest will do the work for you. Eventually, you will be able to eye your 401(k) account or an IRA and quickly pick mutual funds with the ease you would in following a recipe. And if you do it, you will feel comfortable that you won't live like a pauper now or when you retire.

Get Real

People are great at deluding themselves—at telling themselves everything will work out when it won't.

In 2004, Towers Perrin surveyed people within 10 years of retiring. Among those who had saved nothing, 58 percent not only were confident that they would have everything they needed in retirement but expected to be able to take trips and buy luxuries, too.

This delusional thinking gives new meaning to the term "American Dream." We are a nation of optimists, but this takes it a bit too far.

So don't fool yourself. If you don't save, Social Security—alone—won't do it for you, even if the system lasts instead of crumbling the way some analysts are predicting. You won't be buying luxuries. You will be wondering how you will pay for electricity and heat your home or apartment. According to a 2006 survey of seniors done by AARP, half of retirees worry they won't be able to pay their utility bills during the next year.

And it's no wonder. About half of seniors now depend on Social Security to cover at least 50 percent of their living expenses. And the average senior gets $1,011 in Social Security a month.

So let's get real. Think of your lifestyle now, and how you'd handle it if you were living on just $1,011 a month.

But let's take this a step further. Imagine that you have saved what the majority of Americans who are 10 years away from retirement have saved: It's no more than $88,000, according to the latest research by the Congressional Research Service. What would $88,000 give you? If you bought an annuity when you retired—an insurance policy that promises you a certain monthly income for life—you would be able to buy one that would give you about $653 a month.

So that's perhaps $653 from your lifetime savings, and $1,011 in Social Security—or about $1,664 a month to live on.

How does that sound?

Oh, and one more thing. People often think Medicare will cover all their health needs in retirement. But that's not true. The average retired couple has to pay about $330 a month for extra health insurance, because Medicare pays only part of what people need, according to the Medicare Payment Advisory Commission. And then there are prescription drugs. Remember, older people aren't usually as fit as younger people.

Perhaps you've heard that there's a new Medicare program that provides free drug coverage. But that's not true either. It helps pay for drugs. Even with the new coverage, the ordinary retiree will have to spend about $790 a year for prescriptions, according to a Congressional Budget Office estimate.

So now look at a monthly income of about $1,268 after paying for medical insurance and medicine.

Could you handle it?

2

KNOW WHAT YOU'LL NEED

You may find yourself longing for your parents' or grandparents' generation.

When you go to the airport, the golf course, or restaurants, they are there in force—looking tan, relaxed, and well-dressed, enjoying retirement. Yet many of today's seniors didn't have to do nearly the thinking about retirement saving and investing that you must do while you are still working.

This hit me a couple of years ago, when I took my father for his birthday to see a Bill Cosby performance in Minneapolis. We were in a huge theatre, and the audience was a mass of grey and white hair. And I asked myself if Cosby appealed only to seniors. I have no idea about the answer. But the fact is the tickets weren't cheap, and retirees filled the theatre at about $100 a pop for a night of entertainment. The same happened when I took my father to a symphony concert. Clearly, a segment of the older generation has the financial ability to buy expensive tickets, and people under 65 were absent.

Now, don't get me wrong on this. I know that these two experiences are no measure of a complete generation. And as a personal finance columnist, I get plenty of calls from seniors who are having a tough time in retirement and worrying about how they will pay the rent or the heat. But there is a sizable segment of relatively well-off seniors that is doing better than past generations, and a few years ago I set out to find out why.

I wondered whether they'd been disciplined savers and clever investors.

The Retirement Difference: Pensions

So I went to an AARP convention to try to understand how middle-class workers of the 1950s, 1960s, and 1970s had turned into retirees living the good life in the 2000s. After all, if they held the secret to a relaxing retirement, the baby boomers, the Generation Xers, and the so-called millennium generation, or Generation Y, all needed to hear it.

But in interview after interview, these seniors sounded a lot like today's working people with a few exceptions. During their working years, many lived in smaller homes than today's families. They often survived with two bedrooms—cramming multiple kids into a single bedroom. Many said they had dumb luck—retiring and selling their homes just as values happened to skyrocket amid heavy demand from baby boomers starting families. But beyond that, the story of their lives was a familiar one: They said they essentially lived paycheck to paycheck, struggling to raise children and get them through college—just as parents do today. They didn't have money to save. Most were ignorant about investing. A few had turned investing into a hobby after they retired.

But one strong difference emerged: These seniors—even while struggling to raise their families—had a level of comfort that generations behind them do not have or shouldn't have if they think they are going to model their parents' lives.

Besides Social Security, their comfort was often based on one cozy little fact: They figured they could count on their employers to help them out where Social Security left off. The key: After a lifetime of work, they were going to be entitled to old-style pensions from their employer—the type of no-worry pensions that are becoming extinct. In addition, 66 percent of large companies gave employees health insurance for life.

The best pensions, along with Social Security, were designed to pay people about 70 percent of what they had grown accustomed to living on during their last working years. Every month after a person retired, he or she would get a reliable check—a sure thing: money for rent, money for golf, money for a trip.

Employers took on the entire responsibility to make sure the money grew enough and would be there when an employee reached age 65 and started to need the cash. The workers themselves didn't have to know a thing about investing money. The pros in the pension office were doing the heavy lifting for them.

With a deal like that, people didn't have to save much, if anything. They didn't need to know how to select a mutual fund. They didn't have to worry if money sat in an account and barely budged year after year. They didn't have to wonder whether they needed to put aside 5 percent or 15 percent of each paycheck into a 401(k) or an IRA.

If they didn't save at all, they could still get through retirement quite comfortably. Their old employer would make it happen for them.

In the 1970s, almost half of all working people looked forward to having their employers help them with that form of easy, dependable retirement money. Then, 44 percent of workers with pensions were entitled to that no-brainer type, in which their employer put away money for them, promised to manage it wisely, and guaranteed them that when they retired they would receive a decent paycheck on the button every month. Not all of them were going to get a hefty sum, but they were going to have some amount of dependable money besides Social Security.

Working men and women could concentrate on doing their jobs and raising their kids while their employer's pros managed their eventual retirement money. But these so-called "defined-benefit pensions" got expensive for employers. They had to devote talent and money to making sure that the investments were wise and had to fill the pension fund with enough money to cover the monthly paychecks that retirees were expecting. And so if you still have one of these delightful treasure chests, consider yourself one of the lucky few. Now only 17 percent of workers have them. Even those that do can no longer count on them—as demonstrated through United Airlines' recent bankruptcy.

Today's Responsibilities Are Yours

Today, instead of offering the carefree pensions of the past, employers have shifted the responsibility to their employees. Half of Americans now have retirement savings plans at work that have uninviting names like a 401(k), 403(b), or 457. By offering employees these savings plans, employers have taken themselves off the hook. They no longer have to invest money wisely for thousands of people. They guarantee employees nothing at the end of their working lives. It is up to you and other employees to do the heavy lifting and make these retirement savings plans count.

Now, whether you have a 401(k), 403(b), 457, or none of those choices at work, the idea is the same: Your destiny clearly is in your own hands. If you use a 401(k) or an IRA well, you might end up on the golf course, at a concert, or in an airport at 70. Skip it or choose the wrong mutual funds, and you had better like your own cooking instead of restaurant food, and television shows instead of a vacation.

At the end of 2000, 42 million American workers had 401(k) plan accounts.

So, now, the masses of Americans—not their employers—have to figure out how to invest money so that it will grow enough to pay for the food, medicine, and entertainment they need and want during their retirement years. As a part of their life's routine, they must remove enough money from every paycheck and deposit it into a 401(k) or 403(b) so that retirement doesn't creep up on an empty account.

Confusion Reigns

Most Americans don't have a clue about whether they are handling this responsibility wisely, and an uneasiness nags at them. In a Harris Interactive survey of women in 2006, 46 percent said they worried about ending up like bag ladies later in life. And relatively high incomes didn't help. Among women earning $100,000, 48 percent said they were afraid of becoming bag ladies. While many of these women felt sure of themselves in their jobs and other aspects of their lives, they were unsure of their ability to invest and plan for their financial futures.

It's not just women who are worried. In a March 2005 Harris poll, 75 percent of Americans said they were worried about their long-term financial future. Apprehension about retirement was eating at them. They worry about the future of Social Security, and they aren't confident in their ability to invest money wisely.

The evidence of their financial failings is abundant. Confused, about 30 percent of those who could use the retirement plans their employers are offering them are letting the opportunity pass them by even though their employers would give them thousands of dollars of free money—called "a match"—simply for participating. The average person using a 401(k) retirement savings plan is stashing away 6 percent of his or her pay—far below the maximum allowed and too flimsy to allow retirees to keep up the lifestyle they have been used to during their working years. (Retirement planning experts recommend investing 10 to 15 percent of pay. That, of course, can include employer matching money when it's available.)

Young people are missing the most crucial time in life to stash small amounts away and turn meager pocket change into a fortune. About 60 percent of Americans haven't figured out what they will need for retirement. And for the most part, their suspicions about their future are correct—they are falling far short of growing the nest egg they are going to need.

The Employee Benefit Research Institute, after extensive research into the retirement funds amassed by Americans, has concluded that by 2030, retirees will run $45 billion short of what they will need for basic living expenses. And when I say basic, I'm not talking about money for golf course greens fees and restaurants. Basic is food, medicine, lights, and a roof over your head.

What Do You Need?

You can meet those basic needs if—when you retire—your savings can give you about 50 percent of your pre-retirement pay for each year of retirement, according to the Center for Retirement Research at Boston College.

But with that 50 percent and Social Security, there will be little for indulgences. It's a standard no-frills approach.

And if you are like half of Americans, you have saved less than $36,000, according to the Congressional Research Service. That's hardly the level of savings you are going to turn into half of your salary for every year until you reach 80, 90, or even 100.

Still, there is time to improve the outlook as long as you get serious now. If you are in your 20s or 30s, you can make it fairly easily without living like a pauper. Consider a couple, both spouses 35 years old and earning a total of $55,000 a year.

The couple will need to accumulate about $700,000 to keep up their modest lifestyle in retirement. With $900,000 they should be comfortable, although that's still not luxury living.

I know that $700,000 and $900,000 look like overwhelming numbers. But they are less shocking when you consider how you get there. If the 35 year old couple starts devoting about $390 a month to a retirement savings account like a 401(k) and then follows up—paycheck after paycheck—by continually investing 8.5 percent of pay, they should be able to amass a livable nest-egg of roughly $800,000.

I'm assuming they get modest raises of 2.5 percent a year and their investments earn about 8 percent a year on average. If they are lucky with the stock market, and their investments average a 10 percent return per year, they should cross the $1 million threshold. If they get matching money from an employer, and it boosts their savings over 8.5 percent of their pay, all the better.

But what do you personally need for your future to keep living the way you want—$100,000, $500,000, $1 million, $2 million?

Answers vary depending on the number of years until you retire, whether you will get a guaranteed old-style pension, how long you are likely to live, how much Social Security and Medicare you will get, how you invest, and the lifestyle you expect. I'll help you think through this in the rest of this chapter.

For now, keep this in mind: With $625,000 in savings, you could remove $25,000 to $31,250 during your first year of retirement for your living expenses. Then, year after year, you could increase the amount slightly to cover rising costs from inflation, and you'd probably have enough in your nest egg to carry you through 30 years of retirement. With $1 million, you could provide $40,000 to $50,000 and be fairly confident that your nest-egg would last for 30 years of retirement.

The key now: Don't close your eyes. Looking ahead prepares you for the future you want.

How Financial Planners Evaluate
Your Needs

Sheryl Garrett is an Overland, Kansas, financial planner who started working with a couple in their late 40s a few years ago. They are a typical two-income, upper-middle-class couple. They came to her for advice because they were uneasy about their future. But they had no idea how vulnerable they actually were.

Good intentions to save had been put on the back-burner over and over as they were generous with their children and charities. They put their kids through college and then helped them get their feet on the ground after graduating. Steve and Carol weren't spendthrifts. They were devoted parents who didn't want to say "no" when they saw that their children clearly needed help.

But the result was tough to bear: With 17 years to go before they planned to retire, they had $87,000 in retirement accounts. Yet they were used to living on $121,000 a year and had never contemplated a drastic cut in their lifestyle.

To be able to live as they had on $121,000 a year throughout retirement, Garrett calculated they would need about $1.5 million. But they had only 17 years to get there. And the news about what that would take was shocking: If they truly wanted to have enough money to keep up with the lifestyle they'd known on $121,000, Garrett calculated they were going to have to save $39,360 every year until retirement and invest it smarter than they had in the past.

For Steve, that would mean taking more risks with mutual funds because he'd been overly conservative with bonds—not giving his hard-earned savings an adequate chance to grow. For Carol, it meant she'd have to be a lot more conservative than she'd been. One reason she had so little saved for retirement was that she had been ignorantly swinging for the fences with dangerous mutual funds she thought were solid in the 1990s. She paid the price of being overly aggressive. In 2000 to 2001, the stock market crashed— cutting her hard-earned retirement savings in half.

It was the suspicion that they were blowing it as investors that prompted Carol and Steve to go to a financial planner. And it's often that impetus, or the search for the elusive *right* mutual funds, that leads people to a financial planner's doorstep.

But Garrett, like most trained financial planners, didn't start by trying to pick the *right* mutual funds. Instead, she started by trying to figure out what Steve and Carol would need at the end of their working years because everything the couple had to do as investors would flow out of having that one piece of information.

Garrett had to do a calculation for Steve and Carol.

Saving Enough?

And this is where you should start too—calculating what you will need for retirement.

This may sound daunting. I have found in talking with many people over the years that even the simple word "calculation" prompts some to start to sweat.

But there's no need for a bout of math phobia, thanks to the Internet. The Web is full of calculators that walk you step-by-step through the process of calculating what you will need for retirement, and you don't have to do the math. They simply tell you what information is required, and you put in the data from your own life. Some calculators are better than others. Several of my favorites are at www.choosetosave.org. Try the "ballpark estimate" found on the right side of the home page, and then click on Interactive Ballpark. A more in-depth calculator is the "retirement planner" found at www. smartmoney.com. If you have the patience, go with this one simply because you will learn more. Find it by clicking on Personal Finance and locating the Retirement worksheets.

You can also try "Are You Saving Enough" at www.kiplinger.com. To find it, click on Personal Finance and then Your Money. Or one of the easiest to understand is "Retirement Planner" at www.msnbc.msn.com/id/9746069. There's also http:/flagship2.vanguard.com/VGApp/hnw/RetirementSavings.

There are hundreds of other calculators on the Internet. I am referring you to a few that are easy to understand and don't distort your view. I don't like calculators that leave Social Security and old-style pensions out of the calculation. If you qualify for a pension, that's real money that will help pick up from where your savings leave off. Social Security should be considered, too. It's true that the future of Social Security is in question, but I would not ignore it completely.

As you try various calculators, don't be upset when you see somewhat different numbers. All these have built-in assumptions and are designed to give you a glimpse of the future rather than being precise down to the last dollar. Also, as the Web changes over time, some of the calculators I've mentioned may slip from view. Try www.gailmarksjarvis.com, and I'll keep you current.

But before starting your calculations, read the rest of this chapter. I'm going to help you have all the information you need at hand so that when you sit down to do the calculation, it will be simple and useful.

If you do the calculation I am suggesting, it will take you two minutes if you do the short "ballpark estimate" version at the Choose to Save site and about 10 minutes with the more thorough versions. When you are done, you will know whether you are on the right track or whether you need to make adjustments. And the rest of this book will tell you how to optimize those adjustments instead of flailing around like most Americans do.

Don't Let Fear Sidetrack You

Don't skip this step because you are afraid of the results. Carol and Steve found out they needed to save over $35,000, a year, which, of course, was a terrifying proposition—impossible to fulfill. But now that they have done a reality check, they are starting to think about what they can still control: If their health holds out, they now plan to work a few more years beyond age 65.

If they work to 70, they will get more Social Security—so they will need less of their own savings to cover living expenses. But don't make the mistake of assuming that Social Security payments will carry you through retirement. Americans get an average of $1,011 a month—hardly a cushy lifestyle. The amount depends on your income. At the minimum wage level, Social Security replaces about 60 percent of a person's earnings. Average wage earners get about 42 percent of their monthly pay, and people earning over $90,000 can expect only about 26 percent. Carol and Steve figured they'd get about $3,316 a month together in today's dollars. You can figure this out for yourself at www.socialsecurity.gov/retire2/. Try a fast calculation at www.ssa.gov/ OACT/quickcalc.

By deciding to work longer, Carol and Steve did more than increase their Social Security. They also gave themselves three more years of saving in earnest. They started looking for sources of cash to save and invest. With their children grown, they thought about moving to a smaller home with smaller mortgage payments and devoting the entire savings to retirement accounts. They are cutting back their lifestyles a bit without living like paupers. Just skipping Starbucks on the way to work provides about $780 a year. Skipping one meal out a week saves about $2,600 a year, and with the kids grown, they can slash their life insurance.

They are determined now to save with gusto during the next 17 years. Instead of putting away what's left at the end of the year, they start with a disciplined approach—putting away a high percent of each paycheck from the start. Wishful thinking is gone. Realism and action have taken over.

They have calculated the impact of more years of working, rather than guessing. They have decided that rather than having 100 percent of what they had while working, they will settle for 70 percent—cutting what they need to save down to about $16,320 a year. So they no longer have butterflies as they wonder whether they will survive.

You, too, can experiment with the effect of more working years on an Internet calculator. When using the ballpark estimate at www.choosetosave.org, see what would happen if you worked until 70 instead of 67 or held a part-time job after retiring. Consider how you would end up if you decided to replace only 70 percent of your salary instead of 100 percent. You can try the calculation with a lower replacement rate—maybe 60 percent. But keep in mind that if you go much below 70 percent, you aren't likely to live as you do now.

Don't Save Too Much

Maybe you are saving too much, and you should know that, too.

Some financial planners would advise me not to say this. They would argue that, with the uncertainties of inflation and a strong probability that people with good genes will live into their late 90s, there is no such thing as saving too much. They would also urge anyone who is young to save at a high level in case something unforeseen—like a job loss, family emergency, a tax increase, or a brutal stock market cycle—sneaks up on them later and undermines their ability to save adequately.

I agree with this thinking.

But, you may be like Lisa, a journalist I've known for years. Journalists, of course, tend to follow news very carefully. And she had visions of living like a bag lady in her old age every time she read an article about the Social Security system's eventual demise. She was in her 30s, a diligent saver, and because she felt so out of control about the future, she gave up on a lot of small indulgences she would have liked.

When I had Lisa do a calculation, she found that she was saving much more than she had to save. She was able to relax a little, be less hard on herself and spend a little more.

Think of your calculation like going to the doctor. You may dread the bad news, but you will get the diagnosis and prognosis. After you know that, you will be able to take action and repair the damage or improve your financial health for the long run. The doctor can prescribe medicine that will heal you or put you on course for a healthier life.

Your finances are the same: If you know the prognosis, you can put your money on a prescription. In this case, that prescription will come down largely to investments—which ones you will need and how much of each. Perhaps you are relying too much on a savings account or the wrong types of mutual funds. Perhaps you will need mutual funds you haven't had in the past or a different type of IRA. Perhaps you will need to cut back on certain mutual funds.

Understanding your investments is the next step after you calculate what you will need for retirement. I will explain everything you need to know about selecting mutual funds in Chapters 7 through 13—explaining what mutual funds are, how they work, where to get the best ones, and how you can use them so they help you, rather than holding you back. In a nutshell, they will no longer be things with funny, confusing names that move in baffling ways. They will no longer be the things that turn bad every time you think you've selected a winner.

But first: the calculation.

Doing a Retirement Calculation Like a Pro

If you went to competent financial planners, they would all start in the same place: They would ask you for some information so that they could put it into a calculator for you. They would ask about your current income, dreams, and aspirations. They would want to know whether you were likely to stay in your job or move to another that would pay more or less and when you wanted to retire. They would tally your likely expenses in retirement and compare them to today's.

The idea isn't to get friendly with you. The idea is to make a calculation about what amount of money you will need so that it's enough for the lifestyle you want now and through all your years of retirement.

I know it's difficult when you are young to anticipate what you may want in 30 years or more. And if you don't know, don't worry about it.

Remember, the aim of this process isn't to tell you with 100 percent certainty that you will have a certain amount of money or need a certain amount of money when you retire. It's to get close—to give you a ballpark understanding of whether you are currently on course or wildly off course.

As you go through life—especially if you change jobs or make changes such as marrying, divorcing, or having a baby—it's a good idea to go back to the Internet and run a calculation again. Life circumstances change your financial needs and wants dramatically.

Imagine Your Life at 65 and 75

For now, try to think about what you want your life to be like when you are 65 or 75—not in detail, of course. But ask yourself questions like these: Will I be comfortable sitting at home, watching TV or reading, or cooking my own food? Or will I want to indulge myself with restaurant food, trips, or expensive hobbies? Will my mortgage be paid off, or will I still be making monthly payments on it, on a car, and on credit cards? How often will I buy a new car? Is it realistic to think that I will sell my house and retire where housing is drastically cheaper, or is my retirement destination just as costly as where I live now? Even if you plan to stay around the house, puttering in the yard may cost a lot.

A few years ago, I interviewed Rita and Richard, recent St. Paul retirees who had moved south and were shocked at what they were spending during retirement. Richard had spent his life working for a nonprofit organization, and Rita had taught home economics; so they had never been extravagant. But in retirement, Rita took up a hobby of planting wildflowers, while Richard golfed three times a week. And they took a couple of trips a year to visit their children in other cities. With those simple pleasures, they were spending more in retirement than they had while working.

A financial planner told them they'd need to cut back or they would exhaust their savings at age 85. Since they were healthy and their parents had lived long, they knew that running out of money in their 80s would be a problem. A rule of thumb is to never remove more than 4 to 5 percent of your retirement savings a year, if you want it to last.

So when you do your calculation, keep this in mind. The calculator is going to ask you whether—during your retirement years—you will want your savings to replace all or part of your old salary. It will ask you: Do you want to replace 70 percent, 100 percent, or some other amount? Whatever you say reflects the lifestyle you will accept. Rita and Richard thought they could live on 70 percent of what they were making. But the life they wanted meant more than 100 percent.

You may not know what percent to use for yourself. But this might help.

Remember the old-style pensions I described earlier? The best of those pensions are based on a premise: Along with Social Security, the aim is to provide retirees with 60 to 70 percent of the income that they enjoyed while working. That 70 percent is also a rule of thumb with financial planners. The thinking is that if you amass enough savings during your working years to fund an annual income that is 70 percent of your last salary, you will be OK. Many planners would prefer that clients get 85 percent or 100 percent if they can afford it—primarily because rising health-care costs are expected to provide an expensive wild card and because people spend more than they thought they would on fun.

But experiment with numbers. On the calculators I've suggested, you can get a picture of what it means to replace 70 percent or 100 percent with a couple of computer clicks.

Again, I must emphasize that there is no exact number for you. But you are starting to think about a target you want to aim at for retirement.

After you decide on a percent of your old salary that you want, you will see what you will have to do to meet the number. If getting to 85 percent would require you to live too much like a pauper now, maybe you will accept 70 percent or 60 percent later. Just remember that when you say 70 percent for retirement, it shouldn't be wishful thinking. With 70 percent, you will be able to provide necessities, but if you imagine trips and luxuries, then get real. The math just does not work.

If you want more than getting by, this might also help you think about your future: Generally, when people retire, their needs change as they age. At first they like to have fun. Rita and Richard, for example, were so busy with gardening and golf in their late 60s that they wanted to go to a restaurant for dinner once in awhile. And Richard couldn't stand Denny's, so it cost them a little more than fast-food or "family restaurant" prices.

But as people move toward their 80s, they are less active. They spend less on entertainment. At the same time, medical costs can pick up. Most Americans don't realize that Medicare doesn't cover all of their medical costs. But if you are one of them, here's the bad news: Medicare covers only part, and retirees today buy supplemental insurance that can cost about $150 to $250 a month per person, or $300 or $500 per couple. It fluctuates by area of the country. For people who retire before 65, $1,000 a month for medical insurance isn't unusual, so think that through carefully before retiring early.

Health Insurance Is a Black Hole

In 2002, the average American 65 and up spent an average of $3,586 on healthcare. That was 12 percent of their living expenses, according to the U.S. Bureau of Labor Statistics. If your employer offers healthcare for retirees, don't count on it. Only 11 percent do, and 85 percent of those currently offering it say they are looking for ways to reduce the benefit or cut it out completely, according to the Employee Benefits Research Institute.

So plan to pay for health insurance yourself. What might that expense run? Costs have been going up about 7 to 10 percent a year. The Employee Benefits Research Institute has calculated that a person who retires in 2014 and buys top-quality health and drug coverage will need about $202,000 in savings just to pay for that if they live to age 80. If they live to 90, it's $381,000. To 100: $610,000.

Fidelity Investments is suggesting to clients that a couple retiring at 65 today should figure on spending $190,000 over the course of their retirement. With costs rising, Fidelity advises a 45-year-old to anticipate doubling that expense.

Guessing healthcare costs is difficult at a time when the Medicare system is financially troubled and all healthcare costs have been rising at an extraordinary clip. Many financial planners deal with it by not trying to guess. They simply have their clients build up a nest egg, prior to retiring, that will be large enough to cover 100 percent of the last working year's salary for at least 30 years.

This is how Garrett came up with the $1.5 million that Steve and Carol would need. She also assumed that Steve and Carol would live to 100 because both their parents were healthy.

When Will You Retire?

Nearly 80 percent of baby boomers plan to work at least part-time after they retire, according to AARP studies. Most want to work, but 33 percent say they will have to work to pay for necessities.

As a generation, boomers don't see themselves as fulfilled if they simply retire and head for an easy chair. There is a body of medical research that shows they are smart about that. People who work—either for pay or volunteering—after retirement are happier and healthier. The two seem to be interlinked.

So thinking you will work during retirement is well and good. But now—during your working years—you must be realistic about this, too. What happens if you resolve now to skip saving and just plan to work? You may or may not be able to make that happen. If your health holds out, working may be fine.

Yet there's a question about how long you can count on work. McKinsey & Company did a national survey of retirees in 2006 and found that 4 out of 10 people had planned to work longer but were forced to retire—either because of their health or because they lost their job. In 2004, AARP released a survey that measured quality of life for people over the age of 50.

On some measures—especially health—there were great differences between young retirees and older ones (people over 65).

When asked how healthy they felt, 54.5 percent of the younger group said they felt very good. But only 38 percent of the older group did. Think about this: If you don't feel very good, are you going to want to work at 70 because you are running out of retirement savings? Also, even if you are in top shape, is your employer going to let you keep working? Although there's been a lot of chatter about keeping baby boomers in the workplace longer, research shows few employers are set up to do it, and age discrimination is abundant.

Nursing Homes

Here's one last reality check: According to a study by *The New England Journal of Medicine*, 43 percent of people over 65 will spend at least some time in a nursing home. They may be there for a while to recover from an injury or a disease—at a cost of about $200 a day—and then go back home to fend for themselves.

Health insurance doesn't pay for these stays, and Medicare covers only the first 100 days in a nursing home. So this expense can be a huge drain on your savings. Here are a few examples run in "Financial Planning News" and related by Deerfield, Illinois, financial planner Sue Stevens: Cardiac condition 16 months and $75,800, stroke 21 months and $99,500, Alzheimer's disease 96 months and $455,000.

Most people can't save enough to cover all of this. Long-term care insurance might be the answer, but it's controversial because of costs and the stability of insurance companies offering it. Often low-income people can get help with the costs based on financial need, and some financial planners think very affluent clients may be better off accumulating their own savings instead. This is a matter to think through carefully as you approach your retirement years. Financial planner Stevens suggests reading more about long-term care in Phyllis Shelton's book, *Long-Term Care: Your Financial Planning Guide.*

How Long Will You Live?

Next, think about how long you are likely to live. I am stunned by the number of retired people who call me worried about running out of money. When they retired, they envisioned their 70s, but not their 80s or 90s. They lived it up early in retirement, but when they're still healthy in the mid 80s, their life's savings are about to run dry.

Retiring without contemplating how long you might live is like taking a trip across the desert. If it's going to take you a day, you might need a gallon of water. If it's going to be a week, you had better have several gallons.

Of course, you never know exactly how long you are going to live. And some people tell me they would rather not think about when they will die. Instead, they would just like to live each day so that it counts—spending their money while they have it. I wish they could talk to some of the 80-year-olds I have talked with. They would like to live each day so it counts, too. Yet, one had a meals-on-wheels dinner delivered to her house each day, and she made it last all day, eating a little for lunch, a little for dinner, and sometimes a drop of leftovers for the next day's breakfast. To save on energy costs, she kept the food warm on a radiator rather than putting it in the refrigerator and reheating it at night.

Although you don't know with certainty how long you will live, consider how long your parents have lived and then adapt that for your lifestyle and the advances of modern medicine. Life expectancy continues to get longer and longer. When Social Security began, if you made it to age 65, you were expected to live 12 more years. Now, if you make it to 65, the American Academy of Actuaries estimates that men will live to 84.1 years old and women to 86.8. Financial planners who have healthy clients with parents who lived beyond 65 tend to have them plan to accumulate enough savings for a lifetime that extends to age 95 or 100.

They sometimes point to longevity studies that have shown there may be a connection between having enough money and living a healthier, happier life. For example, in one study, men with large pensions lived longer than men with small pensions.

But it's not just money that seems to extend lives. Working does, too. You might want to read research by Ming-Ching Luoh and A. Regula Herzog: "Individual Consequences of Volunteer and Paid Work in Old Age," published in the *Journal of Health and Social Behavior,* December 2002.

For help in calculating your own life expectancy, try the calculator at www.livingto100.com. Again, however, this is simply an educated guess—one that will help you focus on what money you might need as you do your calculation.

Women Live Longer, Need More Money

Women have to be particularly cognizant of their longevity. Typically, they live longer than men, have smaller or no pensions, and receive smaller Social Security checks. Consequently, according to the Administration on Aging, they are twice as likely as men to live their retirement in poverty. And half of the elderly widows now living in poverty were not poor before their husbands died.

If she reaches age 65, a woman has a 41 percent chance of living to 90. Since women tend to marry men older than they are, many married women will be widows for 15 to 20 years before they die. Often widowhood means less money because women exhaust the household's savings caring for dying husbands.

Women frequently end up in a squeeze during retirement because they never envisioned living 30 or 40 years, and simply didn't accumulate enough of a nest egg for such a lifespan. Those who have relied on husbands to do the investing for them can be vulnerable prey for unscrupulous financial consultants.

Over the years, many widows have called me in tears because they have trusted brokers that they should not have.

This is why all women—married and unmarried—should learn the basics about investing that I have explained in this book. And if they are counting on a husband to handle the money, they should discuss investing together and go to brokers or other financial consultants together.

Also, women should know that they are being studied extensively by financial companies, like brokerage firms, because they currently make up about 47 percent of investors and have growing wealth. That research shows that women, as a group, are less confident than men about investing but tend to have better results because they study stocks and mutual funds more thoroughly and are slow to pull the trigger.

There are a lot of finance books written specifically for women, and brokers put on seminars for women. I view many as gimmicky because they create the impression that investing is different for men and women. It's not. When a stock or mutual fund goes up or down, it doesn't know whether you are a man or a woman.

The only thing that makes women unique is greater longevity for females. That means they must run the retirement calculation I have suggested. They must assume that they will need more savings than men. And if married, women need to realize that at some point—either because of a divorce or her husband's death—she is probably going to need to be responsible for handling money.

If you are a woman reading this book, you are taking that seriously. If you are a man, don't leave your partner in the dark.

Dig Out These Records

All the thinking I have encouraged you to do so far relates to thinking ahead about lifestyle and health. Now, to do the calculation right, you will need some information about your finances.

When you retire, your money will come from the following sources: Social Security, any old-style pension you may be lucky enough to get from an employer, your own savings from IRAs, 401(k) plans or other accounts, and perhaps an inheritance.

If you are counting on an inheritance, be practical about what you expect. Although researchers a few years ago were predicting a windfall for baby boomers, it hasn't been happening. With the help of advanced medicine, parents are living longer and spending down their savings. Research by AARP found that the median inheritance recently has been about $30,000.

Here's how to get the figures you will need to put into the calculator at a site such as www.choosetosave.org.

How Much Security Is Social Security?

When you are close to a birthday each year, you get a letter from the Social Security administration. It tells you how much your monthly paycheck should be each month of retirement if you retire at age 62, at 70, or at the typical retirement age—now ranging from 66 to 67, depending on your birth date. People born between 1943 and 1954 must wait until age 66 to retire if they want full benefits. People born in 1960 or later must wait until age 67.

The amount of Social Security you will receive is based on the salaries you have been receiving throughout your working years. This is one reason women tend to get smaller Social Security checks. They often disrupt their salary history by taking time from work to care for children and family members. They also work in larger numbers in careers that provide lower pay.

If you can't find that mailing from the Social Security Administration, you can get the information from 800-772-1213, www.socialsecurity.gov/retire2/, or www.ssa.gov/OACT/quickcalc. To calculate future benefits, at the Social Security site use "Calculate Your Benefits."

You may wonder what figure to use given all the hand-wringing over the future of the Social Security system. In other words, since Social Security is projected to run short of money within the next few years, should you count on Social Security? And if you do count on Social Security, should you figure you will get everything you've been promised?

I don't have a crystal ball on this one. Nor can I predict what Congress might do to reinforce the system or to decrease benefits. I can tell you that over the past few years, I have interviewed players from every end of this debate—from academia, interest groups, the Bush administration, and Congress. At least, for the baby boomer generation, none can see Social Security disappearing completely. The reason is simple: The boomers are a gigantic generation; 77 million people make up a powerful voting block.

So politics alone suggests some kind of continuation of Social Security. On the other hand, second-guessing politics is no easy matter. If you are in your 20s, your generation is large, too—about 84 million. But under the most recent Social Security privatization proposals—which met an early death—some calculations suggested you would have ended up losing about a fourth of your Social Security benefits.

The politics here is a moving target. So my suggestion: Do what some financial planners do—use what we currently know about the system. In other words, in about 10 years the Social Security system is expected to face financial problems, and by 2040 there will be only enough money to pay retirees 74 percent of what's been promised to them. So when you see what you are expected to get in Social Security, remove about 25 percent of it for each month. When you look into your future and use an internet calculator to estimate what you will need for retirement, run the calculation three times: once with full Social Security benefits, once with none, and once with 25 percent less than you've been promised. Then you will see best- and worst-case scenarios and you can plan your saving around them.

This will be easy to do with the "ballpark estimate" calculator at www.choosetosave.org. It provides a link to your Social Security calculator, so you don't have to hunt for the Social Security site.

Olden Days with Old-Style Pensions

If your employer is going to pay you a pension when you retire, you are one of the lucky few. Consider yourself fortunate if you hear the words "defined benefit plan" at your workplace. It means that a guaranteed check routinely will arrive at your home while you are retired. But don't expect it to take care of your every need.

If you haven't spent your full work-life with one employer, your pension probably isn't going to come close to being the only source of money you will need in addition to Social Security. Usually you have to work for 30 years to get the full pension, although you are likely to get a sizable chunk if you have been there for 20 to 25 years.

If you have worked at a company less than five years, you probably aren't entitled to any guaranteed pension. But typically after five years, you will be able to get a modest sum when you retire—even if you left that employer years ago. This, of course, assumes that your employer was offering such a benefit on the day you quit your job.

It's worthwhile to check with past employers to see whether you eventually will be entitled to a guaranteed monthly paycheck from them. And if you currently work for an employer that offers an old-style pension, you can figure out what it will mean to you in your future.

The amount of time you work for the company and your age at retirement will be key to a formula your employer uses to calculate your benefits. Some companies will let you start collecting a pension at age 55, but others say 62 or 65. If you start collecting it at 55, it will be sliced to a smaller amount than if you wait until 62 or 65.

To understand how your retirement age and years of service at the company impact the amount you are due, turn to a document at work called a "summary plan description." You are entitled to see it. Unfortunately, you will probably find it overwhelming, filled with a mass of gibberish. But there are charts that may help you understand what you might get.

The easy way out is to go to your company's benefits or human resources office and ask the appropriate staffer to calculate the amount of your pension for you. This is good to know at any age. When you figure this into your calculation, you will ease your burden about saving considerably.

If you have worked a calculator offered by a mutual fund company, bank, or brokerage firm, they sometimes don't ask you to put a guaranteed pension, or even Social Security, into your calculation. The result is terribly distorted. It looks as though you must save and invest thousands—sometimes hundreds of thousands—more than you must.

Here's a simple example to illustrate the concept. Say you worked at a place for a decade, left, and someday you will be able to get a guaranteed pension of $1,000 a month. That's big money when you look at it in its entirety. Over 30 years of retirement, it's $360,000. So if you also have accumulated $600,000 in a 401(k) retirement savings plan, or in IRAs, and add the $360,000 in pension money, the sum is going to be close to $1 million.

You will have multiple sources of income in this retirement scenario. Without a regular paycheck anymore, you cobble together your income. The first year, you pay yourself $24,000 from your retirement savings accounts, your pension delivers another $12,000, and let's say Social Security provides $20,000. Your total income is $56,000.

The combination may allow you to breathe easier. It's certainly more comforting than considering a mere $24,000 a year from the money you personally amassed. But don't relax too much. Inflation has recently been below the 3 percent average, but it is always a factor in eroding your buying power for the future. Consequently, counting too much on a pension could be a mistake. Pensions often don't increase over time, and $1,000 20 years from now will buy much less than it does today.

The money you have saved and invested on your own will be critical because—unlike the pension—you can invest it and keep it growing. In a fairly conservative investment mixture of stocks and bonds, you might earn a 6 percent return a year. That will allow you to draw out an annual income that will help you keep pace with inflation.

Some pensions have cost-of-living enhancements or raises, so $1,000 could get slightly larger each year. This is unusual, so figure that yours doesn't increase unless you know otherwise.

Also, don't assume you have a pension coming to you from an employer unless you check on it. After all, in the example I provided, having a pension gives you a total of almost $1 million for retirement. Without the $360,000 from the pension, you might need to do more saving before you finish working.

And if you work for a company on shaky ground, keep this in mind if you're counting on a pension: There is a backup if a company collapses and can't pay its pensions. But that's not a full guarantee. The group that is intended to protect your pension is the Pension Benefit Guaranty Corporation, but it has stated that the demands on it are so great it isn't positioned to cover all the potential failures. Even under current conditions, there's a limit to how far the PBGC will help you out. It guarantees only up to about $47,000 a year. If you retire early, the guarantee is reduced.

401(k), 403(b), 457, and Profit Sharing

In the next chapter, I am going to explain how to use these fabulous money-growing machines at work. So don't worry about it now if you are still a bit perplexed by them.

Now, for purposes of your calculation, you need some basic information: Start by finding out how much money you have in a 401(k) or the other similar plans you have at work, with names like 403(b), 457, or deferred compensation. Perhaps your employer also is putting aside money for you in something called a profit-sharing plan.

Whatever these plans are called, check on what's in them or what's called the "current balance." You might find this online through a 401(k) Web site that your employer offers, or you may have received a statement—or letter—at the end of the month or end of the year that will tell you this. If you don't have it, stop in or call your "benefits office" or human resources contact at work. If you don't know who they are, go to the person who gives you your health insurance information. Tell them you'd like to find out how much money you have in your 401(k), 403(b), or other retirement savings plan.

Also, ask—if you don't know—how much money you are setting aside in one of these plans from each paycheck. This is good to know under any circumstance. For Internet calculators, you will need to know how much money you put into your retirement plan each month.

As you search for your 401(k) information, you may discover an unpleasant surprise. You may think you are participating—making money for retirement. But, in fact, you may never have signed up and consequently may not have a penny to your name.

Benefits firm Hewitt Associates did a nationwide survey of employees not contributing to their 401(k) plans and found that people often assume, erroneously, that they are getting the benefit of a 401(k) plan at work when they aren't. About 29 percent of people thought they were contributing to a 401(k) plan when they were not doing it at all. In other words, they thought they were building up money for retirement, and nothing was happening.

You don't want to find this out when you are a few years from retiring. You want to find it out now, while there is still time to call in the doctor and take your medicine for your financial future.

If you have a profit-sharing plan, the information will be fuzzier because precise amounts vary and may come only at the end of a year. Perhaps you can get an estimate from your benefits office.

IRAs and Other Savings Accounts

Again, there is no need now to understand Individual Retirement Accounts, or what are called "IRAs," if you don't have one. I will explain everything you need to know about them in Chapter 3, "Savings on Steroids: Use a 401(k) and an IRA," Chapter 4, "An IRA—Every American's Treasure Trove," and Chapter 5, "IRA Decisions: How to Start, Where to Go."

For now, to do your retirement calculation, you need to know whether you have an IRA. And if you do, find your last statement, which probably comes in the mail shortly after the end of each month. Find out what you have in the account. Look for words like "total account value." If you aren't sure where to look on the statement to find that one number, call the telephone number on the statement, ask them what your total account value is, and ask them to explain where you can find it on the statement for the future.

You will need to know something else about your habits, or practices. Do you put money into the account every month, every week, or once a year when you do your taxes?

If you aren't sure and can't find it on your statement, think about where you went to open the account. Was it a bank, a brokerage firm, or a mutual fund company? Call a central telephone number for the institution and ask to speak to a representative about your IRA. Tell them you aren't sure when the last time was that you put money into the account. Ask them when you did it and what the amount of money was. Ask about previous contributions, too. You will need your Social Security number to access the information.

With this, you will know how much money you put into the account each month or each year. That's a specific number you will need for the calculation.

The Big Guess Numbers

There are two numbers that all calculators will request, and you might not have the slightest idea what number to use. The first number is inflation—or the average rate at which the prices of everything you buy go up each year. Inflation can vary, but I'd use at least 2.5 and maybe 3 percent.

The other number you will be asked is your "rate of return."

What does it mean? It's what you are going to earn on your money. Typically, when people are asked to plug in this number, it's pure fantasy to them. They have no idea what makes sense. During the 1990s, it would not have been crazy to plug in 12 percent for stock market investments. If it was 2005, it was only 5 percent in the stock market. So which do you pick? I'd suggest neither. One year in the stock market is irrelevant because it moves up and down. If a financial planner was doing the calculation, he or she might select 10 percent for your stock market investments such as stock mutual funds. That's because 10.4 percent has been the average annual rate of return in the stock market for the past 80 years, according to respected research firm Ibbotson Associates.

For the foreseeable future, however, Wall Street strategists think growth in the stock market is going to be slower than it's been—maybe a 7 to 8 percent return a year. If you are young, you are investing for many, many years, so some financial planners would tell you to assume 8 percent if you wanted to be conservative and 10 percent if you wanted to follow the historical average of the stock market.

You will feel more comfortable with this item in the calculation after I explain the stock market and mutual funds to you in later chapters.

For now, however, I have to draw a distinction between the various rates of return you might use. If you are only investing in CDs or bonds, you can't assume that you will earn 8 or 10 percent on your money. Historically, the return on U.S. government bonds has averaged 5.5 percent a year, according to Ibbotson Associates. So if that's where your money is, use about 5 percent. If you have all your money in a savings account, you are getting nowhere. You aren't earning much at all—maybe 2 percent.

When you are doing your calculation, try different rates of return to see the dramatic difference that it will make in your nest egg. For example, if you have saved $40,000 and will keep it invested for 20 more years, you will have $154,787 if it grows 7 percent a year. But if you get just one more percent of growth—8 percent—it will be $186,438 (see Table 2.1 for more examples).

In the chapters ahead, I describe how to combine stocks and bonds so that you enhance your returns without taking undo risks. A person who puts 70 percent of his or her money in stocks and 30 percent in bonds might use history to project a possible average annual return of approximately 7 or 8 percent.

Table 2.1

How a $10,000 Investment Grows over Time with Various Rates of Return

Years of Investing	5% Return	6% Return	7% Return	8% Return	9% Return	10% Return
10	$16,289	$17,908	$19,672	$21,589	$23,674	$25,937
20	$26,533	$32,071	$38,697	$46,610	$56,044	$67,275
30	$43,219	$57,435	$76,123	$100,627	$132,677	$174,494
40	$70,400	$102,857	$149,745	$217,245	$314,094	$452,593
50	$114,674	$184,202	$294,570	$469,016	$743,575	$1,173,909

The Easy Calculation

If you feel comfortable with a little math and want to get a glimpse of your future quickly, you can skip the details I have suggested and simply cyeball your money. To estimate what you are likely to have for retirement, you can figure when your current savings will double. This is called the rule of 72.

Here's how it works: You divide the number 72 by your expected rate of return on your investments. So let's say you decide you are likely to earn 7 percent on your money annually. Seven goes into 72 about 10 times. Thus, your money will double in about 10 years.

What does that mean? Consider the person who has saved $40,000 and has 20 years to go until retirement. With this eyeball method, you could estimate that in 10 years, she will double her money and have approximately $80,000. And then in another 10 years—or the full time until she retires—she will have about $160,000.

The trouble with this easy method is that you don't know what you are aiming at. You have a sense of what you are accumulating, but it doesn't help you know what you will need. The Internet calculators I've suggested will help you see the entire picture—what you will need, and the progress you are making to get there.

Still, if you're a paper-and-pencil person, not a computer person, here's a simple calculation provided by Charles Schwab financial planning researchers: If you take your total savings at retirement and divide it by 25, you will see what you can remove for annual living expenses retirement each year. So, for example, if you have $1 million, you could remove $40,000 the first year. That's 4 percent of your nest egg. (Among financial planners, 4 percent is a rule of thumb. They have calculated that generally people can remove 4 to 5 percent of their savings each year of retirement and have enough money to last 30 years.)

You could do this quick calculation in reverse, too. Say you would like to be able to take $50,000 out of your retirement accounts during the first year of retirement. To see if that's possible, multiply 25 times $50,000 or (25×$50,000). You find out you will need a total of $1,250,000 in your retirement accounts. So if you are on course to accumulate $1,250,000, you will likely have what you need.

Schwab has calculated that you will have a 90 percent chance of having plenty of money for 30 years, as long as you remove only $50,000 at first and use no more than 4 percent of your savings each year. If you get more aggressive, drawing more than 4 percent out of your savings each year, you take on a greater risk of running out of money too early in retirement. (I provide more detail on this concept later in this chapter under "Using Your Calculation: The Advanced Lesson.") You might be feeling demoralized at this point. Perhaps you are looking at the meager $50,000 that $1.25 million in savings provides. But stop and think for a minute. The $50,000 comes from your savings. That's only a portion of your retirement money. Let's look at this wholistically.

Maybe at retirement you would like to have an income of $90,000. Is it possible? You check on the Social Security you will be getting and find it's $25,000. You also know you can add another $15,000 from a part-time job or possibly an old-style pension.

Your first year of retirement, using a $1,250,000 nest egg looks like this:

Money from Savings:	$50,000
Money from Social Security:	$25,000
Money from Job or Pension:	$15,000
Total Spending:	$90,000

The next year, of course, the cost of living will rise as it does—maybe about 2.5 percent a year. You will be able to increase your withdrawals from your nest egg slightly each year to cover this modest inflation as long as your investments continue to grow about six percent a year. If you have 60 percent of your money invested in stocks and 40 percent in bonds, that should give you the 6 percent growth you need. But investments are always a wild card. They could do better or worse than you expect. That's why financial planners don't want you to withdraw more than about 4 to 5 percent from your nest egg each year.

As you will learn in Chapter 6, "Why the Stock Market Isn't a Roulette Wheel," you can never guess when you will encounter a bad cycle in the stock market. And if it hits you early in retirement, it could slash your savings. As you will read in that chapter, many retirees had to go back to work after the stock market crash in 2000. Those depending exclusively on stocks lost almost half of their retirement savings.

So the common advice from financial planners is to start retirement by removing only 4 to 5 percent of savings. Then, if you hit a benevolent cycle and your retirement savings multiply at a sharp rate, withdraw a little more as time goes on.

Two Easy Rules of Thumb

There's yet another simple rule of thumb you might want to apply if you only want to eyeball your savings and see quickly how you are doing: For every $100,000 you have in savings, you can remove $5,000 a year for retirement—or 5 percent of your nest egg. With this method, if you think you will need $20,000 a year plus Social Security, you'd need $400,000 on the day you retired. Keep in mind that when you consider your annual income in retirement, you will be paying taxes. Consequently, not every drop of savings is yours free and clear. Also, I need to remind you again that prices go up as years pass, so as you eye your savings, realize that $20,000 in 20 years will buy less than $20,000 buys today. If you doubt this, think about what your first car—or your parents' first car—cost, compared to cars today.

Calculating living expenses for the future is difficult, but the "retirement income" calculator at www.dinkytown.com does the job for you. It builds in inflation and taxes. So use it if you want a sense of what your savings will actually buy at the point when you retire.

If you want to skip all of these calculations, you can fall back on another simple rule of thumb that will at least move you close to where you will need to be when you retire: Save at least 10 percent of your salary—making contributions to your investments from every paycheck—throughout your working years. It's not foolproof, and many financial planners suggest 15 percent because of longevity considerations. But if you are in your early 20s, 10 percent should put you on the road to where you need to go. If you are in your 30s and didn't make the 10 percent threshold in your 20s, you can generally catch up by saving 15 percent of your salary. If you are in your 40s and skipped investing during your 20s and 30s, you have some serious catching up to do. Consider investing 25 percent of your salary.

But if you can't save that much, do what you can, because you will be making more progress than you think. Run a quick Internet calculator such as the "ballpark estimate" at www.choosetosave.org while there is still time to make amends and mold the future you'd like.

How Do You Turn $25 a Week into $1 Million?

How does a person accumulate $1 million simply by investing $20 to $25 a week? It's through the magic of compounding. That's a math term, but you don't have to be a math pro to have it work for you. You saw the power in the earlier numbers.

What it means is this: After you put money aside for retirement, it keeps growing even if you don't add anything else to it. And the longer it stays there, the more magic it works. It's like Rumpelstiltskin spinning straw into gold, only it's not a fairytale. It really works.

Here's a simple example: Let's say that at age 25 you are working at your first job, and you open an IRA at the end of the year. You put $2,000 into it, and you invest it in a stock mutual fund. (I will explain what an IRA is and how to handle it in Chapters 3 and 4.)

For now, I just want you to notice how savings add up to huge amounts without requiring you to dig deeply into your pocket year after year. It's through the magic of compounding. Let's say that by the end of the first year, you have earned 10 percent on your original money. Your $2,000 would now be $2,200. But from that point on you can't afford to save any more. So you just keep the money invested in the stock market, and year after year you earn money on the original $2,000 you invested plus whatever the stock market gives you. So let's assume that year after year you average a 10 percent return on your money in a stock mutual fund.

OK, after the first year you have $2,200—your original $2,000, plus the $200 you earned on the $2,000. So you leave it invested for a year and earn money on $2,200. It consequently becomes $2,420 by the end of the year. You start the next year with $2,420, and by the end of that year it has become $2,662. The next year you start with $2,662 invested, and it becomes $2,928. Now, it's the fifth year. You start out with $2,928, and by the end of the year you have $3,221.

It's going to start getting really exciting now. Remember, you have never added any new money from your pocket. After five years, your original $2,000 turned into $3,221 simply because you left it invested. Now, watch the power of compounding. The same process that I have described keeps happening year after year, so by the end of 10 years, you have $5,187; by the end of 20, $13,455; at the end of 30, $34,899; and after 40 years, $90,519.

That's right. You took $2,000 out of your pocket at age 25, invested it in stocks through a mutual fund, and ended up with $90,519.

But now let's assume that you are 25 and have $2,000 invested. You decide that you are going to keep adding $2,000 in new money to your investments each year. Then, at the end of 40 years, you will be a millionaire. That's right. If you try the "compounding" calculator at www.moneychimp.com, you will see how it works. You actually end up after 40 years of investing $2,000 a year with about $1,064,200.

If $2,000 is too demanding on your pay, you could start investing $20 a week at age 25, or just $1,040 a year. Through the same miraculous power of compounding, that simple investing habit over a lifetime will provide you with about $506,300 by the end of age 64, assuming that you average a 10 percent return on your money annually. Start increasing the amount you save weekly as soon as you get raises, and you can make it to $1 million or more.

Using Your Calculation:
The Advanced Lesson

If you run your calculation now, you will have a ballpark idea about what you are likely to need for the type of retirement you want and what you should save to make it happen.

But keep in mind that none of these calculations is a guarantee. If two or three years after you retire the stock market goes through what's called a bear market—or a scary downturn of at least 20 percent—you could use up your savings quicker than your calculations show. And despite your best efforts, you might have to cut back on your lifestyle.

On the other hand, if you happen to retire at a point when the economy is solid, inflation is controlled, and the stock market is climbing nicely, your savings could mushroom, and you could end up with more than you will ever need.

To illustrate the uncertain impact of your investments on your retirement, the Vanguard Retirement Center provides this scenario: Say you are 65 years old and you have saved $500,000, and you plan to take $25,000 out that year and another 5 percent for each year of retirement. That, of course, is within the range that's considered prudent. During both the first and the second year of your retirement, you have some bad luck. The stock market goes into a bad cycle and your investments lose 10 percent of their value each year—not an unusual occurrence if you look at history. And the third year the stock market remains troubled, and your investments lose another 5 percent. You, of course, have been removing the 5 percent you need each year from your nest egg. Those withdrawals, plus the nasty market, have left you with only about $318,300 in your nest egg. And even though the stock market climbs nicely after that and you earn 7.5 percent on your investments for each of the next 20 years, you will run out of money in the 19th year, when you are 84.

Now assume a different scenario: You retire at 65, and the stock market is very kind to you. For every year during the next 19, you earn a 7.5 percent return on your money. Then, when you are 84, you have over $663,060 left. This happened purely because you avoided a big loss early in retirement. Under this scenario, you can handle a loss in the stock market better. Vanguard suggests that after going through 28 years of retirement, you then lose 5 percent in the stock market, and 10 percent during each of the next two years. And then you die at 95, and have more than $351,000 left to pass to your children or favorite charity (see Figure 2.1 for an illustration of how a bad stock market early in retirement hurts worse than one later).

Figure 2.1

You can't predict cycles: Timing is everything in retirement.

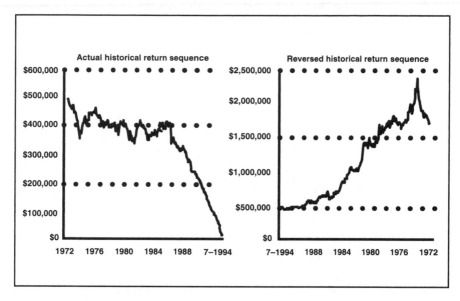

A person retiring in 1973 with $500,000 would have run out of money within 22 years because of the stock market crash in 1973 and 1974 (left), while a person retiring in 1994 would have had the good luck of a strong market at the outset, and his $500,000 would have expanded over 22 years (right).

Source: Ibbotson Associates, a Morningstar, Inc., company

Does this uncertainty make you nervous, or do you feel like I just had you run your saving calculation for nothing? You didn't run it for nothing. It was a good starting point. It gave you a target and helped you think about your future. And if you went to the majority of financial consultants, they would do just the type of calculation I've had you do. They would then send you on your way with an investment plan, and you'd feel nice and secure.

But the best financial planners don't do that. They realize that the averages that are typically used in retirement calculations are flawed. They are based on history. When you go to retire, an average—alone—is not a guarantee. For example, it's true that historically the stock market has gone up on average about 10 percent a year. Yet, you must also realize that some years it falls 20 or 30 percent. If you just happen to hit one of those dreadful times at the beginning of your retirement, you may run out of savings while you'd like to still be enjoying life.

So the best financial planners run what are called "monte carlo" simulations. They use powerful computer programs to analyze a slew of historical events, to jumble them up, and then to predict what might happen to your retirement savings. These simulations can show you whether you are 50 percent likely to run out of money before you retire, or whether you have plenty of money and are 80 percent or 100 percent secure.

This is the type of simulation Charles Schwab researchers ran to come up with the strategy I outlined in the previous pages—the strategy of removing only 4 to 5 percent of your savings during the first year of retirement and then adjusting that only slightly higher for inflation each following year.

The Schwab approach was designed to give you a 90 percent certainty that you wouldn't run out of money during 30 years of retirement. But maybe you don't need 90 percent certainty. Maybe you'd be comfortable at 80 percent or 70 percent. Thanks to the Internet, you can run one of these calculations yourself in about a minute's time. Again, you don't need to know any math or be a computer whiz. The complex data is all behind the scenes. So go to the "Retirement Income" calculator offered by T. Rowe Price at www3.troweprice.com/ric/RIC.

Again, you will put in information such as your age and when you plan to retire and for how long. There are a couple of items I need to explain so that you'll enter the right data. You will be asked for your "retirement assets." That's the money you have accumulated for retirement.

When you are asked for your portfolio, they are asking what combination of stocks, bonds, and cash you will have. After you have read Chapter 11, "Do This," you will understand what that's about. If you want to try the calculation now, however, you could select the "portfolio" that's identified as "60/30/10." That means 60 percent of your money will be invested in stocks, 30 percent in bonds, and 10 percent in cash. That's a classic, or moderate, investment approach.

Then when you are asked to simulate success, you are being asked to choose how much certainty you want about your savings. Do you want enough money to be 100 percent sure you won't run out? Or will you settle for a 70 to 80 percent chance, which is still fairly reliable? If you drop down to 50 percent, that wouldn't give you much confidence.

Work the calculation and see how you come out. It will tell you how much chance you have of making your retirement savings last—no matter what surprises the stock market might deal you.

Now that you know where you need to be headed, I'm going to tell you how to get there by making wise investments.

3

Savings on Steroids: Use a 401(k) and an IRA

If you are like a lot of people, when you hear the word "saving," the image of some sort of miser shoots into your head—maybe a pale, humorless guy hunched over a table, painstakingly ticking off numbers on a detailed budget with a pointy pencil...or maybe a penny-pinching parent or relative admonishing you to give up something fun.

You may want to shout: "I'm young, leave me alone! Saving for retirement is for old people—plenty of time for that stuffy behavior later in life."

Repeatedly, as I have written about saving for retirement over the years, people with that miser image in mind have said to me, "If I don't enjoy my youth while I'm young, when will I?"

That may explain why employee benefits firm Hewitt Associates found that only 46 percent of people in their 20s use 401(k) retirement savings plans at work.

But no matter what your age, I'm not urging you to deprive yourself. You might take a more modest vacation than you intend, but you can still take a vacation. You might run a car longer than you'd prefer, but you will still get around. You might settle for a closet with plenty of shoes instead of one stuffed with them. Maybe you will watch a movie at home with friends instead of going out. You might brew your own coffee in the morning and fill up a mug for the road, instead of dropping $3 at Starbucks.

All you need to do if you are 22 and in your first job is come up with $20 a week, add more when you get raises, and you should eventually build up $1 million. Make it just $15 a week throughout your working years, and you could still accumulate around $500,000. Or if you are 35 and saving for the first time, invest $50 a week and get close to $500,000. Add another $20 a week, and you should approach $700,000. Yet, people often don't try investing small amounts because they don't understand the power they have over $10 or $20 a week. When the Employee Benefits Research Institute asked Americans of all ages and all income levels a couple of years ago whether they could afford to save $20 more a week, most said "yes." They just didn't think it would do any good.

Of course, $20 does a tremendous amount of good. But you can turn nickels and dimes into hundreds of thousands only if you are smart about investing it. What's unfortunate is that too often people get the hard part down: the act of saving—or yanking money from their pocket and setting it aside for another day.

And they get the easy part wrong: the act of sticking their small savings in the right place so that investing transforms a pittance into thousands.

This is a shame, and absolutely unnecessary.

You have a couple of simple strategies available to you. And if you have an elementary-school education, you can master them with very little effort.

I'm talking about two tools that work almost like alchemy, turning pocket change into a pot of gold over time. One is an IRA, a savings account designed specifically for growing money into a retirement nest egg. (You usually have to set up an IRA away from where you work.) The other may be right under your nose where you work. It may be called a 401(k), a 403(b), a 457, or some other equally uninviting name. They get their names from tax laws. All of these are retirement savings plans, and I will explain step-by-step how to handle them a little later.

First, I want to get past the off-putting names, or perhaps the incessant nagging from someone who has made you want to ignore them. They may sound as unfriendly as the miser. But they are powerful money-making machines. Choosing whether to use them or not is like choosing between driving a car and walking to a destination that's ten miles away. You may very well be able to walk ten miles, but you'd be silly to try to do it if you were in a hurry to make an appointment in half an hour. If you drive a car instead, the trip will take a few minutes.

Likewise, you can either build up retirement savings the hard way through devices like savings accounts at banks, or the easy way—through IRAs and 401(k) plans. Too many people make life hard on themselves because they don't choose the easy investing way.

The Hard Way

If you don't use a 401(k) or an IRA, it's going to be like walking a long distance, and you may never get to your destination because it will take an extraordinary, laborious, unfulfilling effort. You will have to deprive yourself either during your savings years or after you retire. But if you use the two simple tools I'm advocating, it will be the opposite. You will feel the difference very quickly between the futile efforts you've been making and the smarter approach.

It will be like driving a car. You will speed toward your destination with very little effort if you start early enough. You will not have to live like a pauper while saving or during retirement.

This will help you understand: Let's say you are 35 years old. You have been pulling hard-earned cash out of your paycheck for the past 15 years and diligently saving it in the bank. You have $30,000 and 30 years to go before you retire. When that day comes, you know you are going to need at least $500,000 to keep up your modest lifestyle. But times have turned rough, and you aren't in a position to save any additional money for retirement. So the key for you will be to let your existing $30,000 grow effectively.

If you leave that money in a savings account in a bank, what will you have on the day you retire at 65? About $46,000—probably not enough to get you through more than a handful of years of retirement.

Now let's look at that same original $30,000 one more time. Only this time, let's assume that you've been smart, and instead of using a savings account, you have put it all in either your 401(k) or 403(b) savings plan at work, or an IRA, and, invested the money wisely in stock mutual funds. And let's say that you earn 10 percent on the money on average a year for the next 30 years.

By using either the 401(k) plan at work or an IRA away from work, your $30,000 should become about $539,000 by the day you retire at 65—not the puny $46,000 that would have happened in a savings account.

So, you see, amassing money doesn't have to be about deprivation. It has to do with being smart about where you stick the money.

What's the Difference?

Why is there such a dramatic difference in what $30,000 can become in a 401(k) or IRA rather than a savings account?

Let's start with the 401(k) because it gives you three huge advantages over a savings account—stock market investments, enormous tax savings, and potentially thousands of dollars in free money from your employer.

When you have a savings accounts at a bank, you will never make much money. You might earn about 2 percent a year. But in 401(k) plans, people can invest in mutual funds that select stocks. I will explain these in Chapter 7, "What's a Mutual Fund?" and you will learn how to use them easily. For now, I just want you to know that, historically, money in the stock market has grown 10.4 percent a year on average, according to Ibbotson Associates. That's not a specific guarantee for the future, but if history repeats and you are using good stock mutual funds in your 401(k), you could make 10 percent a year on average, rather than the 2 percent in your bank account. That's a tremendous difference over many years of investing.

That's not all. Employers often give you free money when you participate in the 401(k) plans they offer you at work. They give you what's called "a match," or "matching money." For you, it's like getting a raise every year—maybe $1,000 or more simply as a reward for participating in the company 401(k). What could be better? It's free money, and it's a reward for doing what's already good for your future.

Employers don't do this out of the kindness of their hearts. They need a lot of participants in their 401(k) plans so that they can handle all the paperwork and administrative tasks economically. They also provide matching money because, under federal rules, they have to get people of all income levels to be involved in their retirement savings plans. If lower-income people shrug off the 401(k), employers have to cut back on the benefits they give management. Of course, employers don't want to do this because they won't be able to recruit sharp people. Talented managers are well aware of the value of a 401(k) plan, and they want to get everything they possibly can from it.

But don't think of the company "match" as some kind of plot with weird strings attached. You aren't being unfairly manipulated. What you see offered to you by your employer is real and good. Don't be like half of workers 25 to 34 who ignore the 401(k) they are offered. Take a lesson from the savvy managers at your firm. They are using their 401(k) benefits to the hilt, and you should, too.

Get the Match

Getting free money from your employer is a great deal—one you'd be crazy to pass up. Imagine if your boss came to you and said, "We'd like to give you another $1,000 a year for working with us, and you don't have to work one extra hour or take on any more responsibility to get it."

Would you even consider telling the boss you weren't interested in the money? I doubt it.

Say you make $50,000 a year on your job, and can qualify for $1,500 that year in matching money under your plan—or 3 percent of your pay. If you were 35, did what you needed to qualify for the full match each year, received 3 percent raises a year, and earned an 8 percent return on your money in your 401(k), you would end up with about $237,300 at retirement simply from the free matching money alone—not from any money you personally set aside from a paycheck. Now, that's a deal!

That should be a huge motivator—a sure thing. It's certainly better than betting on the lottery. Still, according to a survey by the Consumer Federation of America, 21 percent of Americans think the "most practical" way to accumulate a few thousand dollars is to win the lottery. Only 26 percent think they can save $200,000.

You did it simply with your employer match. And with your own money, plus the free matches, you ended up with a grand total of $712,000...An even better deal!

The Power of Warding Off Taxes

There's still another advantage to using a 401(k)—perhaps the top advantage of them all: A 401(k) keeps the tax man away from your money year in and year out. You don't pay taxes on the money you put into a 401(k), and you don't pay taxes on the money that builds up in your 401(k) account over the years. Eventually, you pay taxes after you retire and start spending the money you saved. But the impact of delaying taxes is tremendous. I'm not talking chump change. It's potentially hundreds of thousands of dollars.

Avoiding taxes legally is one of the smartest tactics at your disposal to spin tiny savings into gold. Every wealthy person with a financial adviser uses this trick to the fullest. This is how they turn a small fortune into a cushy lifestyle, luxury vacations, and trust funds for their kids. But you don't need an adviser to make your way through the same terrain.

One of the common man's most delicious tax breaks is served to employees at work each day on a platter. It comes through the company

401(k) plan. When you see a 401(k) plan, it is like posting a "keep off" sign on your money to ward off the IRS. And it should beckon you…it says to you, "Put your money here, and Uncle Sam won't touch it." Years can go by, and your original $30,000 can become $50,000. And Uncle Sam won't make you share any of that $20,000 gain with the government. More years can go by, and your original $30,000 can become $500,000. And Uncle Sam still keeps his hands off.

In fact, the way it's possible to amass that $500,000 is by holding Uncle Sam at bay. If, each year, he was showing up at your doorstep and making you share some of the money you had gained with him, you would have ended up with nothing near a half a million dollars.

If you put all your money into a savings account, none of it is protected from taxes. Uncle Sam shows up every year at tax time and says, "Give me some of that interest money you have made." You have no choice but to pay because you have put the money where it's open season for the government.

So let me show you the contrast in real dollars. Let's go back to that original $30,000 sitting in a savings account in the bank. Look at what taxes do to it if you are in the 25 percent tax bracket. Remember that if you kept that money in a savings account until you were 65, you would have roughly $46,000. If you had been able to keep the IRS at bay, it would have been better—still nothing to rave about, but better. Instead of $46,000, you would have had about $54,000 when you retired.

So let's leave the bank savings account and look at another equally vulnerable approach to saving.

Mutual Funds Get Taxed

Let's assume that you jumped ahead in this book and learned that mutual funds can do a lot more for your future than a savings account. But let's say that you skipped this chapter about the tax advantages of a 401(k) plan. So you ignore the 401(k) plan at work and also an IRA. You go straight to a mutual fund company and plunk your $30,000 into a solid fund that invests in stocks, and you don't protect it from taxes.

Year after year, you earn good money in that mutual fund—let's say the same 10 percent annually you would have made in your 401(k). Except outside your 401(k) or IRA, there is a dramatic difference.

It is Uncle Sam. He shows up every year for his take—each year making you fork over part of the money you made on your mutual funds. The result: On retirement day, you would have roughly $262,000, not the $539,000 you would have had if you had simply invested the same $30,000 in your 401(k) plan at work. (I assumed a 25 percent tax rate and took a couple of liberties with this example. With an actual 401(k) you would not have been able to invest $30,000 in a single year, but rather could have done it over two. But I wanted you to see the comparison with the earlier savings account example in which a person invested $30,000 and ended up with only $46,000 at retirement. Meanwhile, if you want to see the impact of your tax rate on savings, try the calculator I used: "How will taxes and inflation affect my savings" at www.choosetosave.org.)

So amassing money isn't just about digging deeper into your pocket and depriving yourself so much that you feel like a pauper. It's simply about being smart about where you put the money.

It's knowing one simple fact: If you aren't paying taxes on your savings year in and year out, the money can grow vigorously. It's like putting your money on steroids. It's the only way to turn $20 a week into a sum close to $1 million. And Uncle Sam wants you to do it so that some day you aren't a destitute old person and a burden on society.

Of course, when you are retired, you will have to pay some taxes on money you remove from your 401(k) for living expenses. By that time, if you have invested well in the ways I describe in this book, you will have amassed a tidy sum and be able to afford to pay the tax. Also, because you won't be working then, the tax rate you pay might be smaller than what you pay now.

An IRA Instead?

But what if you don't have a 401(k) at work? Only about half of Americans do.

You still have another option that is just as good at keeping the IRS at bay so that you can turn meager savings into a retirement treasure chest.

It's an IRA—or an individual retirement account. Using one takes a slightly greater effort than using a 401(k), because you usually can't take care of the paperwork right at work. But it's not hard to do, which you will see in Chapter 5, "IRA Decisions: How to Start, Where to Go."

For now I just want you to understand that if you had that very same $30,000 in an IRA and used the very same mutual funds as in a 401(k), the result would be identical after 30 years: At retirement you would have about $539,000 because Uncle Sam would have had a hands-off policy for your money during the full 30 years you needed to grow it.

Why not just use an IRA and skip a 401(k)?

There would be nothing wrong with that approach from a tax perspective. But there are three reasons you shouldn't turn your back on your 401(k) at work: The first two, I have already provided. If you don't use your 401(k), you in effect tell your employer you don't want the free money that is being offered you, and that's just plain stupid. Also, your 401(k) is easy and convenient—sitting there at your fingertips every day you go to work. If you will just take about 10 minutes filling out the paperwork, you have set the groundwork for making thousands—maybe hundreds of thousands—of dollars.

Lastly, though, there are limits on how much money you are allowed to stash away for retirement without Uncle Sam raiding your account. Based on federal rules, a typical 401(k) will let you put up to $15,500 a year away, or $20,500 if you are 50 or older. But you can only put $4,000 into an IRA—or $5,000 if you are over 50.

More about those limits later, but now I want you to understand that in the best of all worlds, you would not choose between a 401(k) and an IRA. You would use both—your 401(k), if you have one, and an IRA. This is especially important if you are approaching retirement and have saved very little. In that case, stashing away just $4,000—or even $5,000—a year probably isn't going to be enough. By putting as much money as possible in both your 401(k) and an IRA, you can make up for some of the lost years. And Uncle Sam will help you out by keeping his hands off while you save.

How to Use Your 401(k) or 403(b)

First of all, make sure you are really using a 401(k), a 403(b), or a similar retirement savings plan offered by your employer.

That probably sounds like a ridiculous statement, but it's not.

A couple of years ago, benefits consultant Hewitt Associates surveyed employees at large companies about their 401(k) plans. What the researchers found was disturbing: A full 29 percent of people who weren't participating in their company 401(k) plans thought they were.

Somehow someone got some wires crossed—maybe because many employees find 401(k) plans so confusing, and maybe because employers often fail to give their staff understandable information. Regardless, for these workers, a disaster was in the making.

If these people thought they were building up retirement money for their futures, they were going to have a rude awakening on retirement day. They were on their way to having nothing because they weren't putting a penny into the 401(k) plan, and their employer wasn't doing it either.

So don't assume that you are in your 401(k) plan at work simply because you have heard your company has the plan. To participate, you usually must take action. In many companies, you have to notify your employer that you want to participate. You do this by signing a form, or saying "yes" on your company's intranet site. They will probably call this "enrolling." When you do it, you are telling your employer to remove some money from your paycheck on each payday and to keep the money for you in the 401(k) plan.

Notice I said, you "usually" have to take action by enrolling in your 401(k). Since a new law passed last year, more and more companies are beginning to sign employees up for the 401(k) plan without asking for their permission. This is good, not bad. The idea is to get more people to take part in this critical preparation for retirement.

Just make sure that either you or your employer has signed you up. Don't guess. You don't want to miss out on this.

After you have enrolled in your 401(k), every time you get a paycheck, a little money will be removed—as much, or as little, as you want. But don't feel trapped on this. You are the boss. You can change your mind at any time about the amount. You can even stop contributing anything if you want.

Changing Your Mind

If you tell your employer to remove $20 from each paycheck, that's what your employer will do. On each payday, instead of putting the $20 into your paycheck, your employer will put it into a 401(k) account with your name on it—like a bank account, only with all the advantages I just described.

If a month later you decide $20 is too much, but you think you can afford to give up $10 from your paycheck, you tell your employer to drop your old request and start putting $10 into your 401(k) account on payday instead. It's simple to do. You contact the person or office at your company that handles benefits like health insurance, fill out a form, or do it on the Internet site provided by your employer. It literally will take less than a minute to do.

If you put $10 aside for several months, and you are paying your bills, having some fun, and decide you can afford to stash more into the 401(k), you just tell your employer you'd like to make a change. You could up the amount to $15 per paycheck if you wanted, and go higher and higher over time—especially when you get raises.

Whatever feels comfortable to you is fine. Making changes is all perfectly acceptable. Your employer expects them. At many jobs you can change the size of your contributions every day if you want, although they won't show up until the next paycheck.

If you suddenly get strapped for cash and decide you need every penny from your paycheck, you go back to your employer's benefits office and say you'd like to stop contributing to the 401(k) plan for a while. Even if you would like some more fun-money for a few months, you go back to your employer and stop contributing. No one is going to ask you why you made a change. They are going to do what you request.

Meanwhile, any money you have already contributed will stay in an account with your name on it. Your employer will be just like a bank and hold onto the money for you for as long as you want.

As months and years pass, the money in your account will keep earning interest—or what is called "a return." As the years go by, your return will make the pot of cash grow larger and larger. So when you retire, and no longer get a paycheck from a job, you will pay yourself out of that pot of money you were kind enough to provide for your own future.

Getting Started

To get started for the first time in your company's 401(k), you simply need to call or visit the person or office at work that handles benefits. If you don't know where to go, think about the last time you received information on health insurance. It probably originated at the same place that handles the 401(k), or at least there will be someone at that office who will point you to the right person. You can also ask your boss or coworkers. It's not a dumb question.

When you contact the benefits staff, tell them you'd like to start contributing to the 401(k) plan. They will give you a short form to fill out or tell you where to find it online. On that form, you will have to say what percent of your salary you want to put away for retirement each time you get a paycheck.

You don't have to figure out a dollar amount. All you need to state is what percent of your income you will put aside. Some people just pick an amount that feels comfortable—somewhere between 1 and 15 percent, or maybe even more. But if you'd like to know what a percentage will mean to you in the dollars you will take home with each paycheck, an Internet calculator will give you the full picture in a few minutes.

Large employers often offer you dandy calculators over the Internet to figure out what to do with 401(k) plans. If yours doesn't, simply go to www.choosetosave.org, click on Calculators, and scroll down to "How do 401(k) salary deductions affect my take-home pay?" You can play with different percentages to see what feels right to you.

For example, if you are making $35,000 a year and get paid every two weeks, the calculator shows that if you have your employer put 5 percent of your pay into the 401(k) plan, your take-home pay will be reduced $59.50 every time you get a paycheck. That means each week you will have only $29.75 less to spend than you normally would. And if you are in your early 20s and keep it up, that small weekly sacrifice could eventually turn into $1 million—and almost certainly would become that if you add part of each raise in the future.

While you are at the calculator, give yourself a chance to see what would happen if you devoted just a little more of your pay to the future. Redo the calculation to show what 10 percent would do to your take-home pay. In the case of the person making $35,000 a year, giving up 10 percent would mean $119 less in spending money every two weeks. That's $59.50 a week. But the larger amount greatly increases the chances of building up a comfortable nest egg, especially for a person who never saved anything during his or her 20s.

There's a rule of thumb that if you put 10 percent of your pay into a retirement account, starting with your first job, you will have what you need later in life. Some financial planners feel more comfortable with 15 percent because healthcare costs are growing so much and could drain savings fast for a retiree.

There are limits, however. If you have a 401(k) in 2007, you can put as much as $15,500 into it for the year and get the full tax benefits. If you are 50 or older, you can add another $5,000—for a total of $20,500.

The limits change from year to year based on inflation and tax policies. As of this writing, Congress is looking at ways to induce people to save more. So look for alterations in 401(k) and IRA limits each year and adjust your contributions to the times. Table 3.1 provides the most recent limits.

Table 3.1

Limits for Retirement Accounts

Retirement Savings Plan	Eligible Individuals Can Contribute Up to These Limits	Employer Contributions
Traditional (tax-deductible) IRA	2006–2007: $4,000, or $5,000 if 50 years old or older 2008: $5,000, or $6,000 if 50 years old or older	None
Roth IRA	2006–2007: $4,000, or $5,000 if 50 years old or older 2008: $5,000, or $6,000 if 50 years old or older	None
SIMPLE IRA	2007: $10,500, or $13,000 if 50 years old or older	Typically 2% to 3% of pay
SEP IRA	$0	Up to $45,000, but not more than 25% of pay
401(k)	2007: $15,500, or $20,500 if 50 years old or older	Employer match varies; often is 3% of pay
Profit Sharing	$0	Up to $45,000, but not more than 25% of pay

Source: RIA

More Tax Help Than You Imagined

If you did the "take-home pay" calculation I suggested in the preceding section, you may be a little perplexed at this point.

You may see that when you contribute 5 percent of $35,000 to your 401(k), you give up $59.50 in take-home pay. But you are actually putting $72.92 into the plan for your retirement.

How can that be? You might assume that your reduction in take-home pay would be exactly the same number as your contribution to the 401(k) plan.

But you have just uncovered one of the truly delightful parts of using a 401(k) plan. I told you previously that Uncle Sam doesn't touch the money you make within the plan. But it gets even better than that.

The government is so worried that you won't save enough for retirement that it gives you a tax break right up front every time you put a penny into the 401(k) plan. This, too, should come as delicious news for you, especially if you are worried that your 401(k) contributions will immediately slash your ability to pay your bills. What it means is this: You aren't really sacrificing nearly as much today to save for your future. Because Uncle Sam immediately cuts your taxes on anything you put into your 401(k), you are still keeping more take-home pay than you would have imagined.

In the case of the person earning $35,000, the government reduced taxes on her paycheck by $13.42 cents. If she contributes the same $72.92 to her 401(k) on every payday, she will save $13.42 on taxes each time. For the year, that's about $348 in tax savings—not bad at all. It makes saving for retirement cheaper than you think

Here's a quick way to envision your tax savings: If you are in the 25 percent tax bracket, every $1,000 you put into your 401(k) cuts your federal taxes by $250 that year.

So you aren't really doing without $1,000 of your pay. You are simply doing without $750, because Uncle Sam is letting you keep a larger chunk of the money you have earned.

So when you use your 401(k), it's like buying a better future for yourself by using a 25 percent discount. You aren't stashing away your money at full price. Instead, it's as though you are making use of a "25 percent off" coupon. That lets you acquire a better future without living like a pauper.

Take Baby Steps

Increasingly, employers are not asking their employees whether they want to participate in the 401(k) plan at work. Instead, these employers just put you automatically into it. As I said previously, don't assume that you are in or out of your company's 401(k) plan without asking your benefits office.

Yet, if your company has an "automatic plan," your employer might be removing 3 percent of your pay—or some other amount—and putting it into an account for you every time you get a paycheck.

If that is the case, you are fortunate. You are taking a step in the right direction. Don't simply turn your back on your 401(k) and consider the deed done, however. You still must think about what you will need for retirement, and 3 percent of your pay isn't going to do it for you.

Consider moving your contribution up to 5 percent or 10 percent of your pay. If you have never saved for retirement and are in your 30s, 40s, or 50s, this is especially critical. You would go to your benefits staff, request a form, and simply change the percent of pay they will take from each paycheck and save for you. If you want to know what this will do to your paycheck, try the www.choosetosave.org calculator I mentioned. If you don't have a computer, you can use one free in a public library.

If you don't think you can afford to put 5 or 10 percent of your pay into the 401(k), experiment with a lesser amount—knowing that you can up it later. If you can't decide what you can spare from your paycheck, don't wait to figure it out. Indecision is your enemy. You could lose valuable months and years procrastinating.

Jump in now, and promise yourself to think about it again later. Write it on the calendar so that you actually do it.

Can You Spare a Dime?

If you are terrified about getting by if you save some money in the 401(k), start with a low number—even 1 percent. If you'd like to prove to yourself that you can survive without a little money, try an exercise: Every day empty spare change from your pockets or purse and put it in a jar next to the sink. At the end of the week, add up the amount. That's the money you lived without during the week. Did you survive without it?

You probably did just fine. So make use of that revelation. Go to your benefits office immediately and start having your employer remove that amount from your paycheck.

I have been suggesting this to people for years in my columns and have asked people to let me know if saving that amount of money each week was ever too much. I have never heard anyone say it was impossible to get by, and a lot of people have said it was just the assurance they needed to get started.

If you start out in your 401(k) with a very small contribution, ask yourself in a few weeks how you are doing. "Are you paying your bills and putting food on the table? Are you still having a little fun in life?"

Put a date on a calendar so that you don't forget to ask the question.

If you are doing just fine, go back to your benefits office and up the amount—maybe go to 5 percent. Don't wait, because days will turn into months, and months into the lost power of compounding—thousands of dollars.

If you are already at 5 percent, go to 7 percent. Also, promise yourself that when you get a raise, you are going to put half of it into the 401(k) plan. Don't wait for the first paycheck reflecting the raise. Get a 401(k) form as soon as you hear that the raise is coming, and up the percent so that you deploy some of your raise to your retirement future from day one.

That's often the most painless way of increasing retirement savings, because people don't miss money they never were used to having.

Finding Cash

Over the years, numerous people have contacted me to tell me where they have found money to save—painless ways that don't require them to live like a pauper or cut out the things they love.

Here are some of their suggestions.

- Dump one cell phone in a two-cell-phone family. Save about $480.

- Dump caller ID on the land-line phone into your home. Save about $90.

- Use calling cards instead of a long-distance carrier. Save about $100.

- Get rid of the second phone line into your house. Save about $275.

- Grocery shop with coupons, or shop for food at a cheaper store. Save about $780.

- Carry higher deductibles on home and auto insurance. Save $300.

- Eliminate one coffee-shop coffee or one alcoholic beverage a day. Save $730.

- Stop smoking. Save about $1,450.

- Cut out two restaurant meals a month. Save about $350.

- Use the library rather than buying books. Save $180.

- Cancel cable TV. Save $600.

- Order prescriptions through the mail. Your insurance company is likely to charge a lower copayment than for a drug store.

Also, beware of missing credit card payments. Often, you are hit with a $29 charge, and your interest rate can rise if your payments are late. In addition, be aware of the money you waste when you carry a credit card balance from month to month. The money you are paying in interest could have gone toward savings. To get rid of credit card debt, pay some amount above the minimum and get techniques from reading Liz Pulliam Weston's book *Deal with Your Debt* (Prentice Hall, ISBN 0131856758).

If you have raised children and they are now on their own, you may find additional savings simply by cutting back life insurance. For more saving ideas, try www.americasaves.org.

Then, try to look for small savings in your own lifestyle.

For the next two weeks, carry around a pocket notebook. Every time you buy something—no matter whether it's a trip to the candy machine, a magazine counter, or whatever—mark down the item and price.

At the end of two weeks, look the list over and put a check by the items you wouldn't really have missed. Tally it up. The dollar amount is what you could save. Let's say it's just $5 a week. If you invested that amount week after week for about 40 years and earned a 10 percent return, you'd have over $138,000. Try it yourself with the "Quick Savings Calculator" in the personal finance section of www.money.com.

Qualifying for the Match

Although I told you to start out by contributing only 1 percent if that is the only way you can feel comfortable, there is a better way if you can possibly swing it.

That's to make sure you put enough of your own paycheck into the 401(k) each payday to qualify for every penny of matching money your employer provides.

It's impossible for me to tell you how much you need to put aside to get all the free money your employer is willing to give you. That's because different companies use different formulas. You can ask your benefits office what you must do to qualify for the maximum matching money your employer provides.

Look at why it matters. Assume that you are 25 and making $35,000. You get a very common match from your employer—50 cents on every dollar you contribute up to 6 percent of your salary. So at age 25, you decide to put in the full 6 percent of your salary—$2,100. And your employer provides the full match—$1,050.

Every year for the next 40 years, you contribute 6 percent of your salary so that you get the largest match possible from your employer. The result: With that matching money, your contributions, and an 8 percent return annually in your 401(k), you have about $1.2 million when you retire. And your employer's matching money was not chump change in the outcome. If your employer hadn't been giving you any match and you had been socking away the same 6 percent year after year, you would have had only about $809,000 at retirement.

As you decide what to put into your 401(k) plan, know what you must do to get the maximum matching money from your employer. If you contemplate passing up some of that money, picture your boss standing in front of you with outstretched hands brimming with $400,000 in cash. He says to you, "I'd like you to have this." As a $1,000 bill falls from the pile and floats to the ground, do you say, "That's very nice of you, sir, but I think I'll pass"?

Instead, try calculating the impact of your employer's match using the calculator I just used. Go to www.bloomberg.com. Under Investment Tools, find Calculators and then the 401(k) Calculator. Incidentally, besides a starting salary of $35,000, I figured in raises of 3 percent a year for each of the 25-year-old's 40 years of work.

Procrastination—Not Money—Hurts

So now you have a decision to make: Just how much money will you put into your 401(k)?

Don't back-burner that decision now, because if you do, all the research into 401(k) behavior shows you will put the decision off for months and maybe years. You will get busy with your job, carrying out the garbage, or driving the kids to music lessons and soccer games and forget about it. Instead, go to your benefits office right now while you are thinking about it, and if you start with a small contribution, mark on a calendar when you will make yourself consider upping your 401(k) contribution.

Don't let yourself think of this as a sacrifice, or you may not get started. Instead, look at it as helping yourself. You are making an investment in your future, not depriving yourself. Think of the kindness you are showing yourself by starting now. Consider that an 18-year-old can become a millionaire by retirement simply by investing about $20 a week. Yet a 35-year-old who wants to be a millionaire, and has done nothing about it, has to give up a lot more of his or her paycheck to get there—a little over $100 a week. For a 50-year-old, it's $510 a week.

So no matter what your age, move into action now, telling yourself that if you get into gear now, you are going to remove the chance that you will deprive yourself later.

If you are like 36 percent of people who don't participate in their 401(k) plans, you may be saying to yourself, "I just can't spare a dime."

But the evidence shows you can. Hewitt Associates studied thousands of 401(k) plans and found that inertia—not money—seems to be the biggest deterrent to saving.

The consultants looked at what people do when they have to sign up for 401(k) plans and how that differs from the few companies that don't require people to sign up. In about 10 percent of companies, people aren't required to sign up for the 401(k). Their employer simply enrolls them automatically and starts removing a little money from their paycheck.

Now, here's the interesting part. In companies that just put people into the plan automatically, workers have to go to the benefits office and fill out a form if they *don't* want to be in the 401(k) plan. In other words, it's the opposite process of the usual. The action step is to fill out a form saying "no," rather than filling out a form saying "yes." In that case, guess what happens?

Very few people bother to say "no." Hewitt found that only about 10 percent of people decide to opt out of the 401(k) plan when their employer just puts them into it automatically. So somehow they get by financially with a tiny contribution coming out of their paycheck each month for retirement.

What's the explanation for this huge discrepancy—only 10 percent saying they can't put away retirement money versus the 36 percent who don't when it's up to them to make a decision? Hewitt's answer: procrastination, not money.

Most of us can give up a little of what we have earned to provide for our future. In fact, Fidelity investments has calculated that a

25-year-old who earns $35,000 and gets a 1.5 percent raise over the cost of inflation each year will make $1.9 million over a lifetime.

So don't let valuable years go by for you. If your employer doesn't enroll you automatically in the 401(k) plan, go fill out your form now.

And if you think you are already using your 401(k) plan, ask the benefits staff to confirm it. Ask for a statement that shows how much money you are putting into the plan and where it's going. You might get overloaded with material at this point. You are probably going to see a befuddling mix of gobbledygook. But don't worry about that now. By the time you finish reading the chapters on mutual funds and investing, this stuff will never be vexing to you again. You will look at today's mess of 401(k) choices with the same familiarity you look at the list of flour, salt, and sugar in a recipe.

For now, I just want to encourage you to start putting money into the 401(k) if you haven't already done so.

Leaving Your Job

If you change jobs, all the 401(k) money you accumulated at your old job will continue to belong to you. You will have some options: You can either take the money with you, or leave it in the 401(k) plan at your old job.

If you take it with you, do not spend it, because you will pay dearly for that mistake. Uncle Sam will show up and will charge you a 10 percent penalty, plus taxes. In addition, you will cut off your future by losing the power of compounding to make your money grow huge.

So, if you leave your job, do one of three things: Leave your money in your old 401(k), ask your employer to transfer it to the 401(k) at your new job, or open an IRA (as I will describe in Chapter 5) and have your old employer transfer your old 401(k) money directly into the IRA.

Make sure you follow the rules, using an official transfer, or "rollover." Only that will insulate you from getting slapped with a shocking tax bill.

Leaving your money in your old 401(k) is the easiest approach. If you don't like your investment choices there, moving it to an IRA will give you all the choices you could want. Uncle Sam will continue to keep his hands off your money so it can grow.

Emergency Bailout

If you have a 401(k) and run into an emergency—or just need cash—you can borrow money from yourself in your 401(k).

I want you to know this because it should enhance your level of comfort, knowing that if you are in financial trouble, you have options.

But I also want to tell you not to raid your 401(k) if you can possibly help it. If you do, there are stringent rules. You generally can borrow money at any time, but you also must repay the money with interest within five years, or Uncle Sam will tax you hard—not just the taxes you'd normally owe, but a penalty, too.

Meanwhile, borrowing will work in reverse on the power of compounding. You could slash thousands of dollars from your future. So, resist friends who tell you your 401(k) is an easy source of cash for something you *want,* rather than *need.* If they are dipping into their 401(k) plans, they are undermining all the hard years of saving they have put into it.

If you have a home and want to borrow for a home improvement, a home equity loan is usually a smarter approach. If you are sending children to college, dipping into your 401(k) could reduce financial aid grants—or free money offered by colleges.

Students and parents can borrow money for college through low-interest federal loans available in college financial aid offices. These are better options than robbing your future by tapping a 401(k).

4

An IRA—Every American's Treasure Trove

If you have earned any money working this year, you can open an IRA or a Roth IRA. And you should.

If you haven't worked for pay but have a spouse who has, you can still open an IRA or a Roth IRA. And you should.

In fact, even if you are in elementary school and mow lawns, wash cars, baby-sit, or do anything else for money, you can open an IRA or a Roth IRA. And if you do, you will be setting yourself up to become a millionaire.

That's because IRAs, and in particular Roth IRAs, are powerful money-making machines. And the earlier in life you start one of these miraculous individual retirement accounts, the wealthier you will be.

Nothing makes the point more clearly than an illustration often used in seminars to educate financial planners: Jack Surgent, a Devon, Pennsylvania, certified public account who trains planners, explains how one of his clients is turning a child into a multimillionaire.

It all started when the child got her first IRA when she was only about two years old. Here's what's happened.

Surgent's client is a businessman who used photos of his toddler in business promotional materials. Then he paid the child $3,000 for being a model and put the entire paycheck into a Roth IRA for her.

It was perfectly legal. Although the toddler didn't know it, she was doing work for pay. That's the criteria that must apply when opening an IRA or a Roth IRA—a close relative of a regular IRA.

Now, look at the impact of this creative strategy: Surgent notes that if the parent repeats the same process of paying his child $3,000 a year for modeling for each of the next three years and puts the money each time into the Roth IRA, the child will be a millionaire when she retires in 60 years. Actually, it's a lot better than a millionaire. It's not far-fetched to anticipate $4.2 million if she averages a 10 percent return per year.

And here's the shocking part. The child will use only a total of $12,000 of her own pay—just $3,000 a year for four years—to amass that fortune. If she never adds another penny of new money to her Roth IRA after she is 5 years old, she is likely to accumulate her $4.2 million fortune.

So if finances get tight later in life or she gets busy sending her own kids to summer camp and college as she ages, she won't have to worry at all about saving for retirement.

Keep in mind there are no bizarre get-rich-quick investment strategies or hot stock tips involved here. Surgent isn't suggesting anything other than a simple investment in a stock mutual fund that invests in the entire stock market. I will explain how to make such an investment in Chapter 13, "Index Funds: Get What You Pay For." But if that investment simply earns 8 percent on average a year, the toddler-model will go into retirement with about $1.4 million.

How can this be? How can you turn $12,000 into $1.4 million without any slick tricks whatsoever?

It happens for two reasons: First, it is possible because the child is so young that she has years upon years to earn interest on that $12,000—using the magic of compounding described in Chapter 2, "Know What You'll Need." Second, an IRA—whether a traditional IRA or a Roth IRA—doesn't get taxed at all while the money sits in the account growing bigger and bigger over the years.

I will explain the difference between a traditional IRA and a Roth IRA in the next chapter, but for now just think of the two IRAs as brothers—similar in many ways, but with a few unique characteristics when it comes to profoundly helpful tax savings. Both will shield your tiny savings from taxes so that you accumulate hundreds of thousands of dollars—or after many years even millions. So when I refer to IRAs, I am referring to what either a Roth IRA or a traditional IRA will do for you. And a little later I'll explain the fine points and help you select one or the other.

Now, I want you to understand that like the 401(k) I described in the preceding chapter, an IRA—whether a traditional IRA or a Roth IRA—has a "keep out" sign on it meant specifically for the IRS. So Uncle Sam stays away from the interest—or "return"—you earn during all the years of saving and investing. The toddler's money can turn into $50,000, and the IRS won't touch a penny of the earnings. It can become $500,000, and the "keep out" sign will keep turning the IRS away. It can even turn into $5 million, and at tax time each year, the government still won't show up and ask for anything.

In fact, if you use a traditional IRA correctly, the only time Uncle Sam shows up with an outstretched hand is when you retire and start taking some money out of the account. Then you pay taxes just like you would on a paycheck. But you pay taxes only on the amount you take out of the account per year. The money in the account can still keep growing, untouched by Uncle Sam. That's valuable.

Here's an example. Say you save your entire life in a traditional IRA and have $500,000 in it when you retire at age 65. You aren't getting a paycheck from a job anymore, so you are going to start using your IRA to give yourself a paycheck for living expenses and fun. So you take $20,000 out of the IRA for the year and pay taxes on it—just like you would on a regular paycheck. Meanwhile, the $480,000 left within the IRA is still growing, nicely protected from taxes.

Roth IRAs are even better than this. Uncle Sam stays away forever—even after you've retired. But more about that later.

The key is this: With any IRA you get a fabulous deal—one you cannot get with a savings account, or a mutual fund that isn't protected in an IRA or a 401(k). Remember, Uncle Sam anoints both IRAs and 401(k) plans with tax protection. If you save your money anywhere else, Uncle Sam shows up every year at tax time and requires that you give him some of the money you have earned. So don't do it because you will be throwing the easy money away.

How much? Say you are in the 25 percent tax bracket, you have $10,000 invested for retirement, and you earn 8 percent a year on the money for 35 years. If the money is protected in an IRA, you will amass about $148,000. If you have invested the same money in an account that Uncle Sam can access, you will end up with only about $77,000.

As of this writing, Congress is worried about the lack of saving by Americans and is considering other inducements that will help you save without paying taxes. In the future, you may encounter more tax-protected types of accounts that will work as well as today's IRAs or 401(k) plans. No matter what the government ends up calling these future accounts, whether it's a traditional IRA, a Roth IRA, a 401(k), or a newly designed account with a name like "Lifetime Super Duper IRA," they will be valuable to you for one key reason: You can build up savings without paying taxes. That's potentially worth hundreds of thousands of dollars to you. If you bypass any of these accounts and depend instead on those without tax savings, you will short-change yourself thousands of dollars.

Let's go back to the lucky two-year-old, who put her $12,000 in modeling money into a Roth IRA before she could even read. If her father had put that money into an account that would have been taxed every year, she would have ended up at retirement with only about $1 million instead of the $4.2 million.

So the message is irrefutable: Save money in a traditional IRA, a Roth IRA, a 401(k), or a combination of them, because they are protected from taxes, and if you are young enough you might even be able to turn $20 a week into $1 million. Certainly, saving this way is the easiest route to building up retirement money without living like a pauper when young or old.

More on the Magical Power of Compounding

While you have the rich toddler on your mind, I want to return briefly to the miraculous principle of compounding I explained in Chapter 2, because watching compounding turn $12,000 into $4.2 million should be a constant motivator from this day forth.

Hopefully, it will entice you at any age to put whatever cash you can possibly spare to work in an IRA so that you make compounding work for you. Starting now gives you a jump on the future.

Ignore compounding, and you will have to live more like a pauper late in your savings years or during retirement than you would have if you had simply started saving—or saved more—a few years earlier.

Let's look beyond the toddler. Imagine a 16-year-old with a job and a benevolent grandparent. If she puts $2,000 a year into a Roth IRA, does the same thing for the next six years, and never deposits another penny of new money, the 16-year-old will have $1.1 million at age 65 if it grows by 10 percent a year on average. That's $1.1 million for what? Just $2,000 for each of seven years—or a total of only $14,000 out-of-pocket.

Compare that to the person who doesn't start a first IRA until age 32. That person can contribute $2,000 every single year until retirement and won't come near the $1.1 million. Even if she earns the same 10 percent a year as the younger saver, she will have less than $500,000. She took a total of $66,000 out-of-pocket to end up with about $600,000 less at retirement than the 16-year-old with a helpful grandparent.

Now let's look at it a little differently. Let's say you are like most people, and your father wasn't working with a financial adviser clever enough to put you on the road to becoming a millionaire when you were a toddler. And granny wasn't capable of throwing $2,000 your way when you were a teenager.

So, instead, you open your first IRA when you are 25 years old. Your paycheck is much too small to allow you to put the maximum of $4,000 into an IRA. But you decide to dig down deep and come up with $3,000. You open your first IRA, and every year for the rest of your working life, you put another $3,000 into the IRA. And let's assume you average a 9 percent return on the money each year—a more modest expectation than I used for the 16-year-old.

When you retire at age 65, you will have about $1.1 million. And what did it take to get there? Only $3,000 a year, or $250 a month. In other words, to have $1.1 million, you only had to take a total of $120,000 out of your pocket for the full 40 years. Not bad! Compounding did most of the heavy lifting for you, and because the money was in an IRA, Uncle Sam kept his hands off too. Consequently, you didn't have to sacrifice and live like a pauper when young, and you won't have to when retired either.

Let's say you didn't start at 25 because rent was killing you. Ten years pass, and you are 35. You are now suffocating from house payments and haven't stashed away a penny for retirement. But the news stories about the demise of Social Security are starting to make you worry. So you kick yourself into action and put $3,000 into your first IRA. You've got the commitment in place now, so for every year until retirement, you put $3,000 into an IRA.

But the 10 years you lost between your 25th and 35th birthdays were very valuable. Instead of having the $1.1 million that you would have had if you had started stashing away $3,000 a year at age 25, your $3,000 a year in savings is going to end up as less than $500,000—even if your investments make the very same return as we assumed for the 25-year-old—9 percent a year.

You can fix this, of course, but it will cost you. If you would like to amass $1 million, you will have to save about $6,730 a year every year until retirement instead of $3,000. So for the next 30 years, you will remove almost $202,000 from your pocket, put it into your IRA, and average a 9 percent return annually on your investments. You won't get to the $1.1 million that the 25-year-old amassed by giving up a mere $120,000 over her working years to build a future, but you are still accumulating a nice sum without causing yourself great pain.

But now let's look at the painful way of saving for retirement. Perhaps the house payments and the wear and tear on the paycheck from everything from rising energy costs to soccer equipment for the kids have made saving seem impossible for the past 20 years. You are 45 now, with nothing saved for retirement. Soon the kids will be starting college, and you gulp at the $80,000 four-year college price tag. But you tell yourself that saving for retirement is now or never.

So you come up with $3,000, open an IRA, and do the same thing year after year until you retire at 65. Like the 25-year-old, you are making a 9 percent annual return on your money. But the outcome is nowhere near $1.1 million. Instead, on retirement day you will have accumulated only about $167,000.

If you decide at age 45 that you still want to shoot for $1 million, you might still be able to do it. You might not have to live like a pauper, but you are definitely going to have to dig deep into your pocket and make some sacrifices. To get to $1 million in 20 years, if you earn a 9 percent return on your investments, you will have to stash away about $17,900 a year. That's going to be a total of about $358,600 out-of-pocket for 20 years. Compounding is still doing the heavy lifting for you, but with only 20 years—rather than 40 before you retire—even magic has its limits.

5

IRA Decisions: How to Start, Where to Go

I would imagine that just about any American with a TV set has heard the term "IRA" because brokerage firms and mutual fund companies tout the savings devices in their ads. That's not surprising. Besides the fact that IRAs (individual retirement accounts) are invaluable for individuals saving for retirement, they are a $3 trillion business for financial service companies.

One out of every four retirement dollars is in an IRA, according to the Investment Company Industry, the mutual fund industry's trade group. About 40 percent of U.S. households have an IRA. We're talking about 45 million households.

Despite a familiarity with the term "IRA," most Americans aren't sure what to do with them, which may be why the majority of households still aren't taking part.

Over the years, I've received numerous calls from people like Jessica, who called me one day because her grandmother had sent her one of my columns urging people to open IRAs. Life was a struggle for Jessica's grandmother. Her husband had died years earlier, and she was living only on Social Security. There was no pension and no savings.

Obviously, Jessica's grandmother hoped for a better life for her granddaughter, so Jessica listened when her grandmother suggested she start an IRA. Immediately, Jessica appreciated the logic.

Jessica was 23—years away from retiring—but she told me she didn't want to end up like her 76-year-old grandmother, "sitting in a La-Z-Boy in front of a TV without the money to do anything else." Jessica knew she would need savings for a better life. Yet she couldn't imagine finding enough cash to open an IRA. My column said people could put $4,000 into an IRA. On an income of $25,000, Jessica said coming up with $4,000 was about as plausible as "looking in the mirror and seeing Paris Hilton."

She had made a common mistake. You don't need $4,000 to open an IRA. In fact, you don't even need $2,000—a frequent misconception that dates back to the early days of IRAs. Then, people were allowed to put up to $2,000 in an IRA each year. But $2,000 was the maximum yearly contribution allowed by the government, never a minimum.

Today, the maximum level is $4,000 a year for people under 50 and in 2008 the limit becomes $5,000. But there is no minimum whatsoever, and there never has been.

Tiny amounts of money are perfectly acceptable. The U.S. government—which sets the rules for IRAs—wouldn't object if you opened an IRA with just a few pennies. Financial institutions, however, might not want to bother with such a small amount because it would be a bookkeeping nightmare for them. Some mutual fund companies, such as Vanguard, want you to come through the door with $3,000.

Still, a lot of money is not necessary. Some very fine mutual fund companies let individuals open IRAs with as little as $50 if the person promises to put an additional $50 into the IRA every month. I told Jessica that if she invested $50 every month—or less than $12.00 a week—for the next 43 years in a solid mutual fund that invested in the stock market, she would probably have close to $400,000 at retirement.

That, of course, would have put her in a lot better condition than her grandmother, but not good enough. "Get started with $50 a month," I said, "and then as you get raises, add at least half of that amount to your IRA."

I would have told her to do the same thing with a 401(k), but she didn't have that choice at work. That made opening an IRA vital to her future because it was her only tax-efficient way to save for retirement.

If you are looking for a firm that will let you start an IRA with $50, consider T. Rowe Price. I suggested Jessica open the IRA and invest the money in the T. Rowe Price Total Equity Market Index mutual fund—a simple investment in the full stock market, which I will discuss further in Chapter 13,"Index Funds: Get What You Pay For."

First, I want you to be aware of other common misconceptions about IRAs so that a misunderstanding doesn't keep you from making yourself wealthy the easy way. And I will explain, as I did to Jessica, where to go and how to open an IRA.

Married, with No Job

Too often when people are married, and one spouse stays at home while the other works, they miss out on an IRA. That's not necessary. They assume— incorrectly—that the spouse who isn't working cannot open an IRA.

It's understandable that they would make this mistake, but it's especially unfortunate for women who stay home to raise children. Statistically, such women are likely to end up in poverty or tough times late in life because their sporadic work history leads to low Social Security payments. Also, family savings often get decimated caring for a sick husband while a wife outlives him by 17 or more years.

So whether a spouse is working or not, both married people should open an IRA and fill it to the max each year, if possible. As a rule, a person can't put more money into an IRA than he or she earns on a job or from a business. But there is an exception for a person who has a spouse who is working. Both spouses can have IRAs, and they can each put $4,000 into the account. So for a couple, that's a total of $8,000 a year as long as one or both spouses have earned at least that amount.

If you are over 50, you can stash away even more—a total of $5,000 a person, or $10,000 per couple. In 2008, it will be $6,000 a person or $12,000 a couple.

The federal government recently raised the limits for 50-plus-year-olds, because Congress is well aware that people are far behind with their retirement savings. Political leaders are hoping that if they give people a chance to catch up after their kids have finished college and moved away from home, parents will go into action when the financial pressures of a family have eased.

If you are among them, don't breathe a sigh of relief the day you see your child in a cap and gown, and figure you can start spending the thousands that were landing in the bursar's office over the past four years. When you return home after the graduation ceremony, open an IRA or increase what's in your IRA. And while you're at it, increase your 401(k) contributions, too.

If you forget, go into action the day you get the graduation photos back from the film developer. As you gaze proudly at the pictures of your child, think: "I'm now going to be proud of myself for taking control of my future." Then, get thee to your neglected IRA.

Where Do I Go; What Do I Do?

There are many places to go to open an IRA: your bank, a company that creates and sells mutual funds, a financial planner, or a brokerage firm.

If you use a local bank or brokerage firm, you'll walk into the office and say you'd like to open an IRA. If you deal with a mutual fund company instead, you will contact them on the telephone through a toll-free number or over the company's Web site. (I supply several names and contact information in later chapters, and you can find any name through a Google search on the Internet or through help in the "business" section at a public library.)

Other than the difference between phone contact and direct human contact, the process of opening an IRA is virtually the same everywhere.

It's an easy, quick task, similar to opening a bank account. You tell the firm's agent you'd like to open an IRA, and they give you a short form to fill out. You provide basic information: name, address, Social Security number, and "beneficiary" (the person who you want to give the money to if you die). Then you have to specify whether you want a traditional IRA or a Roth IRA—a decision I will walk you through later in this chapter.

After completing the form, you write a check that will go into your IRA account—maybe as little as $25 or $50; maybe as much as $4,000.

After you have done that, you will have an IRA. But you aren't done.

Opening your IRA is only the first step. At that point, your money is just sitting there, doing nothing. You were smart to open an IRA for yourself. But the money isn't going to grow until you take the second step—a critical one. You must decide how you want to invest the money you just put into the IRA account. You will fill out a second form stating what investments you choose. Your choices could make the difference between ending up with little more than you originally deposited or having hundreds of thousands of dollars later in life.

If you haven't finished reading this book, making investing choices might make you nervous. Don't worry, though. In the chapters ahead, you will become as wise as many financial planners, and I will give you specific mutual fund names that will help you choose.

Meanwhile, as you open your first IRA, be assured that you don't have to decide right there on the spot how to invest your money. Request a list of mutual funds to consider, and take it home with you if you need time to think. As a temporary move, you can tell the person who opened your IRA that you'd like to park your money in what's called a "money market fund"—a safe choice that's almost like a savings account but generally pays a little more interest.

Don't leave the money that way for long. You won't make enough interest on it to harness the power of compounding and make your savings blossom. Instead, you are going to need to select mutual funds, including some that invest in stocks. I will tell you exactly how to do that in the chapters ahead.

Now, however, I just want you to be comfortable opening an IRA so that nothing stops you.

You might feel most confident opening an IRA at a bank because you have been there before and can walk in and talk with a human being. If you need that security for your first step into an IRA, go for it. Yet I want you to understand other options that might seem a little less comfortable at first but are actually as simple and ultimately could be much more lucrative.

Too often banks aren't the best place for an IRA, because they charge high fees. They may charge a $25 so-called "maintenance fee" each year, just to keep your money in an account. And then, mutual funds offered to you by the bank might include extra fees called "loads." On the face of it, these fees might look like small numbers, but over time they erode your savings by thousands. I will explain this in detail in Chapter 12, "How to Pick Mutual Funds: Bargain Shop." For now, just understand that fees matter a lot.

Ask about fees, and try to open your IRA at a bank, broker, or mutual fund company that won't charge you a fee to open the account or an annual "maintenance fee." There is no need to pay such fees, because equally good institutions don't charge them.

If you want human contact, you can do it through a brokerage firm or financial planner, as well as a bank. Perhaps you have heard of firms like Merrill Lynch or Charles Schwab. These are brokerage firms. They sell stocks, bonds, and mutual funds. But they differ greatly by the fees they charge.

Merrill Lynch, Citigroup Smith Barney, and other so-called "full-service brokers" charge fairly high fees. In theory, the fees are supposed to be the broker's compensation for giving you advice. But keep in mind their advice can be good or bad. Brokers are hired to sell, and too often that means they sell what enriches them the most, rather than you—a topic covered in Chapter 15, "Do You Need a Financial Adviser?"

Charles Schwab—and other so-called "discount brokers" like Scottrade or TD Ameritrade—generally charge lower fees, which is why I prefer the discounters. There are many of them—too numerous to list. (Search "discount brokers" on the Internet, comparing the fees they charge and the ease of contacting them.) When you go to a discount broker, you need to know what you want. If you are still at the stage where you feel you need a significant amount of guidance, you won't get it there.

My goal with this book is to give you the tools you need so that you don't need much advice and can consequently save tremendous amounts of money by keeping your fees low at a discount broker or "no-load" mutual fund company. Still, if you feel like you need a helping hand, in person, to get started, do not stew and let valuable time pass by. Go to a broker at a bank or brokerage firm, or find a certified financial planner. In Chapter 15, I tell you how to find qualified advisers who will work for you, not against you.

On the other hand, if you have the comfort level with mutual funds that I hope you get from Chapters 7 through 13, you can go directly to a low-cost mutual fund company like Vanguard, Fidelity, or T. Rowe Price. I provide many other examples in later chapters. You can also use fund "screeners" that will help find funds. Try www.morningstar.com, or at www.moneycentral. msn.com, click on "Investing" and "Funds." Morningstar's website offers Picks and Pans to find long-standing quality mutual funds. If you search most screeners by "low minimum," you find funds which will let you start investing with $250 or $500.

Can't I Wait Until I File My Taxes?

When I first told Jessica to open an IRA and deposit $50 into it every month, she was perplexed. She, like many people, assumed you are allowed to open IRAs only once a year at tax time—part of the process of filling out a tax return.

Again, it's understandable why people would make this mistake. Often people open IRAs when they complete their tax return so that they can use a tax-deductible IRA to reduce their taxes that year. Also, brokerage firms turn up the volume on advertising around tax time because they know accountants will be advising clients to cut taxes with IRAs.

Still, there is no need to wait for the end of the year, and you shouldn't. By investing earlier in the year, you start earning money on your investments immediately. The magic of compounding begins to turn pennies into dollars.

For purposes of doing your taxes, it doesn't matter whether you have contributed to an IRA early in the year, every month, or once a year. You just tally up all your contributions for a year and write the total on your tax return so that you can reduce your taxes.

Under tax laws, people are allowed to open an IRA every year, and they can put up to $4,000 into an old, or a new, IRA for the 2007 tax year, or $5,000 in 2008. The deadline for contributing the money comes at tax time—April 15. That's simply the cutoff date. For example, if you sit down to do your 2007 taxes in April 2008, and you haven't contributed anything to an IRA for 2007, you have until April 15, 2008 to open an IRA for the 2007 tax year.

In Jessica's case, all those $50 deposits would add up to $600 for the year. Then, while preparing her tax return, if she wanted to boost the amount a little, she could. If she had an extra $100, she could add that to her IRA. If she had an extra $2,000, she could add that. She could add any amount as long as she didn't put more than $4,000 into the IRA that year. In future years, she would have to pay attention to new limits by the government—for example, $5,000 for the 2008 tax year.

The flexibility to save small amounts throughout the year and then add more at tax time should give you the impetus to open an IRA now instead of waiting for a stash of money that might never materialize. You can go to a bank, mutual fund company, or brokerage firm, fill out the form to open the IRA, deposit whatever amount you want, and then figure out the amount you could instantly add every time you get paid. For Jessica, it was $50; for you, I hope it's even more.

Regardless, ask to be put on what's called an "automatic" system, in which the institution will remove your $50, or any other amount, from your checking account on a specific schedule. It might be once a month or every payday. Then you will constantly be adding money to your investments.

The nice feature about using an "automatic" plan is that you don't have to trust yourself to come up with $4,000, or even $600, at tax time. You are making sure that the money starts going into your retirement account from the moment you have good intentions. Given human nature, this is the one approach that seems to work most often.

Of course, you also want to put compounding to work. When there is zero in your account until tax time, you are going to go through a full year without earning a return on your money. As soon as you put your first dollar into the account, compounding flexes its muscle. So why would you wait?

If you don't think a few months matters, just remember that time is your best friend if you start early and works against you every day you wait. If you doubt it, remember the toddler who amassed $4 million on $12,000 in IRAs.

The Choice between Traditional IRA and a Roth IRA

Too many people suffer from IRA paralysis, because they can't figure out whether to choose a traditional tax-deductible IRA or a Roth IRA. I don't want you to succumb, because behavioral studies suggest you will then let months or years go by without ever deploying your first $1 into one of these money-making machines. Simply because you are mulling the choice of IRAs, you may cost yourself thousands of dollars in potential retirement money as you leave savings gathering dust in a savings account.

Consequently, if you see that you would qualify for either, and you find yourself in the throes of procrastination, take out a quarter. Call one side "Roth IRA" and the other side "traditional IRA." Then flip that quarter in the air, and whichever side turns up, go for it.

I say this because both IRAs are tremendous choices—huge tax savers, and consequently a no-brainer for growing your money. On the other hand, understanding the variations is not difficult. In a nutshell, the choice comes down to this: In addition to years of tax breaks, do you want an extra serving of tax help at the time you contribute money to an IRA, or do you want to delay it until you are retired?

The Traditional Tax-Deductible IRA

Let's start with a traditional tax-deductible IRA, because there was a time when there was only one IRA—the traditional IRA. When the first IRA was introduced several years ago, people were sold on them as a way to cut their taxes each year. And that's still the appeal today. You can open a traditional IRA, deposit money up to the government's limit for that year, and use that contribution to reduce the amount of taxes you owe Uncle Sam at tax time for that particular year.

Say you earn $20,000 a year on your job, and you decide to put $3,000 into a traditional IRA this year. Because you did this, you are going to reduce your income when you fill out your tax return for this year. In effect, you tell the government at tax time that you didn't really make $20,000. Instead, your income was only $17,000, because you removed $3,000 to start the IRA.

Since your income is no longer $20,000, the government is going to tax you on only $17,000. So instead of having to pay $1,355 in taxes, you will pay only $905. By opening an IRA, you cut your tax bill down by $450. If you want to try this calculation, go to www.dinkytown.com and use the tax estimator.

To look at it another way, because you saved $450 in taxes that year, it only cost you $2,550 to open your IRA—not $3,000.

Getting the tax break in a single year is a good deal. Of course, if you contribute again the next year, you can cut your income and taxes again. You can do this year after year—every time you make a contribution you reduce your taxes at year-end.

But the benefit is so much more than that. Year after year, Uncle Sam also keeps his hands off everything that's invested in the tax-deductible IRA. If your $3,000 earns $100, you will have $3,100 in your IRA, and you won't get taxed on any of it. If, years later, it's grown to $50,000, you still won't need to pay taxes on it. Consequently, your savings—free of taxes—will grow with gusto thanks to the power of compounding on a pot of money that never gets whittled away by taxes.

That original $3,000 should turn into about $49,000 tucked away in your IRA for 35 years, but if you hadn't held the tax man at bay, you would have accumulated only about $24,000. (I'm assuming you are in the 25 percent tax bracket and earn 8 percent annually on your investments.)

Now, here's where that traditional IRA takes a turn you might not like. The gig comes to an end when you retire. That's when Uncle Sam's bill starts coming due. Remember, you have been saving throughout your working years in an IRA so that you could start giving yourself a paycheck each year of retirement. As you go into that period of your life, Uncle Sam starts showing up every time you pay yourself. There's nothing you can do about it. He will tax any money you remove from the IRA. Of course, if you don't need the cash early in retirement and you just leave it in the IRA, you still won't owe any taxes on your savings.

But Uncle Sam wants to make sure he gets a piece of the action, so he won't let you duck him forever. Once you turn 70½, he will require you to remove a portion of your IRA money—whether you need it or not—every year. Then Uncle Sam will take his share of that money, taxing it just as he would a paycheck. Still, the money remaining in your IRA—no matter how large—continues to grow without getting taxed.

So that's how a traditional tax-deductible IRA worked when it was first introduced and still works today. It starts out with a tax break the year you contribute, it protects you from taxes throughout your savings years, and then in retirement you start giving some of the money back to Uncle Sam and your state tax coffers, too.

The Roth IRA

All said, the traditional IRA is a great deal for saving. But a few years ago, along came something even better—the Roth IRA. I think of it as the new and improved IRA.

Now, assuming that you meet the income levels and other criteria explained throughout this chapter, you have a choice between a traditional tax-deductible IRA and a Roth IRA.

With a Roth IRA, you do not get an upfront tax break the year you open one or when you make a contribution. So if you were earning $20,000 and put $3,000 into a Roth IRA, you would not cut your taxes by $450 that year. You would miss out on the basic attraction of a traditional IRA—that easy opportunity to cut your taxes in a single year.

On the other hand, after your money is in a Roth IRA, you get the same goodies as with a traditional IRA. In other words, year after year the pot of money grows and you pay no taxes on the money in the account. If $3,000 turns into $3,100, you pay no taxes. If it turns into $30,000, you still pay no taxes, and so on through the years.

Now comes the really terrific part. When you retire, you still pay no taxes. It is here that the Roth IRA starts to act very differently from a traditional IRA. It becomes the Superman of IRAs—delivering a stupendous deal.

Everything you've built up in the Roth IRA is yours free and clear, forever. You will never owe taxes on any of it. You could have $1 million or $10 million at 65, 85, or any age. Every cent will be yours.

Uncle Sam won't make you take a penny out of your Roth IRA at age 70½, or ever, because he has no claim on it. If you remove $1 million a year, it's all yours. If you remove $100, or $3 million, it's all yours. If it stays invested, it's all yours. Even if you die and it goes to your spouse, children, or any heir, they won't have to pay taxes on any of it either.

Now, that's one magnificent deal! When you are retired and living on a fixed income, you won't have any control over whether your property taxes shoot up or whether your medical bills triple or quadruple, or whether car prices go through the roof and your old wreck breaks down. But you will have one sure thing: your Roth IRA. No matter what you have accumulated in it, every penny will be there for you—with no tax man dipping in each year for a cut.

I think that certainty alone makes the decision between a traditional IRA and a Roth IRA simple: Go with the Roth.

Some accountants have done elaborate calculations to help people decide whether they'd be best off with a traditional IRA or a Roth IRA. The simple rule of thumb is this: If you think you will be in a lower tax bracket when you retire than you are now, you should go with a traditional IRA and get your tax break up front instead of when you retire. You can use Internet calculators to see where you fall. Do a Google search for "which IRA is best" and try the calculator at www.smartmoney.com.

But here's the catch with the calculations: They assume that current tax rates stay intact and that you can anticipate what percent of your income you will owe in taxes when you retire. I am persuaded by Ed Slott, a certified public accountant and IRA expert, that planning based on today's tax system will probably be folly. With a large federal budget deficit, Congress is likely to raise taxes at some point. Even if you anticipate low taxes during retirement, that may not be correct. Consequently, Slott tells everyone—regardless of income—to select a Roth IRA and insulate themselves from the possibility of high taxes during retirement.

His argument convinced me. Of course, some skeptics argue that the government could also renege on its promise to keep its hands off Roth IRA money years from now, but people familiar with the public-policy process tell me that would be a broken promise with gigantic ramifications from unhappy voters. People realize that tax rates are not guaranteed, that government can tinker with them whenever they want. Yet breaking an outright promise—like the one attached to a Roth—is fraught with trouble.

So if you want a simple solution, rather than flipping a coin, go with the Roth IRA, leave your money in it until you are 59½, and enjoy tax-free savings for all the days of your life.

Slott, in his book *Parlay Your IRA into a Family Fortune,* calls Roth IRAs "The Ninth Wonder of the World."

He told me once that he thought young people were foolish to be sucked into the small tax savings they can get upfront from a tax-deductible IRA. Maybe they save $450 on taxes one year on their first $20,000-a-year job, but when they are retired and it's turned into $41,000, they could end up giving away 30 percent of that in taxes.

Consequently, why not just go with this: There is nothing better than no taxes after you are retired. And that's precisely the deal that the Roth IRA offers you.

The Choice between a 401(k) and a Roth IRA

In the best of all worlds, you would be so well paid and have such a commitment to keeping up your lifestyle when you retire that you would use both of these fabulous tools to the hilt. I'm not delusional, however. Only 10 percent of people hit the $15,500 limit on their 401(k)s.

Most people can't, or won't, do more. On average, Americans put 6 percent of their income away in 401(k)s—enough to survive with a roof over their heads and food on the table, but not extras. Many could do more, which is why I wrote this book—to nudge and help you through it in easy ways.

Remember, when the Employee Benefits Research Institute asked people of all income levels whether they could afford to put $20 *more* into a retirement account each month, the majority said yes.

Still, many Americans cannot put $15,500 into the 401(k) and also maximize a Roth IRA, so inevitably that raises a question: Which one do you use?

There's a simple process to follow: First, don't leave money on the table if your employer is offering it. Contribute at least enough to your 401(k) to get every drop of matching money possible. The only exceptions would be if your 401(k) plan is a mess—with an array of awful mutual funds and high fees, or if you believe that your employer may not be putting the money into the 401(k) as required by law. Fraud is unusual, so there's no need to fixate on this. You would get hints if it were happening to you—money not showing up on time or incorrect and late statements from your account.

Assuming your 401(k) is solid, you proceed to the next step after you have put enough money into your 401(k) to get matching money for the year. At that point, with your match intact, you could stop contributing temporarily to the 401(k) and start routing money into a Roth IRA. When you've met the $4,000 maximum contribution for the Roth, then you would return to the 401(k) and fill it to the hilt. In other words, if the limit in your 401(k) plan is $15,500, go for it. Some people skip this last step, thinking there's no benefit because their employer isn't matching the contributions. They are wrong: The goal is to build up a nice retirement stash with the help of the tax system. So that means putting as much as possible into both a 401(k) and an IRA.

The route I've laid out—using a 401(k), then a Roth IRA, and then back to the 401(k)—will work only for a disciplined person who will, in fact, follow up by opening a Roth IRA and feeding it regularly. If you can't trust yourself to do that, fill the 401(k) to the brim before doing anything else because it's there at work. You can set it up once and simply make contributions without thinking about them. In addition, when you hear you are getting a raise, it's easy to tweak the 401(k) forms at work so that part of that raise goes immediately toward funding your future.

The most important consideration for you is to make sure you get the money into a tax-sheltered account such as an IRA or 401(k) so that you don't spend it, and also so that it grows free of taxes.

If you have been kind to yourself by funding both a 401(k) and a Roth IRA, when you retire you will have the best of all worlds. The Roth will provide a pot of money that won't be taxed no matter how long you live, and your 401(k) will be another reliable source of money—but one that will require you to pay taxes. Every time you withdraw 401(k) money during retirement, you will have to pay taxes on it just like a regular paycheck.

Pushing IRAs and 401(k)s to the Limit

After you have a fully funded Roth IRA, if you can put any additional money aside—and you should—devote it to your 401(k). The additional money won't earn you a greater match from your employer, but it will give you a break on your taxes and continue to let compounding do its magic for you while holding Uncle Sam at bay.

And for people who have incomes too high to open Roth IRAs, it's critical to use a 401(k) to the maximum—putting up to $15,500 into it this year, or up to $20,500 if you are over 50.

Rules You Must Live By

One of the reasons IRAs are so confusing for people is that Congress keeps changing the rules. Today's rules may change later, so before opening an IRA, make sure that your age, income, job benefits, and other factors still permit you to take the actions you want. You can read all the current rules in the IRS Publication 590 at www.irs.gov/publications/p590/index.html or a simple version at www.rothira.com.

The following lists the main rules you must follow—rules that will either give you the right to proceed or hold you back on one or both IRAs. I am using 2007 limits to explain how the rules work, but keep in mind that the numbers you see in the examples will change in future years as the government adjusts them for inflation.

Can You Get a Tax Deduction from a Traditional IRA?

Not everyone can get a tax deduction by opening a traditional IRA. It depends on your income and whether you have a pension, profit-sharing plan, 401(k), or other retirement savings plan at work.

Most employers don't offer pensions. And half don't offer a 401(k), 403(b), or similar retirement savings plans. So if you work for one of these companies, you are free to open a traditional IRA and deduct it from your taxes. The reason is simple: You are on your own to provide for your retirement, so the government gives you an incentive to help yourself.

But if you have the benefit of some type of pension or retirement savings plan at work, the government is less interested in helping you out. So your income level counts. You can't deduct a contribution to a traditional IRA for 2007 if you are single and making over $62,000. And if your income is somewhere between $52,000 and $62,000, you can contribute, but you can't get a deduction for the full amount typically allowed for an IRA contribution—or $4,000 in 2007.

If you are married, this gets a little more complicated. If a couple's combined income is $103,000 or over, and they each have either pensions or retirement savings plans at work, they cannot deduct traditional IRAs from their income. And at $83,000 they have to start cutting back on what they can deduct. But if one spouse has a pension or retirement plan at work and the other doesn't, the spouse without the plan doesn't have to worry about the $83,000 to $103,000 cutoff. He or she can open an IRA and deduct the full amount if the couple's income is no greater than $156,000. If it's higher than that, the spouse might still qualify for a reduced deduction. But when a couple's modified adjusted gross income is over $166,000, no deduction is allowed.

What a maze of numbers! I wish I could make it easier, but Uncle Sam requires that you live within the rules.

Just to make things more complicated, these income levels aren't actually what your salary is. Instead, they relate to income levels after certain deductions occur. That means your salary is probably higher than the cutoffs, so you might have more leeway to use an IRA than you think. If you use a tax preparation software like "Turbo Tax," it tells you where you stand so you don't have to wonder about your income level qualifying. Of course, an accountant or www.irs.gov can also help. And since the government can change income limits, check on them each year.

Is Your Income Too High for a Roth IRA?

One of the reasons I like Roth IRAs is that the rules are so simple. Instead of running through a maze of do's and don'ts about qualifying, there is just one simple question to answer: Is my income within the limits? And very few people have to worry about this, because the maximum income is fairly high for Roth IRAs. So if you have been thinking about opening a traditional IRA and have a workplace pension plan that will interfere with a deduction, just turn to a Roth IRA. Remember, if you have a pension, 401(k), or other retirement plan at work, you are free to open a Roth IRA, and you should.

Given 2007 limits on contributions, you could put up to $4,000 into a Roth IRA for the year if you are single and have a modified adjusted gross income no higher than $99,000. Between $99,000 and $114,000, you would have to ratchet back the amount you put into a Roth, but you could still make a contribution of some amount. With married people, you would start ratcheting back a full contribution when your income crossed the $156,000 threshold. Yet, you could still contribute some amount to a Roth as long as your income stayed within the maximum $166,000. Under current tax laws, the limits are supposed to be adjusted annually based on inflation, so as the years go by, search the IRS website to see how far you can go with each year's contributions.

There's also a formula behind how these so-called phaseouts work to limit contributions after a person's income crosses from the low end of the range—such as $99,000 for a single person—and approaches the high end, or $114,000. You can find it at www.irs.gov. But I'll give you a quick understanding here. It has to do with where your income stands between the complete phaseout point and the start of the phaseout. Say, for example, that you are married and file your taxes jointly with your spouse. Together, the two of you have a modified adjusted gross income of $161,000. That's half of the way up to the $166,000 cutoff from $156,000. So your limit on what you can put into your Roth IRA is cut by a half. Instead of putting $4,000 into one that year, you can put in $2,000.

How Much Can You Contribute?

The answer: Only as much as you earn from a job.

For example, if you are in junior high and have been mowing lawns this year and will make $75 for the year, you could put the entire $75 into an IRA. But if you've been putting gifts from relatives into a savings account for years and have $4,000 in it, you can't pull the $4,000 out of the account and open an IRA with it. You are limited to the $75 you earned from working.

But let's say you earn something more than $4,000. Then you have to stay within the $4,000 limit. Example: You make $20,000 on your job and don't need any of it to live on because someone in your family is bankrolling you. Perhaps you'd like to put the full $20,000 into an IRA. But you can't.

Watch these limits, though. Congress is always changing them. As of this writing, the limits for IRAs are supposed to jump in 2008 to $5,000 for people under 50. For people 50 and up, it will be $6,000.

Do You Meet Age Requirements?

There are a couple of ages that are key: 70½ and 59½. But just to drive you nuts, the ages don't apply in the same way to traditional IRAs and Roth IRAs.

After age 70½, you can no longer contribute to a regular IRA, and you must start taking money out at that point. But 70½ doesn't apply in any way to a Roth IRA. As long as you have any income from working—even income as small as working as an election judge once a year—you can make a new contribution to a Roth IRA, no matter what your age.

Then there's the issue of removing money from an IRA. Typically, anyone can start removing money from a Roth IRA after age 59½. But there's another rule tagged onto the 59½ age. The money must also have been in the Roth for five years before the earnings on it are removed.

So if you put money into a Roth IRA at age 50 and want to remove it at age 59½, that will be fine. But if you open a Roth IRA at 58, you have to wait until you are 63 to remove anything beyond your original contribution.

Last-Minute Regrets: I Want My Money Back

I hate to tell you the following, because I don't want you to use it. But I also know that this could make you a lot more relaxed about putting money into an IRA or Roth IRA. So here goes.

If you find out you can't live without the money you put into your IRA or have second thoughts about the amount you deposited, you can change your mind under several common circumstances.

If you find out you need the money to pay for college for yourself, your child, or a spouse, feel free to dip into the account. It doesn't matter what your age is. You won't have to pay the typical 10 percent penalty the IRS charges if you take money out of an IRA before you are 59½. You will just have to pay taxes on the money you have removed.

The same holds true if you are buying your first home and need the cash. You can take $10,000 out of the account. Married people can get their hands on a total of $20,000 if they each have their own IRA.

And if you lose your job and need to buy health insurance, you can tap your IRA penalty-free, too.

People with Roth IRAs have even more flexibility. Besides the right to take money out of IRAs for college, homes, and health insurance, they can yank any of the original money they deposited and use it for anything at any time.

Say you are 35, and you put $4,000 into a Roth IRA today, and a week from now, a friend finds a great fare over the Internet to Europe. You can remove the entire $4,000. You won't have to pay a penalty or pay taxes because—unlike a traditional IRA—you never got a tax break upfront with the Roth IRA. You put the $4,000 in your Roth after paying taxes on it.

So it's yours—free for the taking at any time.

If, however, you had the $4,000 in your account for a few months, and it had grown to $4,100, you would not be able to remove the $100 for your European vacation. That's because you didn't pay taxes on the $100, and your deal with Uncle Sam is the following: Leave all earnings from your Roth in your account until you are at least 59½. As a result, if you removed the $100, you would have to pay both a 10 percent penalty on it and income taxes.

So relax about missing your money in an IRA, and especially a Roth IRA. It's more accessible than you might have thought.

Special Help for Low-Income People

If your income is low and you don't think you can scrounge up anything to put into a retirement account, don't give up.

I have a deal for you—a gift from the federal government, or free money...maybe as much as $1,000 if you put $2,000 into an IRA. Lesser amounts are also OK, but if, for example, you come up with $500 for an IRA, the government won't give you $1,000. Maybe you will qualify for $100 in free money.

Depending on your income (after certain deductions) and the amount of money you put into an IRA, the government might give you 50 percent, 20 percent, or 10 percent of the money you have deposited.

Anytime you can get free money, it's worth pursuing, especially when it's for a good cause—your future.

This free money comes to you via the "Saver's Credit." You ask for it when you prepare your tax return at the end of a year. The government wants you to save for retirement, so the IRS will give you a refund if you contribute to either an IRA or your 401(k), 403 (b), or other retirement plan at work.

That, of course, depends on your income. If you are single, your income has to be under $26,000. If married, it must be under $52,000. (And, of course, check as the years go by in case the government raises the limits.) Also keep in mind that you need to be working, not a full-time student.

Often young people qualify when starting their first jobs because their incomes are low. Sometimes they can borrow from a parent or relative, fund an IRA, and get money from the government so that their financial commitment is pretty small.

Even if your income is slightly higher than the limits above, you might be able to squeeze into this deal. Remember, earlier in this chapter I explained that when you put money into an IRA or 401(k) you cut your income down. So conceivably a single person could have an income around $28,000 and contribute $3,000 to a traditional IRA so that their income would be less than the $26,000 cut-off. Then they could get a $300 Saver's Credit refund.

Anyone who can't come up with cash out of their pocket to fund an IRA might also try this technique: Complete your tax return a couple of months before the April 15 deadline, and report on the return that you are opening an IRA.

Perhaps your plan is to put $1,000 into the IRA. You would report a $1,000 IRA on your tax return. But you wouldn't put any money into the account then. Instead, you would wait until the government processed your return, gave you the Saver's Credit, and sent you a refund. After the refund arrived, you could use it to fund the IRA. Just be clear on this: You will face a penalty if you don't actually put the money into the IRA by that year's April 15 tax deadline. So don't forget or change your mind in midstream.

For more information on the Saver's Credit, get IRS Publication 560, Chapter 5 and Form 8880.

Even if you don't qualify for a Saver's Credit, paying your taxes early is a good way to come up with cash for an IRA. If you are entitled to any refund, don't spend it. As soon as the check arrives, put it into the IRA. This way, you will never miss the money and it will turn into thousands.

Help for Affluent People

What if you make too much money for a Roth IRA?

If your income is too high for a Roth IRA, there is still a way to keep Uncle Sam at bay so that your retirement savings will blossom. Just open a taxable IRA. They are called "non-deductible IRAs."

At first this might seem worthless because you don't get a tax break at the outset, and you don't set yourself up immediately to get the beauty of tax-free money when you retire. You do, however, get to keep Uncle Sam from taxing any money you earn in that IRA while it stays invested over the years.

And through a new law that goes into effect in 2010, you are going to have options that people at your income level never had in the past. Starting then, you will be allowed to convert a taxable IRA into a Roth IRA, no matter what your income is.

You will have to pay taxes on the money in the IRA when you make the conversion. After that, however, you will have all the benefits of a Roth IRA. You will never have to pay taxes on the money growing within that Roth IRA, and when you retire, every penny will be yours. If it's worth $20,000, $2 million, or even more, Uncle Sam will never touch a cent in the account or anything you remove during retirement.

There is another alternative, too.

Some employers are offering what is called a Roth 401(k) alongside your regular 401(k) at work. If your employer offers it, there are no income requirements for using the Roth option. So even if you make too much money to open a Roth IRA now, you can use a Roth 401(k) at work. And if you do, all the money you make in it over the years will be yours free and clear when you retire. Uncle Sam won't touch a penny, ever.

That's very different from a regular 401(k). When you remove money from the typical 401(k), you must pay taxes on the money you withdraw.

So if you have a Roth 401(k) at work, this is an attractive choice as long as you can live without the immediate tax break you get with a regular 401(k). You can put up to $15,500 for the 2007 tax year into a Roth 401(k), or $20,500 if you are over 50. But be aware that before making those contributions, you pay your taxes on that income in full. Your tax break comes during your retirement years, not the year you make your contributions.

What Comes First: College or Retirement Saving?

In the best of all worlds, parents would save for their children's college education in addition to retirement.

College is expensive—currently about $80,000 for four years of tuition, room, and board at a public university, and over $160,000 at many private colleges. Few parents can save enough for the full package. If you have limited resources and must choose between funding your retirement and funding college, emphasize funding your 401(k) and IRA over the college account.

There are good reasons why: If you have spent a good chunk of your savings on your children's education, and you are 75, can't work, and have depleted your retirement savings, you can't go to a bank and take out a loan for food, utilities, and medicine.

But for college, students can get relatively large low-interest, federally subsidized student loans to pay part of the cost. So, obviously, loans can help make up for what you can't handle.

That, of course, could leave your children with debts as they begin their working years. The average college student with loans leaves college with about $20,000 in student-loan debt, which is a hefty sum. It's understandable to want to save your children from such a fate, and you should if you can. But keep in mind that college graduates have at least 10 years after school to pay off the low-interest loans. And during their working years, they generally will be in a better position to handle that burden than you will be to handle the life of a 75-year-old without savings.

Beyond that fact of life, however, there are other reasons to place retirement saving first, and college saving second.

If you have retirement saving well under control by the time the children start college, you can cut back on saving somewhat while they are in college and use a larger portion of your paycheck to pay for tuition during those few years.

Also, most students need some financial aid. But based on the quirky college-aid formula that is used to grant aid, families with large college saving funds can erode their opportunities for sizable aid packages. Yet, typically, colleges do not reduce aid based on well-endowed 401(k) plans or IRAs. So making retirement saving a priority can make college more affordable for middle-class families.

Don't take this for granted, however, especially if your income is well over $100,000. Then, you might find financial aid in short supply, and you will need all the savings you can accumulate. You can check now to see how likely your family might be to qualify for financial aid. Try the How Much Aid Can You Expect worksheet at www.smartmoney.com. Find it under Personal Finance and then College Planning.

If You Operate a Small Business

Often, small-business people get buried in the ongoing stress of running their businesses and feeding their families. They promise themselves to think about retirement saving "soon," and then *soon* can come decades later.

Since planning for retirement too frequently comes late in life, alternatives that are available need to be used to the max. So putting $4,000 or $5,000 a year into a Roth IRA is going to help. If you open a Roth for a spouse that will be even better. But you need to go further.

Consider the following options, but keep in mind that for a business, the decisions are more complex than for an individual. You must consider not only your income, but matters such as how many employees you have, what you might be able to contribute in good years and bad years, and the ease of handling a business retirement savings plan.

Talk to a certified public accountant to understand what matches your business and personal needs best. (Details are available in IRS Publication 3998 at www.irs.gov, and the American Institute of Certified Public Accountants provides information at www.aicpa.org. Search for "IRAs and 401(k)s: How to Pick the Best Plan.")

Here's some basic information to get you started.

Individual 401(k) or Solo 401(k)

If you are a sole proprietor and long for the days when you worked for someone else and had a 401(k) at work, long no more. You can treat yourself to the very same thing.

They are relatively new, but tax laws have been allowing self-employed people since 2001 to create what are called Individual 401(k) plans, or Solo 401(k) plans, or Single-Participant 401(k) plans. These can include a Roth 401(k) feature, so you can save money and know that it will be yours free and clear of taxes when you retire.

The problem with starting a 401(k) plan for an independent business-person can be costs and IRA reporting requirements. Administrative fees are relatively high. Yet the benefit can be tremendous, because people can shelter huge amounts of money from taxes. That, of course, lets the person who ignored saving for years build up a nest egg quickly.

Self-employed people can save more than with most alternatives, because they have two ways of stashing away money without paying taxes on it. A person's total contribution can be as much as $45,000 currently, and can ratchet up annually with inflation. There are also "catch-up," or extra contributions, allowed for people over 50—$5,000 a year.

You get the maximum amounts through two different contributions. As a self-employed person, you are like anyone else with a 401(k). You can have money withheld from your paycheck. So in 2007, that would mean as much as $15,500, or $20,500 if you are over 50.

Then you can boost that again, as your own employer. In that role, you are entitled to contribute another 20 percent of your net self-employed income. So if you happen to make $147,500, you could contribute $29,500 to your solo 401(k). With that, along with the $15,500 you took out of your paycheck, you would reach the $45,000 maximum allowed.

Because of the large sums of money, the plans are attracting a wide range of financial companies. Among those offering them are Fidelity Investments, T. Rowe Price, and Charles Schwab. Make sure you compare costs, because they can seriously eat away at the potential for your money to grow. And pay attention to the calendar. To make a contribution this year, you must set up the plan by December 31.

Also, revisit the maximum contribution limits I have provided, because the government adjusts them on the basis of inflation.

SEP-IRA Simplified Employee Pension Plan

If you can't afford to stash away a lot of money and want an easy-to-handle plan that won't require annual filings, there are special IRAs for businesses that may be just the ticket.

With a SEP-IRA, or Simplified Employee Pension, you can contribute up to 25 percent of your business's net income as long as you don't exceed the $45,000 limit.

In lean years for your business, there is no requirement to make any contribution whatsoever. But if you have employees—even part-time employees—you must make contributions for them, too.

You don't have to do much thinking ahead to contribute to a SEP. If you are approaching an April 15 tax filing deadline and realize you'd like to shelter income, you can respond at the last minute.

Having a SEP is similar to having a traditional IRA except that you can contribute a lot more and shelter it from taxes. To get started, simply contact a mutual fund company, brokerage firm, bank, or other financial institution.

SIMPLE IRA (Savings Incentive Match Plan for Employees)

The name of this IRA tells all. It truly is simple to open, is inexpensive, and doesn't burden busy business owners with IRS reporting requirements.

Unlike with the other plans, however, business owners have to pay attention to the calendar. You must open a SIMPLE IRA by October of the year you want to contribute. (Use IRS Form 5304-SIMPLE or Form 5305-SIMPLE. Financial institutions will process most of the paperwork for you.)

And if you have employees who have earned at least $5,000 a year, you must allow them to contribute to a SIMPLE plan and provide matching funds between 1 and 3 percent of compensation.

Although this IRA is indeed simple, the drawback is the limit on contributions. You cannot shelter as much income from the IRS. This year, the limit on contributions is $10,500, although you can go to $13,000 if you are over 50.

The Next Step

Now that you are stashing away good sums of money into IRAs and 401(k)s, the next step is to make sure your savings harness their full growth potential. That means investing well. And the next few chapters will enable you to do it.

6

WHY THE STOCK MARKET ISN'T A ROULETTE WHEEL

Before I help you invest your money, I have to talk about a billboard I saw over a busy Minneapolis freeway a few months ago. It was for a casino. And it was aimed straight for the ordinary American's underbelly with giant-sized words asking passing motorists: "Does your 401(k) need some more Ks?"

The obvious solution posed by the billboard, of course, was to stop worrying about your meager little retirement fund and head for the casino, win, and then fill that 401(k) to the brim. No fuss, no muss...Voilà, instant retirement!

Too bad it doesn't work.

As much as we savor the fantasy of instant riches, we know that if we spend $1 at the casino, we might get $1 worth of fun and maybe even a few bucks, but no Ks for the retirement account. The trouble is that we aren't sure what the alternative might be to build up those Ks by the time we need them.

For most Americans, investing in stocks, bonds, or mutual funds is a treacherous experience that doesn't make sense and doesn't feel much different from tossing some coins into a slot machine or choosing between red and black on the roulette wheel.

At work, employees are given a bizarre-sounding list of mutual funds for their 401(k), and somehow each person is supposed to make sense of the gobbledygook descriptions. Sometimes, the employer brings in an investment expert who yaks for an hour in a foreign language and shows a befuddled audience some pie charts. At the end, the strange mutual fund words are just as confusing. So perplexed workers eye their list of mutual funds the way they would a roulette wheel, selecting one or a few. Then they spin the wheel and hope luck is on their side.

Too often, black turns up when they cast their lot with red. So they lose money and decide to spin again. They ask people, who know as little as they do, how to win. And when they follow the leader and choose black for the next spin, the stars have realigned, and the investor loses yet again. Only this time, retirement is months closer than the last time lady luck failed to pay their 401(k) a visit.

The entire process seems like a mystery—fraught with danger. And so some people joke helplessly that their 401(k) has turned into a 201(k)—in other words, cut in half. And then they naively move on to repeat the same mistakes with their retirement funds that decimated them in the past.

It doesn't have to be this way.

Investing is very different from gambling. And the stakes are high. Blowing $100 at a casino is entertainment. But if a 25-year-old blows $100 in his retirement account, he will be sacrificing about $4,500 by the time he retires. That's right, just a $100 flop is likely to cost $4,500 about 40 years later because of the power of compounding.

And it gets a lot worse if the individual inadvertently makes a habit of blowing $100 each year. If a 25-year-old destroys just $100 a year every year through ill-informed gambling moves in a retirement account, that's potentially a loss of $53,000 from his nest egg. Again, the power of compounding magnifies the impact of a $100 annual mistake repeated over and over for 40 years.

So eyeing your list of 401(k) funds and then throwing up your hands in frustration and deciding to just spin the roulette wheel is just plain idiotic. If I told you today that it wouldn't hurt you to throw $4,500, or $53,000, into the trash over the next 40 years, you'd look at me like I was crazy.

If you really invest money—rather than gambling with your IRA or 401(k)—you will be doing yourself a huge favor. You will give yourself a chance to make every $100 work for you instead of having to dig deeper into your pocket for another $100 to make up for the messes you have already caused.

If you have been investing in your retirement account for some time and have no idea why the money just sits there gathering dust or evaporates shortly after you've poured your cash into the account, you owe it to yourself to understand the harm you are causing yourself so that you can easily fix it.

You don't have to know math. You don't have to know how to pick a stock. You don't have to understand the Federal Reserve's tinkering with interest rates. And you don't have to understand the chatter on TV investing shows.

But you must know one important fundamental point that is yanking at your money at all times when it's in stock mutual funds in your 401(k) or IRA: The stock market, and pieces of the stock market, move in cycles.

Taking Control of Cycles

Those cycles are what have been bashing your savings. And they can be cruel if you don't understand them. They are why your mutual funds shock you and hurt you. They are why the mutual funds you might have loved in the 1990s turned into the mutual funds you hated in the 2000s. They are why your winners turn into losers and why, long after you have dumped a loser in disgust, it suddenly looks like a keeper again. It could be why you figure luck is rarely on your side when it comes to investing.

Cycles are inevitable. You cannot stop them, but you can tame their impact on your money. I'm not going to get technical on you now. But I want you to know that cycles will hurt you much less if you come to expect them the same way you expect the seasons of the year to change. Just as I can assure you that the leaves on trees will change as summer gives way to autumn and then winter, I can guarantee you that no matter what is happening to your money in stock mutual funds now, it, too, is destined to morph as it goes into a new part of a cycle. If you have a winning fund, it will turn into a loser. If you have a loser, it will—at least—become more of a winner later. The perplexing question for you will be, how much later?

Often it takes so long for cycles to change that people figure it will never happen. When life is good, when you are making money, it seems like it will continue forever. That's where people make mistakes and lose money ignorantly in the changing cycles.

In the cycles, the stock market as a whole, or certain types of stocks or mutual funds, look boring or even downright scary for a while. Then, after some time has passed, the once-ugly investments start looking better and better. They become increasingly popular with investors, eventually seeming like the hottest, smartest investment anyone could buy. This is usually when ordinary investors pile in, thinking the hot investments are a no-brainer that will make people rich forever.

But with more time, the entire group of hot stocks cools off—maybe because business conditions change or maybe because smart investors decide the stocks became so expensive they are no longer a good deal. The shrewd pros look for a better investment—something cheaper, with more chance to take off in the next phase of the cycle. So, they sell the once-hot investments, and suddenly the ordinary guy is holding onto a stock mutual fund wondering what in the world happened to it. His beautiful investment of yesterday has turned into an ugly money loser and is turning uglier with each passing day—seemingly for no good reason.

Because there are about 40 different varieties of mutual funds, each type will behave differently during specific times in each cycle. Funds are designed that way on purpose so that investors can buy a variety and be prepared for anything. Yet, given the funds you have selected, at any moment in time you might feel brilliant or like a supreme idiot. If you have a mixture of funds, you will always like one more than the other, and as the cycle changes, your favorites will always be alternating.

The 1990s: From Stock Lovefest to Disaster

So let me illustrate what I mean by cycles. I want to take you back to the end of the 1990s, one of the most vivid examples of a dramatic change in cycles since the Great Depression.

The end of the 1990s was a period of euphoria for the ordinary investor. People could throw a few bucks into a 401(k) or an IRA and make mounds of money almost overnight. Peering into a 401(k) account was pure joy. Many Americans made a hobby of treating themselves to the pleasure at their computers every day. Most didn't realize it at the time, but they were simply riding a cycle up—a cycle that was bound to move from hot to cold, destroying trillions of dollars in the process.

In polls, individual investors naively said they thought the good times would last. They were expecting to keep making 20 percent returns on their money every year, even though Wall Street's old-timers knew that the 1990s were extraordinary and 10 percent returns in the stock market are the average. Even some investing professionals—who should have known better—were equally mesmerized by the moment, leading clients to destruction. They thought the economy and stocks were in a new era—where old rules about cycles no longer would apply.

Investing magazines had covers posing the question "Are You Rich Yet?" CNBC's constant stock market news was on TVs everywhere—from golf courses to Burger Kings. Giddy with their new-found wealth, people borrowed money on their homes so that they could invest in the most dangerous stocks. Many who had never analyzed a stock in their life quit their jobs to trade stocks at home computers. The mood was like the "Roaring Twenties" all over again—you couldn't lose in the stock market.

At the time, John Brennan, the chairman of a mutual fund company named Vanguard, discovered how far the mania had gone. He stopped in a Burger King one night after jogging, and a senior citizen recognized him from some stock market comments he'd made on TV. The man was almost trembling with excitement about the stock market and told Brennan that he, his wife, and two friends went to the Burger King every night to watch the stock market news because they didn't have cable in their homes. And the man asked Brennan to autograph his Burger King coffee cup.

That's when Brennan was sure investors had gone crazy over the stock market, and a cruel downturn was sure to come.

Readers of my column would call me at my newspaper office to giggle about the stocks they'd bought that doubled or tripled in value in a few weeks. Ordinary people who told me they once begrudged the rich were calling me to get information about tax shelters because they'd made so much money.

People who knew nothing about picking stocks felt like geniuses when they selected stocks like Cisco—even though they had no idea what technological gizmos these companies produced or what would make customers want to buy them. They didn't realize until it was too late that they'd paid about 10 times more for many technology stocks than they should have, and that ultimately set them up to lose almost everything when the game ended. Technology stocks as a group crashed about 70 percent, and many beloved Internet companies went bankrupt—leaving stocks worthless.

But before the crash, there was one investing game in town—buy either individual technology company stocks or mutual funds that super-sized their exposure to technology stocks. Anyone who had those investments won and felt like smart investors—that is, until summer turned into autumn and ultimately a two-year piercing-cold winter took hold.

Everyone Played the Game

You may not have realized any of this in the late 1990s. You may not have even imagined that you were a part of it—riding a cycle, speculating on insanely priced technology stocks. But if you had money in a 401(k), an IRA, or any mutual funds and liked the way they were behaving, you were probably part of the mania. Unbeknown to you, the money you were making was coming from gigantic bets on technology stocks by the people who were running your mutual funds.

Amid such merriment, being cautious was the ultimate sin for a mutual fund manager. Individual investors had no patience for mutual funds that were climbing 10 percent a year while their workmate or neighbor was making 25 or 50 percent, or even more, in funds brimming with technology stocks. In 1999, the funds that invested in only technology stocks climbed an average of 134 percent—probably a once-in-a-lifetime occurrence that should have warned investors that trouble was on its way, that the cycle would have to change.

Some of the nation's most renowned professional investors, who shunned technology stocks and respected the precepts of good investing (in other words, buy only cheap stocks) paid a dear price: Their clients resented cautious investments and abandoned the thoughtful professionals so that they could give their money instead to flashy, young upstarts caught up in the tech craze.

At the time, long-time investment pro Al Harrison, of Alliance Capital, spoke at a luncheon of other investment professionals and complained that young investment managers in his office were admonishing him for his cautious approach to hot stocks, saying: "Get with it, granddad." A few years later, his fund got with it too much, getting almost decimated with Enron stock.

In the midst of the hot cycle, individuals who bought anything other than technology felt like jerks. Investments in companies that made machines, produced oil, or provided home mortgages—or virtually anything that wasn't technology—couldn't measure up. They were the ignored orphans of the stock market. Funds that invested in gold and real estate went out of business because investors wanted nothing to do with them; then five years later, as the cycle changed, investors couldn't get enough gold or real estate.

A bond, too, was nothing but a four-letter word. After all, why would people buy such a lethargic safe investment when they could double or triple their money overnight with hot technology stocks and mutual funds full of tech?

Everyone was caught up in the mania—novices and professionals alike. I went to an investors' conference for pension fund managers back then, and the presentation on bonds drew fewer than 20 people into a giant hotel ballroom. The sessions on technology stocks were standing-room-only in rooms holding hundreds.

The ordinary guy unknowingly bought all he could through funds operated by companies like Janus—thinking the managers were brilliant. But Janus funds were simply riding a hot cycle for technology stocks. In 1999, the Janus Twenty grew investors' money about 65 percent by sinking large sums into technology stocks. During the next three years, investors didn't know what hit them as they lost everything they'd made, and then some. Before that happened, readers got angry at me when I warned them against buying too many technology stocks and mutual funds like Janus that were super-sizing exposure to those stocks. I will never forget one who called me and stated angrily: "You are as stupid as Warren Buffett."

Obviously, I am no Warren Buffett—one of the most renowned investors of our time. But I knew something that every ordinary investor must know—that cycles happen, moving up and down, or from hot to cold. So technology stocks couldn't keep giving investors returns of over 100 percent a year.

The Game's Up

Then it happened. The cycle started to turn in March 2000, when astute investors decided the game was up. They came to the realization that they had paid way too much for technology stocks, and the stock prices wouldn't keep going higher every day. These savvy investors started dumping the stocks. That made stock prices nose-dive. The little guy didn't know what was happening and held on waiting for a return of the good ol' days. But while his 401(k) was slipping lower every day, many of the pros weren't riding it out with the ordinary little guy. They were selling technology stocks before they lost fortunes and buying cheap stocks in many industries that had long been ignored during the tech craze.

The market was being set up for a new cycle—a healing phase that, at first, would hurt many who clung to the past: The cheap nontechnology stocks had become cheap because no one wanted them when technology investing was driving the cycle. Yet sharp professional investors who snapped up all the solid stocks people had been ignoring knew that with time the cycle would change and their bargain-hunting would pay off.

It took longer than many expected, but eventually the cycle changed—just as it always does. The bargain stocks that no one had wanted amid the technology craze just a couple of years earlier soared in price, and investors who had them in their retirement accounts made money almost overnight. Waste Management, for example, a company that deals with collecting garbage, was unpopular with investors as it dealt with lawsuits over its accounting in the late 1990s. As the cycle changed, Waste Management stock shot up 42 percent in a few months. And Nabisco, another stock people ignored in the technology craze, climbed 183 percent as the cycle changed.

Meanwhile, investors who loved Amazon—the Internet bookstore—in the hot technology stock cycle of the late 1990s lost 67 percent in just a few months in 2000 as the cycle turned cold. Investors who put $10,000 into technology mutual funds like the Monument Digital Technology fund at the beginning of 1999 gleefully watched their money turn into $37,300 that year and then gasped when they checked their account in September 2001 and found only $4,888 remaining.

If, in 2000, you were lucky enough to have a mutual fund in your 401(k) that held stocks like Nabisco, Philip Morris, and Waste Management, you would have been feeling pretty good after technology stocks started blowing up. Mutual funds with those bargain-priced stocks in them soared over 25 percent. But if you were like the ordinary investor, you probably didn't know what hit you. All of a sudden, your hot funds of the late 1990s mysteriously turned into losers—many destroying 50 percent or more of investors' money.

Those holding onto the past—expecting the technology cycle to continue—were being slaughtered. Internet companies went bankrupt. Retirement funds bled cash. People already in retirement had to go back to work because savings were cut in half. The overall stock market crashed because, during the mania, it had become heavily dependent on technology stocks.

Taming the Herd

All this happened because of cycles. Several economic factors cause the stock market to go from hot to cold and cold to hot over time. But simply put, there is a human factor that plays a major role in driving cycles: Investors tend to run in herds.

Both professionals who should know better and the common investor pile into certain types of stocks that look hot. For a while, popularity alone makes stocks rise. And the managers who bought the hot stocks for mutual funds look brilliant, when all they are doing is running with the herd. Then, at a certain point, reality catches up with people.

Stock prices ultimately are based on more than popularity: Profits are key, and if smart investors realize profits aren't going to measure up to the prices people paid for a stock, they dump the stock, the stock price falls, and people lose money.

Or, to say it another way: When investors look out from the herd on some level-headed day and see that the herd is crazed and corporate profits can't possibly live up to investors' expectations, the herd panics and starts stampeding to dump stocks.

The old cycle cools, and ordinary investors get hurt. They hold onto their old stocks and mutual funds waiting for them to come back. As months pass, the statements from their 401(k) and IRA look uglier and uglier. And finally the little guy says: " I've got to stop the hemorrhaging, or I'll have no retirement left."

He sells the ugliest investments at their darkest hour and then puts the money into something else. The trouble is that if he turns to another investment that looks hot—perhaps the mutual fund in his 401(k) list that has made the most money in the past year—he is likely close to the top of a new cycle.

Unknowingly, he is positioning his money to get clobbered again—as soon as the cycle for that new mutual fund cools. And when that ordinary investor's 401(k) bleeds cash, the poor guy chalks the entire fiasco up to bad luck. The trouble is, it's not luck at all—it's being naive about cycles. It's about forgetting the oft-repeated precept of investing: "Buy low; sell high."

It's managing a 401(k) like playing the roulette wheel, but there's a better way.

What to Expect from the Stock Market

With the realization that cycles occur in the market, you may come to the conclusion that you will stay out of harm's way by avoiding stocks or any mutual fund that holds stocks.

I would not suggest that approach for anyone with years to go before retirement. In fact, most financial advisers think that even people late in retirement should have a small portion of their savings in the stock market. Notice I said "small." The amount of money you hold in stocks is key, which I will explain in Chapter 11, "Do This."

Perhaps if you were a multimillionaire, you could stay out of the stock market throughout your life and be fine. You could put all your savings into ultrasafe government bonds and earn 5 percent on your money, and, because you would have so much money in the first place, a tiny "return"—or earnings—on that money might be adequate to provide a decent lifestyle for all the days of your life.

But most Americans can't afford to rely exclusively on ultrasafe investments like bonds or CDs. They need to have a sizable portion of their retirement savings invested in the stock market to earn enough to live on later in retirement.

During the past 80 years, the stock market has been much more benevolent to investors than the bond market. Despite horrible losses in the market at times, investors have averaged a 10.4 percent annual return in stocks versus just 5.5 percent in safe U.S. government bonds, according to Ibbotson Associates, a stock market research firm. That's because the good times outweigh the bad in the stock market as the years go by.

Take a look at it in money: A person who put $1 into the stock market in 1925 would have had $2,657.56 80 years later at the end of 2005, according to Ibbotson Associates. But if that person had put the same $1 into long-term, safe U.S. government bonds for the same 80 years, he would have only $70.85 (see Figure 6.1).

Making about $2,658 with a $1 investment may seem shocking to you if you recall some of the terrifying times in the stock market. For example, Ibbotson's numbers include the Great Depression in the 1930s, a period when an investor would have lost 86 percent of the money invested in the stock market. It also includes an awful period in 1973–1974, when stocks fell 48 percent. Most recently, there was the terrifying period between 2000 and 2002, when common folks quaked as their stock market investments fell 49 percent amid an end to the technology stock craze, terrorist attacks, a recession, scandals in corporations like Enron and WorldCom, and preparations for war in Iraq.

Figure 6.1

What a dollar became invested over 80 years, end of 1925 to end of 2005.

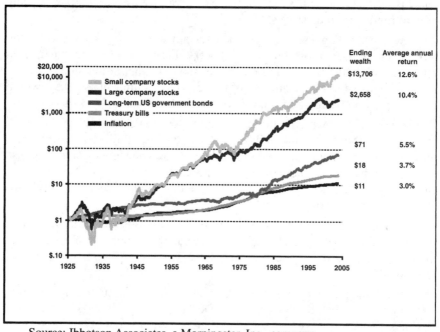

Source: Ibbotson Associates, a Morningstar, Inc., company

Despite all those truly horrifying cycles, $1 in 1925 still turned into about $2,658. And, although no one can predict exactly what stocks will do in the future, analysts see no reason why the U.S. stock market shouldn't continue to rise in the future, because it is based on a solid growing U.S. economy. Simply put, when you invest in the overall stock market through the types of funds I describe in the chapters ahead, you are investing in the overall U.S. economy.

Or as one investment manager once said to me: "The economy goes through recessions, sometimes individual companies go bankrupt; but if a person contemplates his future and presumes that he, his friends, neighbors, and his family are likely to have jobs, and that they will be able to continue shopping at supermarkets and shopping malls, that shows an inherent belief in the U.S. economy. That belief should also foster confidence in the stock market's ability to grow." And then he added, "If the person doesn't think anyone is going to have a job, and the world as we know it is going to come to an end, his problems are worse than worrying about the stock market....So who cares?"

Stocks Provide Risks and Rewards

I don't mean to make light of the possibility of losing money in the stock market. The threat—as many investors learned in 2000 through 2002—is real. But typically the threat occurs when people invest money for short periods of time, panic when conditions turn ugly, don't realize that with time the cycle will turn, and foolishly withdraw their money.

For example, if a person had had $100,000 in stock funds in a 401(k) in March 2000 and put no new money into the account after that, by September 2002 he might have been horrified to see he only had about $51,000 left. The stock market crash would have destroyed $49,000 he once thought was his to keep. But the destruction at that point was on paper, based on a moment in time, and recorded in the records he received monthly from the firm doing the accounting for his 401(k).

He would have made the destruction real and lasting if, at that dark hour for the stock market, he awoke in a sweat one night and said to himself, "I can't take this any longer...pretty soon I'll have nothing left for retirement." If he moved everything the next day to a very safe money market fund in his 401(k), he would have felt safe, but actually would have positioned himself for real harm. Over the next couple of years, his money would have earned only about 2 percent. At that rate, it would take him about 36 years to double his money. And he would have missed a dramatic recovery in the stock market as stocks went into a new part of the cycle.

From the worst point on October 9, 2002, to September 2006, the stock market gained about 76 percent. That's a healing number, especially compared to maybe an optimistic 5 percent gain in a money market fund—or even 5 percent in a CD (certificate of deposit).

So the investor who panicked and fled the stock market at the worst hour locked in his 49 percent loss at the low point of the cycle and won't regain what he lost for years. The investor who was scared but clenched his teeth and held onto the mixture of reliable mutual funds I will describe in the next chapters has gained back everything lost and then some. If he kept adding money during the scary period, his money grew throughout the upward trend in the cycle, and he's well beyond where he was before his friends fled in a panic.

Of course, it's always easier to say what you should have done with your money in retrospect. At the truly dark hour for the stock market in September 2002, no one knew that the cycle was going to turn better soon. During every low point in the market, there is never a clear signal that the worst has occurred and investors will stop losing money and start making it again.

So what's a person to do?

Professionals use history as their guide. They show clients the way stocks have climbed over many years and try to prevent nervous investors from fleeing solid stock mutual funds. History doesn't provide guarantees, but it has shown repeatedly that changing cycles always repair the damage that has occurred if investors give the market enough time to move back into an up cycle. Because the U.S. economy continues to grow, there are rough periods when businesses and investors lose money, but the long-term trend is for the stock market to continually recover from downturns and keep climbing (see Table 6.1 for how long bear markets—or severe market downturns—have lasted and how the market recovered).

Table 6.1
Bear Markets throughout History

		Bear Market Statistics		Performance from Bear Market Low		
	Date of Market Trough	Peak to Trough Performance	Duration of Bear Market	Performance 1 Year Later	Cumulative Performance 2 Years Later	Cumulative Performance 3 Years Later
1	Nov-9-1903	–46%	29 months	59%	93%	122%
2	Nov-15-1907	–49%	22 months	66%	87%	60% **
3	Sep-25-1911	–27%	22 months	28%	13% *	–2% **
4	Jul-30-1914	–24%	22 months	44%	70%	76%
5	Dec-19-1917	–40%	13 months	25%	59%	5% **

		Bear Market Statistics		Performance from Bear Market Low		
	Date of Market Trough	Peak to Trough Performance	Duration of Bear Market	Performance 1 Year Later	Cumulative Performance 2 Years Later	Cumulative Performance 3 Years Later
6	Aug-24-1921	–47%	21.5 months	56%	44% *	62%
7	Jul-8-1932	–86%	34 months	172%	124%*	141%
8	Mar-14-1935	–34%	20 months	81%	127%	34% **
9	Mar-31-1938	–54%	12.5 months	29%	44%	17% **
10	Apr-28-1942	–46%	41.5 months	54%	59%	98%
11	Jun-13-1949	–30%	36.5 months	42%	59%	80%
12	Oct-22-1957	–22%	14.5 months	31%	44%	37% **
13	Jun-26-1962	–28%	6.5 months	33%	56%	59%
14	Oct-7-1966	–22%	8 months	33%	42%	27% **
15	May-26-1970	–36%	18 months	44%	60%	56% **
16	Oct-3-1974	–48%	20.5 months	38%	67%	55% **
17	Mar-6-1978	–19%	17.5 months	13%	25%	49%
18	Aug-12-1982	–27%	20.5 months	58%	62%	83%
19	Dec-4-1987	–34%	3.5 months	21%	57%	46% **
20	Oct-11-1990	–20%	3 months	29%	36%	56%
21	Aug-31-1998	–19%	1.5 months	38%	59%	18% **
22	Oct-9-2002	–49%	30.5 months	34%	44%	54%
Average		**–37%**	**19 months**	**47%**	**60%**	**56%**
Median		**–34%**	**20 months**	**38%**	**59%**	**55%**

* Notes loss in second year of recovery   ** Notes loss in third year of recovery

Source: Adapted from the Leuthold Group data

Bear Markets Maul Investors

During bear markets—or periods when the market drops at least 20 percent —investors get nervous while the bear mauls their savings. In the midst of the downturns, people never know when healing will occur or when they might get back what they've lost.

Yet The Leuthold Group found that during the 20 different bear markets that have happened since 1900, the median time it took for investors to recover the money they lost was two years and three months. In half the downturns, they had to wait longer.

Still, even after the worst periods in market history, investors did recover. That's what you must consider as an investor, or you will be doing yourself a disservice.

Since the Great Depression, when the stock market fell about 80 percent, the next worst period was 1973–1974. Still, after about 7½ years, the stock market recovered completely from a 48 percent loss in the down cycle, and investors went on to ride the cycle to great profits. Over the next 20 years, they would average about a 16 percent annual return in the market.

Novices Choosing Stocks Are Gamblers

Of course, the pain in bear markets is worse if investors select certain stocks or mutual funds. If, for example, in the early 1970s you had put all your retirement savings into 50 of the most beloved stocks of the day—including Avon, Xerox, and Polaroid—you would have crashed so hard it would have taken you 10½ years to recover your money. And the pain would have been particularly difficult to stomach given the assumptions investors had made just before they took a thrashing.

Back in the early 1970s, when investors were loading up on those so-called "Nifty Fifty stocks" like Avon, there was an assumption that the stocks were so strong investors couldn't miss on them. They were supposed to be the stocks people could buy at any price and make money for the rest of their lives.

Those promises, like all hype in the market over the years, however, turned out to be false. Polaroid, for example, fell 91 percent after the herd awoke to reality, and the stock price never went back to what investors had paid for it.

Others, such as Coca Cola—which fell 70 percent then—regained strength and went on to delight investors who held on.

This should show you why you should not try to buy individual stocks unless you can, and will, examine a company's financial records deeply. The stocks that fell hardest were those that were overly expensive. Investors were sucked into the hype, falling for hot tips and promises that the stocks were a sure thing. Whenever investors grab for the enticing story—instead of the laborious number crunching that stock picking takes—it's like going to the roulette wheel and putting your money on red. Luck may be on your side, but you will need luck. You are not investing. You are gambling.

Likewise, during the 2000s, many of the dream Internet stocks of the early part of the decade are gone. The companies were never solid investments even though the technology and ideas were creative and exciting. The companies went bankrupt, and mutual funds that invested in only technology stocks are a long way from recovering. They lost 70 to 90 percent initially, and six years later they were still far under water. A $10,000 investment in a technology fund in February 2000 was worth only $3,500 in March 2006, according to Lipper, a mutual fund tracking firm.

Both the 2000s and the 1970s deliver a harsh but important lesson for novice investors: A company may be popular with investors, and its product may be enchanting, but that doesn't mean the company will survive or that the current stock price is a fair one. And if investors awaken one day and discover that the price is too high, you will get crushed if you hold on as the herd stampedes.

Getting excited about a product or a technology is not enough to carry a stock. The management in that company must also know how to raise enough money, produce a product, position it so that people will buy it, compete effectively against the competition, and survive recessions. Ordinary people who can't or won't analyze corporate financial statements are going to get hurt if they buy stocks based on a tip or a gut feeling.

But you don't have to put yourself in this position. If you buy solid mutual funds thoughtfully, you won't need to do math, and you will insulate yourself somewhat from the brutality of cycles. I will tell you how you can do this very simply in the following chapters. But first, a quick note about time.

Making Money Takes Time

Because cycles arrive unexpectedly in the stock market, you can never put money into any stock investment—whether it's an individual stock or a mutual fund—and assume you will make money in the next months or even couple of years.

Generally, there is a rule of thumb about the stock market: Don't put any money that you will need within five years into the market. The timing is based on the bear market research I mentioned previously. We know cycles can and will happen, but if you look at history, investors who have been willing to sit tight and weather the downturns have generally come out fine if they could give it at least five years. People willing to stay with their investments for many years beyond that have done exceedingly well.

So if you are saving money for a down payment on a house, you wouldn't put any of that money into the stock market if you plan to buy a house within a couple of years. If your child is going to start college in three years, you wouldn't keep money for the first two years of college in stock mutual funds.

On the other hand, if you are three years away from retirement, you can have some money in the stock market because you won't need all of it the first year. On the day you retire, you will still be investing money for 20 or 30 more years, so you can afford to have perhaps 50 or 60 percent of your money in the stock market at first and then cut it back toward 20 or 30 percent as the years go by. (This is something to discuss with a reputable certified financial planner when you are about 5 to 10 years from retirement.)

For now, I just want you to recognize the risk of the stock market but not to fear it when handled wisely. Rushing into the stock market with money you will need soon is foolish. Buying an individual stock on a tip is idiotic. But avoiding the full stock market is equally foolish when you have savings that must grow during the next 10, 20, 30, or 40 years.

History, again, helps to lay the groundwork for thinking. Although the chances of losing money in the stock market are great over a 1-year period or even a 5-year period, when you move to a 10-year period, investors have lost money only once—between 1929 and 1938, which was the Depression. Investors have never lost money over 15 years or longer, according to Ibbotson research.

When thinking about risks, remember that stocks are definitely dangerous if you rely too heavily on them—or cut yourself short on time. You take on tremendous risks if you try to pick them yourself by running with the herd instead of doing serious research on their profit potential.

But there is another risk that is critically important when saving for retirement: the risk of running out of money when you are 70 or 80 and cannot go back to work. So to prevent that risk, you must respect the stock market and use it to your advantage in the simple and effective ways I will now explain.

7

What's a Mutual Fund?

Now that you are aware that cycles in the market will play havoc with your money, you are ready to select mutual funds with your eyes open. Instead of making foolish mistakes that will cripple your savings, you will be able to select certain mutual funds so that they insulate you from cycles, while giving you a chance to make money whenever and wherever conditions are bestowing wealth.

If you are like many people with a 401(k) plan, you can't tell one mutual fund from another. Don't feel badly about this. You are in good company.

A few years ago, two well-known professors, Shlomo Benartzi and Richard Thaler, set out to see how people picked mutual funds in their 401(k) plans. They gave a list of funds to employees at the University of California, and their mutual fund choices were abysmal. The employees, like most Americans, didn't have the slightest idea what they were doing with mutual funds. They didn't understand what the names of the funds were telling them, so they simply chose every single fund they were offered even though some of the funds should have been ignored.

You may do that, too, and if so, you are probably over-exposing yourself to the cruelty of cycles and potentially slicing hundreds of thousands of dollars from your future retirement money.

Other mistakes are also common. Typically, when novice investors are losing money in their mutual funds, or making less money than their friends are making with other mutual funds, they surmise that they've selected a dud and have blown it as an investor.

Neither, however, may be true. You may have a very fine mutual fund that is losing money, or you could be getting richer by the day with a fund that is actually lousy. I know this is counter-intuitive, because if something looks good, we generally assume that it is good. In investing, the opposite often is true.

Your particular fund—through no fault of its own—may simply be temporarily positioned at the top or bottom of a cycle. When that cycle turns, your loser is probably going to seem like a phenomenal choice. Instead of destroying your money, it will start making money. Meanwhile, the fund you cherish because it is making you so much money today eventually could look like garbage. Then months—or even a couple years later—your garbage fund could turn sweet again, and your favorite fund could sour.

Your Fund Is Designed for a Purpose

The reason sweet funds often turn into temporary losers is simple: Each mutual fund is constructed for a unique purpose, and therefore is filled with stocks or bonds that are intended—by design—to be strong in certain cycles and weaker in others. This is no small matter. If you don't know this, you will give some mutual funds more credit than they are due and shun some that deserve to be in your IRA or 401(k) portfolio.

There are about a dozen basic designs, and none is inherently good or bad. Each is simply unique.

Think of a bakery. It sells baked goods, but there is a wide variety intended for different purposes. You can buy muffins, bread, and cake. None of the three is innately good or bad. They are simply different—each perhaps baked to perfection based on a unique recipe. Still, you probably don't want the cake for breakfast, and that doesn't mean the baker flopped when baking the cake. Based on where you are in the day's cycle, the muffin might be best in the morning, the bread at lunch, and the cake after supper.

Just as you will want bread, muffins, and cake depending on where you are in the cycle of the day, you will want a unique mutual fund for each point in the stock market's cycle.

And just as you might have all three baked goods in your freezer, awaiting the point in the day when you will want them, you also do that with a variety of mutual funds. You keep the variety on hand in your IRA or 401(k) at all times—ready for the parts of the cycle when each will perform best.

Unfortunately, people get tripped up in this process. It seems complex, even though it isn't. So, in effect, if they see that everyone wants cake, they make the mistake of buying only cake—for example, mutual funds filled to the brim with technology stocks in the 1990s. But loading up on cake—or a mutual fund that is intended to be the dessert after the main meal—is a disaster for investors.

Want to know whether you inadvertently have been loading up on cake? If you were happy at the end of the 1990s with your 401(k) mutual funds and then hated them between 2000 and 2002, you probably were guilty. You probably were unintentionally eating too much cake at the end of the 1990s, and that made your money sick in 2000.

But it doesn't have to be this way. The strange words you see on your mutual funds are intended to help you understand whether they should be a staple like bread, or whether they are dessert—intended to be consumed in dessert-size portions.

Soon, you will be able to look at a list of mutual funds and know at a glance what each fund is intended to do for you in various cycles. When you reach that point, you will never feel befuddled again as you look over names on a 401(k) list, or a financial adviser starts chattering to you in a seemingly foreign language.

All you need is a little vocabulary. The first step is to understand what your mutual fund manager does to try to make your money grow.

What Happens in a Mutual Fund?

When you select a mutual fund in a 401(k), an IRA, or any other account, you—along with hundreds of other people—are turning your money over to an expert. You know you don't have the expertise to examine more than 6,000 different stocks that make up the stock market. You have no idea how to determine which stocks have the potential to make you money or lose money. Nor can you examine the thousands of bonds available in the market. You'd probably much rather devote your free time to your family, friends, or fun than analyze whether a stock or bond might be a good investment.

So you turn your money over to a professional, called a "fund manager." With that, you are telling him or her to spend every day trying to figure out which stocks or bonds will make you as much money as possible. Each day, the manager will watch the economy and different businesses.

If he or she works for a so-called "equity" mutual fund, the manager will pick many stocks for your fund—possibly 100 or more. The word "equity" simply means "stocks." So every day your mutual fund manager will hunt for the best stocks for you and all the other investors in your fund. Managers will analyze each business they think will make you money and determine whether both business conditions and stock market conditions are in place to stimulate a stock price higher and boost the value of your mutual fund investment. When the individual stocks in your fund are going up in price, your share of that mutual fund will also go up in value, and you will be making money.

If your fund manager is doing a good job, your tiny savings in the mutual fund should start looking like thousands—not in a month, maybe not in a year, but after a few years.

To analyze a particular stock, the fund manager will try to figure out whether the company is producing products well, whether the products are keeping up with the competition, whether new competitors are likely to take customers away, whether the employees are creative about designing new products that customers will want, whether the sales force sells well, whether managers handle money effectively, and whether the company has the money to fulfill its innovative plans and make profits grow.

The Key: Company Profits

Analyzing a company's profit potential is the name of the game. And it's not easy to do. Superficial guesses—the types that ordinary investors make when they try to pick individual stocks on their own—don't work.

Typically, when a company's profits grow—especially if profits grow more than investors thought they would—the company's stock price goes up. So if you own the stock of a surprisingly profitable company, or if your mutual fund owns that stock for you, you make money on it.

When a fund manager spots a company with potential, he may buy the stock, or he may not. First, managers examine the stock price, and compare it to the profits they think the company will generate. Managers will want to make sure they don't pay too much for the stock, and the only way to know will be to scrutinize the company's profit potential.

If the manager thinks the company is going to delight investors with more profits than anyone expected, that's a good sign investors will make

money, and the manager may buy the stock. If the manager spots a threat—
perhaps a new competitor for that company—he or she may not buy the stock
even though it's been a tremendous success in the past. If the manager thinks
a company might have trouble borrowing money at a low interest rate, he or
she might not buy the stock because the company could have difficulty making or selling products if it doesn't have enough cheap cash. The analysis
goes on and on.

Meanwhile, other investors are eyeing the same stock. If many of them
are excited about the company's growing business at the same time, they will
be snapping up the stock, and the stock price consequently will soar. Under
those conditions, your fund manager might decide the stock price is too high,
and he or she won't buy it.

High Stock Prices Can Be Warning Signs

This is often a shocking revelation to novice investors. Why not go for it, if
the stock price is soaring? The manager's decision, however, isn't based
solely on the quality of the company or the delicious gains people have made
on the stock recently. The manager might think it's a phenomenal company
with great products and smart managers, but when stock prices get too high,
stocks are vulnerable. High-priced stocks fall hard—hurting investors—with
the slightest misstep. Managers know that a sudden unexpected turn in the
economy could change the outlook for a hot company, reversing the cycle
that was carrying the stock higher and higher.

So instead of buying a stock at an extremely high price, a cautious fund
manager might determine that he or she would like to own the promising
stock for you, but at a lower price. If you make a point of shopping for
clothes only when they are on sale, you understand this concept completely.
Perhaps you have had your eye on a sweater, but it's expensive. So you wait
to buy it, knowing that the store will offer a sale in a couple of weeks in
which everything is marked down 25 or 30 percent. Then you will buy—you
will get the same sweater you always wanted, but at a more reasonable price.

As you walk out of the store, you will commend yourself for finding
such a "good value." In the mutual fund world, the funds that are conscientious about shopping for "good values" actually alert you to that discipline
sometimes through their names. (I'll tell you how to spot these so-called
"value funds" in Chapter 9, "Know Your Mutual Fund Manager's Job.")

While fund managers are always busy looking for deals—or stocks that
appear to be marked down inappropriately—shopping for them is slightly
different from shopping in a store. That's because the fund manager doesn't
know when the stock will go on sale. It might take months or years.

For an extreme example, consider the terrorist attacks of 2001. After the attacks, investors were fleeing stocks—especially hotel stocks—as Americans stopped traveling. The stock prices were plunging below bargain-basement levels. That's when Oakmark mutual fund manager Bill Nygren loaded up on Starwood Hotel (Sheraton and Westin) stock. He told me then that he couldn't imagine Americans giving up on vacations or one-on-one business meetings with clients forever. As fears eased and people traveled again, the stock became a winner—climbing about 55 percent in 2003 and 65 percent in 2004.

Even when the price of a stock comes down and fund managers consider buying it, they still don't leap immediately. They reexamine the company to make sure that while they were waiting for a good price, the company didn't slip in some way that might stifle profits in the future. Stock prices can fall for many reasons—at times because a company is making mistakes, but at other times it could be something less troublesome, like a temporary down-turn in the economy. For example, stores may see their sales slow down during recessions, but powerful companies like Wal-Mart or Home Depot usually come back to life when the short-term economic pressures subside.

There are no assurances, however. To make sure there isn't a problem hidden in the company, when an attractive stock dips in price, the fund manager will go back to his or her original analysis and reexamine how the company produces and sells its products. The manager will want to know what profits to expect so that he can determine whether the current stock price is a good deal. It doesn't matter what stock price existed in the past or what the profits were like in the past. It doesn't matter that people got rich on the stock last year or during the last ten years. Only one thing matters for the stock's future: what profits the company will generate in the future.

Novice investors who buy stocks themselves often make a major mistake about this: They look at a stock price of $20 and say to themselves, "It's a great deal because people used to buy that stock at $50." But that's flawed thinking. Stocks have no memory. Yesterday's price will never be repeated again unless the company becomes more profitable than investors are anticipating.

Want an example? In the preceding chapter, I mentioned Polaroid, a high-flying stock in the 1970s—investors loved it with the same intensity some had for Amazon in the 1990s or Google recently. Analysts told investors to pay higher and higher prices for Polaroid because it would never go down and dis-appoint them. But you know now that camera products have changed dramat-ically since the 1970s. Polaroid's stock hit a high in the early 1970s, crashed, and never got back to the price that gullible investors paid for it.

When your fund manager looks at a stock, he or she will focus on the out-look for profits at that company for the next quarter, the next year, and so on.

Fund Managers Babysit Stocks

If everything checks out and the manager thinks the company is on the road to being more profitable, he or she will buy the stock. Then, the manager will watch that stock every day—looking for warning signs that the business might be losing its footing. Amid any concerns, the manager will try to sell the stock before it plummets. If the manager fails to pick up on problems early, the stock could fall hard, and you could lose some money.

Besides watching for problems, managers will be equally vigilant about the winners in the fund—knowing that stocks will climb only so far. When managers think that point is nearing, they often will sell the stock and, with that money, try to buy another stock that is cheaper, and consequently more promising for the future.

Before managers buy a new stock, they will look at a list of stocks they've been keeping and try to identify a favorite company that temporarily has a cheap stock price compared to the profits they expect the company to generate in the future.

In other words, they will try to "buy low and sell high"—a comment you may have heard about buying stocks. It's the key precept of good stock investing, and the most often abused because people are emotional. Instead of buying a cheap stock that will soar over time, people get sucked into the excitement and hype over the hot stocks of the moment. They buy expensive stocks just as the cycle for that stock is about to peak and smart fund managers are getting ready to dump them.

What's in Your Fund?

Many mutual funds contain 100 to 500 different stocks. So when you buy a share in your mutual fund with your 401(k) or IRA money, you will end up owning a tiny, tiny piece of many companies. For example, if your mutual fund invests in Wal-Mart stock, you will own a teeny piece of all the Wal-Mart discount stores. If your fund invests in General Electric, you will own a miniscule piece of the company that makes everything from stoves to NBC TV news. If your fund owns McDonald's stock, you will own a smidgen of the restaurants, and you will hope that people continue to want to eat hamburgers or that McDonald's will figure out how to attract customers with other foods.

If, on any particular day, investors think consumers are squeamish about hamburgers or McDonald's has lost the knack for making as much money as it has in the past, the stock price will fall, and your mutual fund will lose money on that stock that day. But you might not lose money overall in your mutual fund, because you will have dozens of other stocks to cushion the

McDonald's blow. For example, General Electric and Wal-Mart might look like they've got their act down, and their stock prices might be rising nicely on the same day McDonald's is losing ground.

When you have a mutual fund, each individual stock is not as important as the mixture of stocks. So your fund manager will intentionally try to blend stocks that act differently from each other during cycles. If your fund manager buys more stocks that climb, rather than fall, you will make money. But you will always have some losers. Some companies will make mistakes in their businesses, so the stocks will turn into rotten investments—maybe temporarily, maybe for as long as the company survives. Your fund manager will try to spot the problems early and sell the stock before you have lost a lot of money on it. But that's often not possible.

There are always shocks that are unforeseen. For example, while investors did well with hotel stocks after the terrorist attacks in 2001, the shock pulled the rug out from under airlines. Many ended up in bankruptcy.

Then there's Merck, which makes prescription drugs. It was a glamorous stock at the end of the 1990s. But in 2004 the stock plunged from about $45 a share to $33 in just one day after Merck pulled its blockbuster product, Vioxx, off the market because of evidence that the painkiller was dangerous. In other words, in a single day, an investor—whether a person or a mutual fund—lost about 27 percent of the money invested in the stock. Amid hundreds of suits over patient deaths and illnesses, the stock continued to drop. Investors lost about half of their money within months. By 2006, Merck stock was climbing again, but many investors had bailed out long before that happened.

Here's the important point I want you to keep in mind about mutual funds: Your opportunity to survive a stock blow-up is tremendously greater if you own mutual funds than if you try to select a handful of individual stocks. If you had a mutual fund that invested in Merck, you lost a little money because of the Vioxx mess. If, however, you had simply purchased the individual stock and decided to flee, you would have lost about half of the money you had invested in it. In your mutual fund, you had protection. You had many other stocks that were great investments at the time of the Merck fiasco, and the strong stocks buffered your loss. You probably didn't feel it a bit.

Cycles Take Stocks for a Ride

Aside from corporate disasters like Vioxx, cycles also work on the different stocks in your mutual fund in different ways. For a while, investors will be enamored with retail stocks like Wal-Mart, and that company, like other retailers, will be on a roll in the stock market—riding the cycle for retail stocks higher and higher. Meanwhile, investors may not be particularly excited about some other type of stock.

For example, investors didn't want anything to do with gold-mining stocks for two decades. Yet in 2005, those stocks shot up almost 33 percent as investors worldwide started stockpiling gold as they feared inflation and geopolitical unrest. Also, throughout the technology craze, investors snubbed energy stocks. Yet in 2005, investors got rich on energy as the stocks climbed 48 percent—a repeat of a strong 2004. Meanwhile, investors dumped retail stocks, fearing that the high cost of gasoline and heat, plus rising mortgage interest rates, would cause consumers to shop less.

Eventually, every cycle—no matter what is hot at the time—will turn.

Mutual fund managers who seek bargains will say to themselves at some point, "Retail stocks aren't popular now, but I can find good deals on those stocks. I'll buy them and hold onto them until they turn popular again, making the investors in my fund a lot of money." Or at some point they say, "People are going to cut back on gasoline if they lose jobs in a recession, so I'm going to sell Exxon and some of my other energy stocks now, while I can still make a good gain."

The mixture of stocks you get in mutual funds insulates you from different cycles and also from a particular company's stumbling. At any time, some stocks in your fund will be falling, but the rising stocks will cushion the fall so that your money keeps growing or shrinks merely a little, recovering a short time later.

When your mutual fund owns a lot of stocks that are going up, you will be making money. If the fund manager makes a lot of mistakes and buys more losing stocks than winners, you will lose money—at least temporarily.

Good Funds Can Be Losers

Picking stocks is difficult—even for the most brilliant fund managers. Some of the nation's top managers have told me they regret about 40 percent of the stocks they pick. They inevitably make mistakes on forecasts for the economy and companies. Because the stock market runs in cycles, there can be times when your mutual fund will lose money even though the fund manager has selected excellent stocks.

Cycles hit certain types of investments, or groups of stocks, without warning. Entire industries—or what are called "sectors"—get hurt as a group. By groups, or sectors, I'm referring, for example, to all energy company stocks, or all manufacturing company stocks, or all retail company stocks, and so on. When people worry that consumers won't be shopping much, for example, everything from Best Buy to Home Depot and Gap might go down together. This is important to know because if, for example, you owned Best Buy stock and were watching only it, you might see the stock price fall and think there was something wrong with your stock alone. In fact, Best Buy might be suffering temporarily in a cycle that will turn.

Cycles also hit various parts of the world at different times. In the late 1990s, investors ran away from Latin American stocks in terror, as companies suffered from economic and political turmoil. Investors swore they'd never put a penny into Latin America or other emerging or developing nations again because they were burned so badly. Yet, if they were still snubbing Latin American companies in 2005, they missed out on an astronomical 76 percent return as China and the rest of Asia hungered for Latin American oil and natural resources.

As an investor, you won't get hurt by any of these cycles if you don't overdose on anything that looks overly enticing—like energy companies amid a boom or Latin American stocks riding the wave. Your future depends on recognizing what's making each mutual fund do what it's doing and knowing that cycles will affect various mutual funds differently. You need to know this whether your funds are bestowing riches at the moment or sucking wealth away from investors.

This might sound like a mammoth task. But there's an easy shortcut I will teach you. It simply involves recognizing some befuddling names that currently make mutual funds appear confusing. You are about to learn how to eye mutual funds quickly and choose them with confidence.

I'm going to start walking you through the process.

8

MAKING SENSE OF WACKY
MUTUAL FUND NAMES

When I started going to physical therapy for a back problem about four years ago, word spread quickly that I was a new patient there. One of the therapists, Mark, told me while strapping me into a weight machine one day that he and other therapists were trying to edge their way onto the schedule so that they could get me as a patient and grab a little investment advice.

He apologized for "taking advantage of a client" but then persevered anyway.

It wasn't unusual. I'm used to being cornered at parties, at doctors' offices, at the hair salon, and even in the gym by apologetic people who are perplexed about investing and desperate for help. I can almost predict their questions before they ask them.

Nothing prepares Americans to invest money for their futures. So everyone, from doctors to hair stylists, commits similar, devastating mistakes that could easily be avoided if they simply knew about stock market cycles, picked up about a dozen vocabulary words, and had a few basic tidbits of information about making mutual fund choices.

So I told Mark I was happy to assist him or anyone else.

At the therapist's office, there was a sense of urgency. The staff, like so many ordinary investors, had been badly bruised by the 49 percent plunge in the stock market in 2000–2002. They had no idea how to rehabilitate their long-lost savings.

Mark, for example, was a therapist by day and a jazz musician at night. When he looked at his list of mutual funds, he saw nothing but "wacky words." None of them made sense, so in the 1990s, he made the same mistake that masses of other novice investors do. He looked over his list of 401(k) funds and saw one that was making more money than any of the others. Figuring that it had to be the *best* one, he put all his money into it.

Picking the big money maker—the fund that looked the *best*— had led him into a dangerous snare. By selecting the champion among his fund choices, he had set the groundwork for a disaster, but he didn't know it. For a while he was ecstatic. Every time he eyed the account, he saw more thousands. The sum was getting so big that at one point he had visions of retiring rich and devoting his time to jazz. Then, one day the cycle changed, and thousands of dollars vanished for some seemingly mysterious reason. Every day he peeked at his 401(k), it was worse. Instead of retiring rich, he began envisioning himself setting up weight machines for sweaty people forever.

When Mark told me about his missed fortune, he looked like he was in more pain than I as I struggled to finish my nineteenth repetition on the weight machine.

Then he asked me the same naive question thousands of others have asked me: "I've lost so much money in my mutual fund. Should I sell it?"

"What fund is it?" I asked. And the answer he gave to that critical question was totally predictable—an area where most investors get tripped up unnecessarily. Like the average person with a 401(k), Mark didn't know the name of his fund, and, of course, didn't have the slightest idea what the fund manager's job was. All he knew was that he was losing money.

"Knowing what the fund manager has been hired to do is essential," I told Mark. "The clue often comes from the fund's name," I said.

Then I delivered the shocker: "I know it's awful to be losing money, but the loss, alone, tells me nothing about whether your fund is good or bad. Your fund may simply have suffered along with others in a bad market cycle."

Poor Mark! He looked like he had just edged his way onto the physical therapy scheduling list for nothing.

Yet when I returned for my next therapy session, Mark was primed. He knew the name of his fund and gave me his full list of 401(k) choices.

"Which is the *best* fund?" he asked. He was making another toxic mistake that virtually every novice investor makes.

"That's the wrong question," I told him as I watched his earnest face turn disappointed once again. "There is no single *best* or *right* fund in your 401(k) plan or anyone else's 401(k) or IRA. If you rely on just one fund again, your retirement dreams will probably implode one more time. Instead, what you have in your 401(k) are several funds that you need to combine.

"Think of it like baking a cake. Flour is one of the *right* ingredients, but if you leave sugar, eggs, and a few more ingredients out, your recipe is going to be a flop. You have a retirement fund disaster now because you tried to make a recipe using only sugar."

"So now look at your 401(k) list," I told him. "I will give you a quick recipe for retirement-investing success.

"To start, I am going to help you understand the wacky words because everyone needs to recognize them. They are invaluable. They tell you whether you are selecting flour or sugar," I explained. "Next, I'm going to tell you how to mix them together. Proportions matter a lot. You can ruin a 401(k) or IRA by using too much or too little of an ingredient, just like you will ruin a cake by using only a tablespoon of flour when the recipe calls for a cup."

Mark was wearing his hopeful, earnest face again. And in less than an hour, I gave him all the basics he, or anyone, needs to be a successful investor in a 401(k), an IRA, or any other retirement account.

This is what I told him, and I offer it as a roadmap for you now and in the next couple of chapters. It is your guide to maneuver through cycles and to make sense of the befuddling language. It's what people pay financial advisers to handle for them. But regular people—no matter what their background—can master it. It's your recipe for a decent retirement. I promise.

Avoid the Traps

When employers create 401(k) plans for their employees, they typically provide about a dozen mutual fund choices, but that doesn't mean they are all for you. Some people like to tinker with their mutual funds more than others. Some want to take more risks than other people. Some will be retiring in a couple of years, and some have decades to go.

Consequently, a few of the mutual funds in the 401(k) will be essential for you, and others are available so that there is something for everyone.

You need to zoom through the mess and focus on what you need—not what looks like a winner.

The mutual fund with the best return is often not the essential one. In fact, you can think of it as a decoy or trap—perhaps distracting you from the mixture of funds that ultimately will be best for you. If you throw all your money into the enticing fund, it will likely hold you hostage from a decent retirement. Falling into the trap seems to be human nature. In a recent study, Harvard students were given a list of mutual funds, and almost everyone fell into the dangerous snare.

Instead of falling for it, when you see the highest return, remind yourself about cycles. The fund that is attracting you is probably riding a cycle that could be about to end. This was the case with Mark's choice—a stock fund on steroids, filled with technology stocks. He was attracted to it when it was on its last legs.

Rather than focusing on the hot fund, there's another way—the only way that works: Make your way through categories.

The Three Main Choices: Stocks, Bonds, and Cash

Having a dozen or more choices of mutual funds can be overwhelming, but while they make your head spin, the pros see it much more simply, and you can, too. Realize that virtually all the funds before you in a 401(k), or available for an IRA, fall into three basic categories: stocks, bonds, and cash.

After you know that, your choices will start to dwindle. Instead of feeling like you have to make sense of a dozen funds with strange names, now you are focusing on just three simple categories.

Even discerning between stocks and bonds on a 401(k) list might seem hard at first because investment pros muck up those easy words by using their own lingo. When they mean stocks, they sometimes use the word "equity." When they mean bonds, they might use the word "fixed income."

The same might happen when you go to a broker to open an IRA. But your choices ultimately come from the same three basic categories.

To the pros, the special language has extra meaning, but just speak English to yourself. Say, "OK, I have a choice between a fund that will buy stocks for me and a fund that will buy bonds for me."

In addition, just about every 401(k) has something in it called a "money market fund." When you see one, consider it like a piggy bank for cash. That's your safe place to store money when you are trying to decide what investment to use next. It's similar to a savings account at a bank, but it pays you a little more interest.

After you recognize the difference between stocks, bonds, and cash, you are half of the way home.

You don't need to use the money market fund. But you will need to put a good chunk of money into stock mutual funds and some into a bond mutual fund. Using both stocks and bonds is what the professionals refer to as "diversification." That's important, and I will explain how to do it right, and simply.

First, I must teach you a few more vocabulary words so that the "wacky words" help you, rather than hurt you, and so that your mutual funds no longer act in mysterious ways. The wacky words sound strange, but they alert you to how each fund will behave in cycles. The words guide you to the variety of funds you need to weather all cycles.

If you put money into a stock mutual fund, you will own stocks—maybe 100 of them, all within that one mutual fund. So when people are making money in the stock market, you will likely be making money in your fund. When people are losing money on stocks in a rough cycle, it's likely that you will be losing, too. This is why it was not relevant that Mark's mutual fund was losing money. It was natural that he would be losing when the stock market was dropping 49 percent. In fact, losing some money—though unpleasant—doesn't necessarily mean a mutual fund is defective.

What mattered was whether Mark's mutual fund was losing *more* money than other funds like his, and whether he'd given himself enough protection from inevitable market cycles by investing in a variety of mutual funds instead of the one. Without knowing the name or the description of his fund, he was in the dark—absolutely unable to make a smart decision. His quandary is almost universal among people with a 401(k) or an IRA.

By the end of my session with Mark, he realized where he'd gone wrong. He had not known about cycles, so in his attempt to be prudent and pick the *best* fund, he had chosen a dangerous one—one posing as a mild-mannered large cap fund but hyped up on an overdose of technology stocks. That overdose made it exceedingly vulnerable to cycles. His fate was sealed the moment he was lured by the tantalizing fund.

There was a better way to pick funds, I told Mark. I gave him all the tools he needed to assess whether a fund is better or worse than others. I will provide you with that same ability. In addition, I started with the most essential of investing lessons: To avoid grief in the future, Mark could not depend only on a single stock mutual fund. He needed a bond fund, too. He needed to start "diversifying." In other words, he needed to start mixing and matching mutual funds into an appropriate combination so that cycles wouldn't hurt him badly the next time conditions turned brutal.

Why You Need Bonds

Sometimes investors who don't understand the vocabulary of mutual funds steer away from bond funds.

They peruse their mutual fund list, and they see some funds in their 401(k) bestowing perhaps 10 percent gains for investors, and then they see another one giving investors just 5 percent. They figure the one paying 5 percent is a bad fund—a laggard among better funds. But that laggard happens to be a bond fund. It's a perfectly good fund, acting like a solid bond fund, doing exactly what it can be expected to do—to grant investors gains of about 5 percent a year, while keeping money relatively safe.

You never should compare the returns of stock funds and bond funds. The comparison is meaningless. You should choose bonds to do a job for you—to cushion the blow from your stock funds when cycles turn against you and make your stock mutual funds act in scary ways.

Here's a clear illustration of how it works, based on actual mutual funds during the period that caused Mark, and possibly you, so much distress. The data comes from a firm named Lipper that tracks mutual fund performance.

Say that on March 1, 2000, you put $10,000 into the average U.S. stock mutual fund just before the market started to crash. During the next couple of years, your $10,000 would have been sliced almost in half, and you probably would have been most unhappy. During the next few years, it improved as the market climbed about 60 percent. Still, six years after that initial $10,000 investment, you would still be suffering. You would have just $8,530 of your original $10,000 left. You would be waiting impatiently to break even. Like Mark, you might have grabbed the first person you saw, hoping he or she could give you a way out of the mess.

Now, look at it differently. See what throwing bonds into the stock mix would have done for you. Say that in March 2000, you decided to take a safer approach with your money than putting it all into a stock mutual fund. Instead, the fund you chose would put about 60 percent of your money in stocks and 40 percent in bonds. You would have lost some money during the harsh downturn: about 9.5 percent in 2002, according to Lipper. But that's mild compared to the awful decline you could have had if you'd relied merely on a stock fund. And, with your stock and bond mixture, you would have recovered more quickly than with only a stock fund. In 2003, you would have begun the healing process, with your stock and bond fund climbing 19.5 percent.

Less than three years after that, your money would be in good shape. Your initial $10,000 investment, which you made in March 2000, would have recovered everything you had lost and then some. You would have

$12,320. Not bad at all considering that you just went through one of the worst stock market cycles in history! And certainly not bad compared to the person who relied on the average stock fund and was still underwater with only $8,530 of the original $10,000 investment.

When you mix bonds in with the stocks, you receive a smoother ride. Bonds become your lifesaver, or maybe you can think of them like a bungee cord. When you are heavily invested in stocks and plunging toward destruction amid a terrifying cycle, the bonds snap you back so that your money doesn't perish.

What's a Bond?

Bonds generally are safer than stocks for one basic reason. When either a person or a mutual fund buys a bond, there is a specific promise made—one that doesn't exist for stocks.

The promise is the following: If you buy an individual bond, you will loan money temporarily to a corporation, to the U.S. government, to a city, or to some other entity. (The entity's name will be on the bond.)

You know the concept if you've ever given a reliable friend a loan and been paid interest for doing it. The bond itself works the same way. It's simply an IOU for a loan you make to a stranger instead of a friend. At some specific date in the future, the loan will end and the corporation or government will give all your money back to you. Until that date arrives, however, you will get a certain amount of interest on a regular schedule. It won't change. It will be like a tiny paycheck that comes regularly.

This is why people buy bonds. They want to earn interest on their money, and they like the safety of knowing the interest check will arrive like clockwork. They want to earn more interest than they would in a savings account. They especially like the assurance that eventually they will get all their original money—or "principal"—returned to them.

If you own an individual bond, you will get your interest payments directly on a specified date. But if you instead invest in a bond mutual fund, your fund will hold the bonds for you and hundreds of other investors in your fund. The interest payments will go into your fund, not directly to you. So, in effect, you will be sharing the interest payments with all the other investors who put money into your mutual fund.

Regardless of whether you buy a bond directly or your fund manager buys a bond for your fund, the same process occurs.

When you loan money to a corporation or governmental entity by buying a bond, that entity tells you upfront when they will return that money to you. It might be 5 years or even 30 years.

Take, for example, the hypothetical Nimble Pots and Pans Company. It needs money to develop some new pan factories around the world. So it decides to borrow the money by selling bonds to many different people. You hear about it from a broker and decide you will buy one of the bonds so that you can earn interest. Nimble sells you a $1,000 bond through your broker. The bond is like an IOU. You turn over $1,000 to your broker, she gives it to Nimble, and then Nimble promises to give you back the full $1,000 on September 15, 2016. Meanwhile, to make it worth your while, Nimble also promises to pay you interest for the next 10 years. In this case, let's say it's 5 percent, paid semiannually. So that's $50 a year, or $25 paid in September and $25 paid in March every year until September 15, 2016.

As the years go by, you rely on Nimble to keep its promise. After 10 years, you assume that you will get your original $1,000—or what's called "your principal"—returned to you.

How to Lose Money in Bonds

Although bonds are your insulation from painful stock market cycles, they are not absolutely safe. You need to know this so that you don't bail out of your bond fund at the first sign of a loss. I've had people call me, horrified, over a dip in a bond fund. "There's something wrong with my bond fund. It's losing money," they'll say—unaware that mild losses occur even in relatively safe bond funds during a few months, or even a year.

Combined with a stock fund over many years, your bond fund will protect your money. The losses in bonds aren't nearly as intense as those in stocks and don't last as long. Whereas the worst single year in stocks has been a downturn of 43 percent, the worst for U.S. government bonds has been 9 percent, according to Ibbotson Associates. With less lost, recoveries come faster.

So expect bumps from bond funds, and understand why they occur so that you don't dump a fund you should hold. There are two types of risks in bonds.

I'll start with what's called "credit risk." You need to know the concept, not the term.

It works like this: When you or your fund manager buys a corporate bond like a Nimble Pots and Pans bond, there is a risk you won't get all your money back. Remember, when you buy an individual bond, you are making a lengthy loan—maybe for five years, maybe longer. Sometimes, during that time, business conditions change and companies can't keep their promise to pay you back. Say that a few years down the road, Nimble has built new factories all over the world, and all of a sudden customers don't like the pots and pans anymore. Nimble's business starts to deteriorate, and eventually the company is having trouble paying its bills. With time, it ends up filing for bankruptcy.

This is one of the scariest prospects for people, or mutual funds, that invest in individual corporate bonds. When companies go into bankruptcy, they usually don't pay back all the money investors were promised. If you are lucky, you might get a portion, but your bond definitely is not the safe investment you anticipated.

When you invest in a bond mutual fund, however, you have a lot more protection from bankruptcies than if you had gone to a broker and bought a single bond. Because your fund manager has selected hundreds of bonds for you, you might not even sense one bad bond. Most of the bonds in your fund will continue paying interest. Your bond fund manager should be studying bonds constantly and steering clear of a lot of dangerous companies, like Nimble, so that blowups like Nimble don't happen often.

Also, if you invest only in U.S. government bonds through what will be called "government bond funds," you don't have to worry about bankruptcies at all. No matter how financially stressed the government gets, it can always raise taxes and use the money to pay you and other investors back. It will do just that, because it needs the entire world to be confident that it will always pay its bills.

Even with ultrasafe bonds like U.S. Treasury bonds, however, you are not completely safe if you invest in a bond fund.

There is another risk you must recognize. It applies even to the safest of bonds, and people who depend on bonds fear it greatly. It's called "interest rate risk." Again, you don't have to learn the term, but you need to understand the concept so that you don't look at your bond fund in your 401(k) some day and panic when you see you've lost a little of your money.

The risk works like this: Whenever you hear in the news that the Federal Reserve is raising interest rates or you notice that mortgage rates or credit-card interest is going up, it usually means your bonds or bond funds are vulnerable to losing some value. Bonds that you purchase today will always lose value tomorrow, next month, next year, or years later, if interest rates end up higher then.

This may sound complicated, but it's not. Think of it this way: Say I want to borrow $1 from you for a week, and I tell you I will pay you either a nickel or a dime when I return the dollar to you. The nickel will be 5 percent interest and the dime 10 percent. I would assume that you'd prefer to make the most money you can. So you'd want the dime—in other words, 10 percent in interest.

Well, when you invest in bonds, you are always examining the interest that bonds will pay you, and you will always hunt for the most interest you can get. That's why you will be disappointed if you buy a bond that is going to pay you 5 percent interest during the next five years, and then a few months later interest rates go up and other investors are able to buy new bonds that will pay them 7 percent interest.

At that point in time, you are stuck with money in a lower-interest bond, and although you can sell it, no one else is going to want your 5 percent bond when he or she can simply buy new bonds paying 7 percent. So your bond is going to lose value. If you wanted to sell it to someone else, that person would pay you less than you paid for it. In other words, you would lose money.

If you keep holding that bond instead of selling it, you might not care that the value has dropped. You will continue to get your 5 percent interest, and at the end of five years, your original money will also be returned to you, as promised. So you won't lose a penny. But the situation is different if you have a bond fund.

If your bond fund manager bought a lot of bonds paying 5 percent, and new bonds become available at 7 percent, your fund manager might want to sell those old, low-interest bonds. At that point, no one is going to pay full price for them. So you are going to look at the bond fund in your 401(k) one day and discover you are losing money.

You may find that unsettling. If it happens, however, do not assume that your bonds are as dangerous as stocks. With time, your fund manager will adjust to the higher interest rates by buying newer higher-interest bonds, and you will stop losing money.

In other words, you are affected by changing cycles in bonds, as well as stocks.

The Trade-off between Safety and Making Money

I want you to understand something very important about safety and investing. It's a fact of life that is at the center of all the investing choices you will make.

When you choose a safer investment, you also choose to be paid less for it than you would for taking more risks. So stocks have the potential to pay you the most—perhaps averaging 10.4 percent a year if history repeats. But they also smack you the hardest—maybe dropping more than 20 percent at times. That's part of the bargain. You are supposed to know it and go in with your eyes open.

Bonds aren't as risky, so they pay you less than stocks. The lower returns from bonds don't just happen by accident. Governments and businesses that sell bonds know they don't have to pay you as much as stocks pay, because they are giving you a special promise instead of big returns—the promise to repay all your money, plus interest.

Stocks, on the other hand, never make promises. You buy a stock for the *potential* of making money. There is never a "sure thing" with an individual stock, no matter what anyone tells you. You can win; you can lose. Of course, with a stock mutual fund, you have a better shot at winning than if you pin your hopes on one stock, because mutual funds hold dozens of stocks.

Although bonds generally are safer than stocks, they come in different varieties. Some are safer than others, and they pay you accordingly based on the risks you take. They don't do this out of the kindness of their hearts. They do it because they know they have to pay you extra to get you to accept greater risks.

The U.S. government doesn't have to pay you much interest on U.S. Treasury bonds, because you can be sure you will get every cent back. So historically that's meant about a 5.5 percent average annual return for long-term bonds. Corporate bonds are more risky because of the possibility of bankruptcy, so they pay more to entice investors to take the risk—about 5.9 percent on average, according to Ibbotson Associates.

If you reach for the highest return in bonds, you will select what's known as a "high-yield bond fund," or what is called a "junk bond." Beware! This fund might say "bond" on it, but it is not mild-mannered. It is almost as dangerous as stocks because it purposely picks bonds from companies that are in financial trouble and might go bankrupt.

You might be attracted to a 12 percent return in a high-yield bond fund when a safe U.S. government bond fund is paying only 5 percent. But since you get paid to take risks, that 12 percent return should serve as a red flag. Instead of picking it for the juicy temporary return, you must try to picture that very same fund losing 12 percent during a bad cycle and ask yourself whether you want to take the risk of losing money in it then. If your goal is to use bonds for safety, you'd be wise to pass up the high return.

An Easy Bond Fund Choice

Here's an easy solution for your 401(k) or IRA. Look through your bond mutual fund choices. You might see a "short-term bond fund," a "long-term bond fund," and an "intermediate-term bond fund." The diversified "intermediate-term" fund is a solid all-around choice. It usually invests in bonds that mature in about 10 years or less, so it generally won't fall as hard as a long-term bond fund when interest rates rise, and it usually yields more than a short term fund. (By "mature," I mean that the loan ends and the government or corporation returns the investor's money—or principal—to the investor.)

If you buy a diversified intermediate-term bond fund, your fund manager will buy a mixture of bonds for you—some very safe U.S. government bonds, some riskier corporate bonds, and maybe a small number of risky high-yield bonds to boost your return just a little. Mixing bonds together cautiously, while relying mostly on safe government bonds, is a sound strategy.

In the words of the investing profession, you will balance out your "risk and return." You are "diversifying" your bonds. That means you will get a little jolt from a small quantity of riskier bonds but protect your money with the safer choices. Such a fund is a good choice for one-stop bond shopping.

You now know how to use bonds to reduce your risks in your retirement savings. You have progressed a long way. You know how to spot a mild-mannered bond fund among 401(k) choices and how to ask for a diversified "intermediate-term bond fund" for your IRA. You are already better off than most people with 401(k) plans and IRAs. If you went no further, you would be to the point where you'd have a healthier retirement. But you can do even more for yourself.

To build up enough money for retirement, you must hold significantly more stocks than bonds.

So next, you are ready to learn how to spot the risks in stock funds, too. Then you can deliberately choose a mixture that will blend different levels of risk and help you weather the cycles that will come your way.

Like bonds, stocks don't come with just one level of risk. Some can give you explosive growth but also can explode into nothing. (Mark had these.) Others are more mild-mannered. You don't have to guess about which are which or find out in the middle of a scary cycle.

Stock mutual funds have specific names that alert you in advance. So, now, onto the "wacky words" that help you spot stock funds you will need, and an introduction to your fund manager's job.

9

KNOW YOUR MUTUAL FUND MANAGER'S JOB

One reason people make so many mistakes with their stock mutual funds is that they and their mutual fund managers have a totally different understanding of the fund manager's job.

This ends up in awful marriages and painful divorces between investors and their mutual funds. Destructive relationships batter retirement savings.

Most novice investors put money into a mutual fund with a dangerous false assumption. They assume that they hired their fund manager to make money for them, no matter what. Consequently, if they start to lose money, investors figure their fund is a flop and they should unload it and find a better one before all their money disappears.

The fund manager, on the other hand, is operating with a totally different mind-set. Managers don't want to lose money, either. They tend to be fiercely competitive people who love to leave other fund managers in their dust. Yet they know that there will be times when losing money will be inevitable simply because of the specific job they've been assigned and the cycles of the market that will temporarily spoil their specialty.

This is no small matter. Fund managers are specialists—hired to pick a precise type of stock and to ignore all other investments. It means that some managers are expressly hired to take on huge risks with your money, and others are hired to take only modest risks. It means that if a manager's specialty is being thrashed by a nasty cycle, the manager usually won't be allowed to pull away and channel your money toward safer stocks and bonds—even when the cycle is being gracious to those alternative investment choices. You read that right: Your fund manager—by design—will have to shun stocks or bonds that could be moneymakers for you.

Under certain cycles of the stock market, you will lose money in particular funds no matter how brilliantly the fund manager handles stocks. That's even true of lower-risk stock funds. All stocks get battered by cycles, but not all stocks suffer at the same time. As cycles change, there will be times when the risky ones get hurt and other times when the safer ones take the beating. In general, though, it's the riskiest stocks that get throttled the most.

Novice investors are usually shocked to find out that there will be times when even the savviest stock-picking pro will fail to save a mutual fund from harm. But your fund managers assume that you know all of this. They figure that you are consciously choosing mutual funds with your eyes open and that you can distinguish one fund from another by recognizing the wacky names most people find so befuddling.

In other words, if you buy an aggressive, risk-taking fund, the manager assumes that you bought it on purpose. With more than 8,000 other funds available, you could have purchased other funds instead. So the manager takes his marching orders from you. When you bought the fund, the manager assumed that you were instructing him or her to take sizable risks for you and that you are prepared for the extreme highs and lows that come with the territory. So rather than fleeing from the strategy in the midst of a scary cycle, the manager forges ahead—completing the job he thinks you want done, preparing you for the next upturn in the cycle.

This is why Mark, the physical therapist I mentioned in the preceding chapter, might have had a perfectly capable mutual fund manager—one worth keeping despite losing thousands of Mark's savings. The manager, after all, was doing exactly what he'd been hired to do—to buy the riskiest stocks. Mark just couldn't stomach the ride down even though it was part of the original bargain—a natural trade-off for the superior gains Mark had loved previously.

Everything would have been fine for Mark if he had understood what he was getting into at the outset. He could have stayed out of the dangerous fund, or bought less of it—using it as spice in his investment portfolio instead of the main ingredient. With a small portion of the risky fund, he could have added larger portions of safer stock funds and bonds. The combination would have insulated his money from the brutality of the high-risk stock fund.

Because he was like most investors, however, Mark naively poured all his money into the one fund that seemed like a winner and got into a position he couldn't stomach.

The Cost of Ignorance

Messes like Mark's are unfortunately repeated over and over again among novice investors, and they are costing people dearly.

In 2006, a mutual fund consulting firm named Dalbar analyzed how mutual fund investors handle their money. The findings were enough to make you cry.

Over the previous 20 years, investors would have gained about 11.9 percent a year on average if they'd simply stuck money into a mutual fund that reflected the stock market and stayed the course. Instead, Dalbar found that people moved from fund to fund, looking for the elusive *better* fund. And they earned a measly 3.9 percent a year.

Take a look at this disaster in dollars: At the end of 20 years, investors would have had about $398,500 if they had invested $5,000 a year in the stock market—or what's called the Standard & Poor's 500—and stayed with it through thick and thin. Instead, by running away from one disappointing mutual fund after another, the ordinary mutual fund investor ended up with only about $153,100.

This is why you must know your fund manager's job before you pick a fund. That way you will be able to discriminate between funds and protect yourself before it's too late. You won't need to bolt when your fund does just what you should have expected.

I'm sure you are wondering now how a person like you can ever know what a fund manager is hired to do. It's actually quite simple, and you don't have to know the intricacies of the job.

You merely have to pay attention to the wacky words in your mutual funds and know what they actually tell you. It's not just gibberish. Fund names and each fund's description usually tip you off to the risks you will take and how the fund will act in cycles.

Although there are more than 8,000 different mutual funds, there are actually only a few specific types, or categories, you must recognize. Just as you gave yourself an easier task by breaking down a list of 401(k) choices into just three categories—stocks, bonds, and cash—you are now going to break down the stock category into a few very manageable types.

When you do that, you will be able to spot what you need fast and know how to mix and match riskier and less risky stock funds so that you can whip up a hardy recipe for your retirement fund and save yourself from grief.

Focus on the Right Words

I'm talking about terms like "small cap" and "large cap"—the stuff they throw at you in TV ads to make investing seem more complicated than it has to be. I'm not talking about company names like Fidelity, or Vanguard, or American, or Janus, or hundreds of others. People get lost in those less critical words. They will call me and say: "I have a fund that's doing badly; should I get rid of it?" When I ask the name, they might say, "Fidelity." But that's totally deficient information.

Names like Fidelity and American just tell you what company is running a fund. That's not where I want you to focus. This illustration will help you understand what I mean.

Picture yourself walking into a large electronics superstore. The variety of merchandise can be almost as overwhelming as a 401(k) plan. The store carries televisions, computers, DVD players, cellphones, and so on. You are in a hurry and want to go quickly to the section of the store you need.

You want a television. So when you walk into the store, you don't want to waste a minute. You go to the clerk by the door and ask her to point you in the right direction.

Do you ask the clerk where to find the Sony? Of course not. Sony makes loads of products. If you focused on the brand name, you could bounce around the store all day, seeing everything from computers to digital cameras, and never find what you needed. With the brand name alone, the clerk wouldn't know where to send you in the store.

What's relevant is to ask where to find the televisions. After you get to the television section, you might want to discriminate between the Sony and Panasonic brands, but the key for you is to at least find, and buy, a television. Even if you picked a television that was somewhat inferior to another, any one of the televisions would do the job for you—it would let you watch your favorite shows.

It's exactly the same with mutual funds. Fidelity, Vanguard, and hundreds of other companies make dozens of mutual funds, but the key to your selection is to find a certain type of mutual fund—one that will do a specific job for you. That's a "small cap fund," a "large cap fund," a "bond fund," an "international stock fund," and so on.

Soon, you will look at a list of mutual funds and be able to focus in on a key term like "large caps" and say instantly and with certainty, "That's like a television. It's what I came to buy."

Or to go back to the investing recipe analogy I want you to keep in mind, you will look at a list of mutual funds for your 401(k) plan, ignore the brand names, and scan the list for the term "large cap." When you see it, you will say to yourself, "That's like flour—the main ingredient for cooking a solid retirement fund. I need a fairly large amount of it." And then you will scan the list a second time, and you will say, "I see a small cap fund. That's like sugar. It will sweeten my retirement fund, but I have to be cautious about adding too much."

This quick recognition will determine whether you make a lot of money or lose it.

So hunt for the following words in mutual funds, and know both the worst-case and best-case scenarios they can deliver—paying serious attention to what they will do for you over many years, rather than one or two.

The idea is to never be taken by surprise—to know what you are getting into so that you can avoid bailing out after losing a bundle at a frightening point in a cycle.

Often you will find the few words you need buried right in the mutual fund's name. Other times you will have to look a little further at the description of a fund. You can always find the description in a booklet called the "prospectus." There's one for every mutual fund, and you are supposed to receive a copy whenever you buy a fund.

Unfortunately, prospectuses are written in too much legalese, so reading them from cover to cover will be impossible. But in a simple paragraph usually labeled "investment strategy," you will spot the keywords I'm about to teach you.

Look for the keywords so that you will know whether you are buying flour or sugar for your retirement fund recipe. Then you will be ready for the next chapter, knowing how to mix and match all the ingredients, in the right quantities, so that you enjoy the brew you've created—even when the stock market is acting cruel.

Stocks Come in Three Sizes:
Know Your Size

Three key words in stock mutual funds relate to sizes of companies: "large cap," "mid cap," and "small cap." Don't be put off by the word "cap." It's an abbreviation for the word "capitalization." It's simply a way of telling you how big a company is. The word doesn't relate to how much a company sells, but rather tells you what investors think the company is worth. It's the market value of the stock—or what all investors together are willing to pay for all the shares of stock in a company.

That might be confusing, but don't worry about it. What matters to you as a mutual fund investor is that "cap" instantaneously helps you identify a category. And that is important.

Categories help us in everything we do. For example, if we are thinking about animals, the word "mammal" helps us start focusing on a certain type of animal. But it's still a very broad word, or category—including everything from dogs to lions. Knowing the specific names of the animals will clue you in to how they will behave.

Likewise, the word "stocks" is very broad—including stocks that act more docile like dogs and those that are fierce like lions. So the fund world tells you more about stocks with more specific terms such as "large cap" and "small cap" so that you can anticipate distinct differences in the behavior of stock categories.

As stocks, "large cap stocks" and "small cap stocks" are somewhat alike but with differences that increase or decrease your risks during various cycles in the market.

When you start recognizing the distinct label for stock categories, it will help you keep track of where your mutual fund manager will be hunting for stocks to buy for you and the risks he or she will take with your money.

That might not sound like much. After all, a novice investor often thinks: *A stock is a stock; I know nothing about them and just want my manager to buy me the best one.* But categories matter.

Different size stocks behave differently, just like different animals—dogs and lions—behave differently. With stocks, those differences come out dramatically during various cycles in the market. The risks between different sizes vary a lot.

In other words, when you recognize categories of stock, you will know whether you are getting into a cage with dogs or lions. In the next chapter, I'll tell you how to corral dogs and lions together to remove the lion's fury. Together they act like man's best friend.

Using the Remainder of This Chapter

Use the next part of this chapter to become acquainted with the categories of stocks. Don't expect to absorb the details all at once. I figure you will familiarize yourself with categories now, learn how to mix and match them in the next chapter, and then come back to this chapter over and over again in the future—whenever you need to choose a fund for an IRA, a 401(k), or some other kind of investment account.

As you go through the categories here, I've put a quick note at the end of each about how to use funds in that category. You will get complete recipes—or step-by-step models to follow—in the next chapter. But in the future as you make mutual fund choices, the quick notes in this chapter should be a fast reminder about how to use each type of mutual fund. If you have a list of 401(k) funds in hand and then compare your funds to the following list, you should be able to make choices within less than five minutes.

Also, you will see some suggested funds. The list doesn't include every fine fund, but I've given you some reliable ideas for IRAs or other investment accounts. If you have a 401(k) plan, do not be dismayed if you look through my suggestions and your 401(k) funds aren't among them. Remember, the most important job you can accomplish with your 401(k) is to use the proper categories—rather than specific funds—and then to mix and match them.

That's what you will accomplish in the next chapter. Now, you will learn once and for all what those wacky words are telling you.

Large Cap U.S. Stock Funds

If you have a fund with "large cap" in its name or description, your fund manager will look only at the very largest companies in the nation. In other words, he or she will sort through companies that are household names—firms such as Microsoft, General Electric, Exxon, Wal-Mart, Johnson & Johnson, Citibank, Coca-Cola, and so on.

These are primarily established companies—those that might be called "blue chips." They are solid firms that aren't likely to go bankrupt. Of course, as time goes by, business conditions change and even great companies sometimes flop. Just consider firms such as KMart or United Airlines, goliaths that succumbed to bankruptcy. However, it's less likely that a large, established company will fail compared to a young, small company that is still trying to figure out how to get customers to buy its products.

Larger companies are considered safer investments than small companies—not as safe as bonds, but among stocks, they are the safest.

Your fund manager must still study them carefully to make sure that each company will be growing its profits and that the stock price will rise. But over many, many years, a mutual fund holding a broad variety of solid large company stocks is likely to behave a lot like the overall stock market—or what you might hear called the "Dow Jones Industrial Average" or the "Standard & Poor's 500" on the news.

Understanding Your Risks in Large Caps

Over the past 80 years, the Standard & Poor's 500—which is just a shorthand way of referring to many of the largest stocks of the stock market—has given investors an average annual return of 10.4 percent. So, with a mutual fund that invests in large stocks, you might anticipate an average annual return around 10 percent if you keep the fund for many years. But don't expect it each year or even the next 10.

Remember the past: Large cap stocks have fallen as much as 43 percent in a year, if you go all the way back to the Depression. They have also climbed as much as 53 percent in a single year, according to Ibbotson. In the past 30 years, the extremes have been less dramatic. The largest loss in a year: 26 percent. The largest increase: 37 percent.

What does that tell you? It's not a guarantee, but if you look at your large cap mutual fund someday and see that you have lost 10 percent, or even 20 percent of your money, and news reports are saying the stock market is down like that too, you should be able to calm yourself and say, "This is within the realm of possibilities for this type of fund. I thought about this when I bought it, and history tells me that cycles will change. If I stick with it, I could still average a 10 percent return—or something like that—over the next 20 or 30 years."

History is used as a guide by investment professionals to anticipate the future. It's not perfect or precise, but it's all we have to go on. You should use the past for insight but realize the future could be somewhat different. Some analysts, for example, are telling investors to expect only about 7 to 8 percent returns on stocks over the next decade.

Also, keep in mind that historical averages apply to large cap stocks in general. Your particular mutual fund might not act just like the average. Maybe yours will be a couple of percentage points higher or lower than the average for funds in its category. (You should check your funds every year to make sure they are roughly on course, and I give you the tools to do so at the end of Chapter 13, "Index Funds: Get What You Pay For.")

What's important now is to realize that your fund isn't going to deviate much from the average fund, because the category of stocks you have tends to dictate how you will do during cycles of the market. One large cap fund will behave much like another. Keep this in mind so that your mutual funds don't seem so mysterious.

When large caps are popular, your fund probably will be making money. When they are unpopular, you probably will be losing money or just crawling along lethargically—not making much or losing much. You will be doing this along with people who have chosen hundreds of other large cap funds.

Their managers might be smart, but depending on the cycle, they probably won't be able to protect investors if it's a losing time for large cap stocks in general. Just as you can't expect a dog to act like a cat, you can't expect a large cap fund to act like a small cap fund or a bond fund.

Still, your fund manager is going to try to pick the best stocks for you out of the bunch—ones he or she hopes will give you an extra edge over the average. If the manager picks a lot of technology stocks like Microsoft when tech is popular, you might do better than investors on average in the large cap fund category. But if the manager guesses wrong about what will be popular, and stocks like Exxon become popular, you might not do as well as the average.

What to Do with Large Caps in Your Retirement Fund

Because large caps are the most stable companies, a large cap fund should serve as your core investment in stocks at all times. By "core," I mean the largest portion of your stock money should go into large caps and stay there year after year. It's your staple—like bread in a meal. Financial advisers frequently rely on a simple guide to determine how much of a client's money to invest in large cap stocks or large cap funds. First, they channel some of their client's money into bonds. Then they focus on the full U.S. stock market. When they consider the composition of the entire U.S. stock market, they see that large cap stocks make up roughly 70 to 75 percent of the total. So when investing in U.S. stocks, they simply put 70 to 75 percent of an investor's stock investments into large caps. You can do the same. I will give you more guidance in Chapter 11, "Do This."

Some Large Cap Funds Ideas

There are hundreds of large caps funds, and an excellent choice is usually what's called an "index fund." You will find the names of several here, and I provide more information about them in Chapter 13. I am also providing a couple of other well-respected fund names so you can make comparisons. Don't worry if you do not see your 401(k) funds here. This list does not include all the quality funds available. Also, remember that whenever you select mutual funds from any list—whether this one or in a magazine, newspaper, or TV—you should check them out using the techniques provided at the end of Chapter 13. Fund quality is not static. It can change over time.

For now, here are some ideas you can use as starting points when digging through thousands of funds: Vanguard 500 Index (VFINX), Marsico Growth

(MGRIX), T. Rowe Price Growth Stock (PRGFX), Standard & Poor's 500 exchange traded fund (SPY), Weitz Value (WVALX), Fidelity Spartan Total Market Index (FSTMX), Vanguard Total Stock Market Index (VTSMX), iShares S&P 500 Index (IVV), or Fidelity Spartan S&P 500 (FSMKX).

Notice the capital letters in parenthesis. These are called the "tickers" or "symbols." They are a short-hand way to look up a fund on the Internet or to order one from a broker. To identify more funds, try the "easy screener" at www.moneycentral.msn.com. Find it under "investing" and "funds." Don't use the screener for "top performers." Being on top for a few months, or even a year, means nothing.

Small Cap U.S. Stock Funds

Small cap funds are the dessert, or the funds you use to sweeten your results. As with dessert, however, you should not rely on them for a healthy diet unless you are very young and can accept a loss as painful as 58 percent in a single year.

In their best years, there is nothing like small caps. As a group, they have climbed as high as 143 percent in a single year, but they've also destroyed a lot of wealth during periods when they have been unpopular. In the worst year, they've dropped 58 percent, according to Ibbotson Associates. Over the past 80 years, all those ups and downs have turned into an average annual return of 12.6 percent—significantly higher than that of the large companies at 10.4 percent.

Small cap funds invest in very small companies—such as Borders Group or Krispy Kreme Doughnuts. You might not think of them as small. After all, Krispy Kreme has about 300 stores and sells donuts in grocery stores and gas stations.

Remember that when I'm talking about size, I'm talking about what investors think a company is worth or what's called their "market cap." For small caps, that generally means companies worth about $1.5 billion or less. That compares to large companies—at about $7 billion or more.

Small companies can be fragile because they are often young, or struggling, and consequently making mistakes. Their products might be hot, but if the corporate leaders can't make the business work out right, all the excitement about what they sell may be for naught.

Consider Krispy Kreme Doughnuts. People loved the donuts, so they paid high prices for the stock in the early 2000s. Then the company had serious operating problems and legal battles with the independent business-people—or franchisees—who ran many of the donut shops. Government regulators also questioned whether investors were misled with faulty financial reports. The stock, which soared in 2003 to about $49, fell below $4.

An investor who got excited about donuts and bought the stock at $49 would have lost almost all of his or her money.

Small cap stocks have a high probability of problems. It's an area of the stock market that can make you very rich if you spot a rare winner like Microsoft in its infancy. But more often than not, small businesses fail. They may depend on a single customer, and if that customer encounters financial trouble and goes out of business, the small company might be sunk. Likewise, if another company offers a better price than a small company, all the customers might shift their business to the competitor, and a great small company could be toast.

In addition, small companies can have trouble getting banks to loan them money, or they might have to pay higher interest to get loans. If interest payments are expensive, the small company may be short on cash and may not have enough money to make top-notch products or advertise and market them. The company might not be able to hire the best employees if it can't afford to pay people what a large company would.

A fund manager for a small cap fund must hunt for companies that will excel—knowing full well that a number of factors could work against them.

Because small caps—like Microsoft in its infancy many years ago—can make extraordinary gains, investors who find well-managed small cap companies can do extremely well. But risks are especially great during downturns in the economy or during some of the cruel cycles that thrash small caps for months or even years.

A large company can trim fat during economic stress, but small companies often don't have fat to cut. Think of Wal-Mart and a neighborhood store. If people lose their jobs in a recession, they might buy less from both types of stores. Wal-Mart might have to lay off some people or cut some advertising; the neighborhood store might not even be able to pay the electric bill.

Consequently, investors should put some money into small cap funds for the extraordinary growth that young upstarts enjoy—but they should do it with care because the downside is dramatic, too. Your fund manager must be exceptional as he or she tries to identify the great firms and survivors. Since the risks are great, avoid a steady diet of small caps. Dessert-size portions will sweeten returns over many years.

What to Do

Financial planners generally suggest investors put about 20 to 25 percent of their U.S. stock money into smaller company stocks. The definition of "small" is somewhat imprecise. Often when professionals talk about small caps, they are referring to the stocks that are smaller than large ones, so medium-size companies might be included in the mix. If a financial planner focuses more specifically on small companies, the adviser might suggest putting only about 12 or 15 percent of your U.S. stock money into small cap funds.

These are all ballpark figures. Some advisers are more liberal with daring investors, if they are confident the people won't panic and flee small caps during a brutal cycle.

How do you know whether you should be more daring? You know that small caps have fallen close to 60 percent in a single year. So look at your money. Maybe you have $1,000. Ask yourself: "Could I stand to lose all but $400, knowing that over the next 20 to 30 years I will be likely to make more money after that loss than I would if I invested only in large stocks?" Then, revisit the issue one more time and think of it this way: "If that $1,000 goes to $400, I won't know at $400 whether it will turn to $200, and I won't know when the bleeding is going to stop." If history still comforts you, then you might have the stomach to hold more small caps than the average person.

One more warning before I move on: The closer you are to retirement, the less you can afford to risk. If you are 20 and lose half your money, you can earn it back—maybe in 5 years; maybe in 15. But if you are 50, you don't have enough working years ahead of you to keep investing new money while waiting for the old money to rebuild again after a substantial loss.

Here's an example: If you would have put $10,000 into the ordinary small cap growth fund in March 2000, you would have lost all but $5,787 by October 2001. By March 2006—or about six years after the crash—you would have regained most, but not all, of your money. You would have had $9,707, according to mutual fund research firm Lipper.

Put that into perspective by thinking of people in various age groups. For a 20-, 30-, or 40-year-old, the effects of the crash would be about gone after six years of waiting, and there would be years ahead to enjoy the high growth that historically has come from small stocks. But if you were 60 and about to retire, having $10,000 turn into less than $6,000 would be a harrowing experience. After you stop working and stashing away new money, catching up is difficult to do. In retirement, you remove money from savings rather than adding to it. You may not have six years to let your original $10,000 come back to where it started.

Some Small Cap Ideas

Consider Royce Special Equity (RYSEX), Masters' Select Smaller Companies (MSSFX), T. Rowe Price Diversified Small Cap (PRDSX), Vanguard Small Cap Index (NAESX), Vanguard Small Cap Value Index (VISVX), S&P SmallCap 600 exchange traded fund (IJR), or Russell 2000 Value exchange traded fund (IWN). For investors with less than $1,000 to invest, it's difficult to find funds, but Buffalo Small Cap (BUFSX) accepts just $250.

Mid Cap U.S. Stock Funds

Now that you understand large and small caps, this one should be easy. These are medium-size companies—those between about $1.5 billion and about $7 billion in capitalization. Examples you might recognize are Coach, Black & Decker, or H&R Block.

Mid caps generally are companies less vulnerable than small caps. The businesses may be more established. They still are not the goliaths that large caps are, however. Some might have been large companies at one time and stumbled.

As a group, the companies tend to be a little more risky than large caps and a little less risky than small caps.

What to Do

A financial adviser might have people put about 14 percent of their U.S. stock money into mid cap stocks if that choice is available within a 401(k) plan. Until a few years ago, advisers simply focused on large and small caps, not considering mid caps as a significant category of stocks. Some advisers still don't bother with mid caps. So if you don't have a mid cap choice in your 401(k), don't worry about it. Instead, put some of the mid cap chunk of money into your large cap choice, and slightly more than you otherwise would into small caps. Keep the basic makeup of the stock market in mind. It's roughly 71.5 percent large caps, 14.5 percent mid caps, and 12 percent small caps. Feel free to copy.

Some Mid Cap Ideas

Consider Ariel Appreciation (CAAPX), Mairs & Power Growth Fund (MPGFX), Fairholme (FAIRX), Selected Special Shares (SLSSX), Vanguard Mid Capitalization Index (VIMSX), Weitz Hickory (WEHIX), or Standard & Poor's MidCap 400 exchange traded fund (IJH). If you have only $250 to invest, consider Buffalo Mid Cap (BUFMX)

Recognizing the Tortoise and the Hare: Growth versus Value

There are two basic ways to make money with stock mutual funds. You can buy funds that try to pick stocks because they are expected to be very fast winners— like the hare in the story the "Tortoise and the Hare." Or you can buy funds that try to pick the slow but steady, dependable stocks—or the tortoise.

When you see a list of mutual funds, you will sometimes see the word "growth" in the name or description. When you do, that's the hare. The fund will try to pick stocks like eBay, a company that has grown its profits at a phenomenal pace and consequently caused the stock to soar.

If instead you see the word "value" or maybe "equity income," that's the tortoise. The fund might pick companies like Proctor & Gamble—a company that's been around for a long time and keeps growing, but at a slower and steadier pace than fast-growers. It makes dependable products for the household, so whether the economy is weak or strong, people are going to need them—a relatively dependable stock.

Stocks that grow at a startling rate can't keep it up forever. So growth stocks tend to be hot for a while and then maybe lose their momentum. At that point, stock prices often drop—leaving investors bruised. Value stocks are less exciting, and may include companies that have seen better days. As a group, however, they tend to be more dependable.

In the famous story, the tortoise wins the race. In investing, academic studies have shown that the tortoise is also the winner when the race lasts for many, many years. But with stocks, the hare wins a lot of sprints—and those short spurts can be very lucrative to investors.

Consequently, most financial advisers have their clients invest in some "growth" funds, which pick stocks that are expected to grow fast, and some "value" funds, which pick relatively cheap stocks that are less likely to nosedive. Neither growth nor value is inherently good or bad. Both behave very differently during market cycles. At the end of the 1990s, investors were infatuated with growth stocks. They climbed about 40 percent a year. But in the 2000s, it was a totally different matter. Growth stocks fell close to 40 percent. Then, investors got scared and didn't want to touch the growth stocks they loved in the 1990s. Then, all they wanted was the safety of the steady value stocks.

Between February 2000 and the end of 2005, the tortoise left the hare in his dust. In other words, value stocks climbed with gusto—up 59 percent. Meanwhile, the hare was out of gas. Growth stocks lost so much money between 2000 and 2002 that investors holding them were still down 38 percent at the end of 2005.

All these statistics can make your head spin. I present them now just so that you realize that what's hot for a while doesn't stay hot, even though you might have the illusion at any point in time that excitement for a certain category will last forever.

When investors are very confident, and love stocks, growth funds tend to soar. When they are nervous, they tend to pick safer, more dependable stocks, and then value clearly has the edge. Since growth funds tend to pick technology and healthcare stocks, and value funds tends to pick industrial and financial stocks, their fate tends to depend on phases in the economy and popularity of those types of stocks at any given time.

Don't drive yourself nuts trying to figure out whether a growth fund or a value fund will be a potential winner in any single year. By having a mixture of growth and value, investors give themselves a chance to make tremendous gains during hot cycles but protect themselves somewhat during down cycles.

How to Recognize the Fund

Growth is likely to have the word "growth" in the name. It also might suggest some forward-looking idea like "new era" or "new millennium." Or it often uses the word "aggressive" or "emerging."

Value often includes companies that pay dividends, because older, established companies tend to pay dividends. (Dividends are small regular payments—somewhat like an interest payment—that are sent to stockholders by some companies.)

So a value fund's name might include the word "income" to reflect the dividend payments. But if you see "income," look at the description to make sure it's talking about stocks. The word "income" often refers to bonds. You won't get the stocks you need for perhaps an 8 or 10 percent a year return if you buy a bond fund by mistake.

What to Do

Let's assume that you put 50 percent of your entire stock portfolio into funds that invest in large stocks. Divide that up half-and-half—with an equal portion in a large cap growth fund and a similar portion in a large cap value fund. So 25 percent large cap growth, 25 percent large cap value.

Do the same with small cap stocks. Say you have 16 percent invested in small company stocks. Divide that equally into a small cap value fund and a small cap growth fund. So 8 percent, 8 percent.

On the other hand, if you get nervous about losing money, no one says you must have riskier growth stocks. Just select value stocks through a small cap value fund. You will still lose money during cycles when stocks are falling, but you aren't likely to lose as much as in growth funds.

If you would rather not have to bother figuring out "value" or "growth," look for a fund that calls itself "blend" or "core." Blend funds mix value and growth for you. Often 401(k) plans offer a large cap "blend" fund.

Because small cap growth funds can be so volatile, and because some research shows small cap value funds have had an edge during long periods, some financial planners use only small cap core funds and small cap value funds—not growth.

Here's what happened to investors during the latest bear market or market crash: An investor who put $10,000 into a small cap growth fund on March 1, 2000 went down below $6,000 in 2001 and in March 2006 had about $9,700. But the investor in a small cap value fund turned a $10,000 investment into about $24,700 during the same six-year period. Does that predict the future? Absolutely not. I use it just to show you that sometimes growth doesn't really grow, and sometimes value isn't as lethargic as you might think.

Some Core Fund Ideas

Consider Vanguard 500 index (VFINX), Fidelity Spartan Total Market Index (FSTMX), Vanguard Primecap Core (VPCCX), Fairholme Fund (FAIRX), Third Avenue Value (TAVFX), Wintergreen (WGRNX), or Muhlenkamp (MUHLX).

Check Value and Growth Funds for Worst-Case Scenarios

Still not sure whether value or growth is best for you? If you want to understand what your mutual fund is likely to do in the worst of times, go to www.morningstar.com, type in the name of the fund in the box labeled "quotes," and when you get to the snapshot of your fund, click on "Performance." Pay particular attention to the years 2000, 2001, and 2002—three terrible years in the stock market. You can get a glimpse of the damage investors endured. It's not a perfect look at the future, but it gives you a recent example of a major bear market. Also click on "risk measure" and notice the "bear market decile rank." (A score of 1 is best, and 10 is worst.)

International Stock (Equity) Funds

When you have an international stock fund, you hire a fund manager to search the world for the best stocks for you.

Perhaps the fund manager will pick Toyota in Japan or Samsung in Korea. If his or her fund looks for small foreign companies, you may not recognize the names of the businesses.

If your fund is a truly broad "diversified" international fund—one not focused on one particular country or region—your fund manager will search for good buys on every continent. That's the type of diversified fund that is best for investors rather than one focused on one country or region. Find it by looking for the word "diversified" in the fund's name or description.

Sometimes novice investors will see news about a booming economy somewhere in the world and think it has to be a great investment. But their timing has been atrocious. They tend to jump in after a cycle has been climbing for a long time, and then their money gets decimated.

New investors are not ingrained enough in foreign cultures to anticipate events that can zap company profits. How your stocks perform depends on the management of particular companies, politics, and economic conditions. A change in political leadership in a country, for example, could bring about government regulations that could turn a profitable company into an unprofitable one. Competition from another country with low-cost labor could take customers away from a country that previously was known for a certain product. Reading a newspaper in the U.S. doesn't provide a deep enough insight.

Stay away from funds that invest only in Japan, only in China, only in Latin America, or in any other single country or region, unless you can tell yourself, honestly, that you know what will happen with the Yuan currency in China or how the next election will turn out in Venezuela. Leave those judgments up to a fund manager who travels the world to spot strong companies in places where political, regulatory, or economic conditions will help them profit. Even the pros will make mistakes on these complex factors.

If you have a good fund manager for a diversified international fund, the manager might move you into Japanese stocks, for example, when he or she sees potential there. Later, when growth seems to be peaking in Japan and there is potential elsewhere, your manager might move some of your money away from the lackluster area to a region of higher potential.

Like the U.S., each country or region of the world goes through economic cycles and times when local stock markets are weaker or stronger. In 1998, for example, underlying problems in overheated Asian economies suddenly became undeniable, and stocks went from red hot to scary losers fast. During just three months, Asian stocks dropped 40 percent. Yet, at the same time, large European stocks climbed 35 percent.

You could have lost 40 percent of your money if you had invested only in an Asian fund then. But if you had a "diversified" international fund that made a practice of investing money all over the world, your European stocks would have buffered the blow you took on Asian stocks at that time.

When investors are given a choice of international funds, they will sometimes see what are called "emerging market funds." Fund managers for these funds invest in less stable countries than the U.S. or Europe—places like

Argentina, Brazil, Indonesia, Lebanon, and Turkey. The economies are developing and move in fits and starts that make them volatile. They soar and crash—often with little warning to an outsider.

If you look at an emerging market fund during a hot period, it may look like the wisest investment at the time—maybe providing a 40 percent return one year. But don't be fooled. These are volatile, and while they might be red hot for a while, they have been known to drop 80 percent.

Consequently, a better approach is to pick a "diversified" international fund in which your fund manager can dabble in emerging markets, while holding a lot more stable stocks to buffer any surprise disaster in a corner of the globe. Typically, they might put 5 percent of your money into the volatile areas of the world—or emerging markets.

What to Do

Search for what will be described as a "diversified" international fund, one with a manager who has been investing in foreign markets for years. This is no area for a newcomer. Check on a fund manager's background by reading a prospectus, or the pamphlet you are given when you select funds. For an easier approach, call a toll-free number for your fund and ask about the fund manager's background. Another easy approach is to go to www.morningstar.com, type in the name of your fund, and read the quick description under Management.

You want your manager to have at least five years of experience running your fund or an international fund just like the one you are considering. Think about it: If managers are new to the international arena, are they going to be equipped to appreciate cultural nuances?

Checking a manager's background should actually be a part of your research on any fund. I bring it up for foreign funds, however, because many fund companies dump managers into these complex funds before they've had adequate experience abroad.

You can put about a third of your stock portfolio into international funds. But you should know that investment managers have been having a spirited debate about the right proportions. Some argue to invest as much as 50 percent of your portfolio outside the U.S. because international markets make up about 53 percent of the world's economy. Others claim there is no need to invest any money abroad because large U.S. companies do so much business in foreign lands.

I have been persuaded by those who argue that it is worthwhile to be invested in the best companies everywhere. And while the economies of the world are intertwined, cycles will play out differently in various parts of the world. So you diversify your stocks by investing at home and abroad.

There will be times when U.S. stocks do better, and others when your foreign funds will be best. That's the idea. Because it's impossible to predict cycles accurately, you don't guess. You simply keep some money in international funds at all times—just as you would with small caps and large caps.

Some International Fund Ideas

Consider Nicholas-Applegate International Small Cap Growth (NAGPX), Oakmark International (OAKIX), Oakmark International Small Cap (OAKEX), MSCI EAFE exchange traded index fund (EFA), Masters' Select International (MSILX), or Vanguard Total International Stock Index (VGTSX).

Balanced Funds

These are easy-to-use funds that allow you to hedge your bets because they combine stocks and bonds for you. Although they are typically called "balanced funds," they might also have a name like "asset allocation" funds. Typically, they invest about 60 percent of your money in stocks and 40 percent in bonds.

Increasingly, employers are depositing their employees' 401(k) contributions automatically into this type of fund. So don't be surprised if you look at your 401(k) plan and see your matching money there.

During good cycles in the stock market, your stocks will help you make money, but you won't make as much money in that single fund as you would if you had chosen a mutual fund that invested only in stocks. During bad cycles for the stocks, your bonds will insulate you—keeping you from having awful losses.

So, for example, 2002 was an awful year for the stock market. If your money was in mutual funds that invested only in stocks, you probably lost at least 22 percent of your money. But when you mixed stocks and bonds together through a balanced fund, you lost only about 9.5 percent.

Then came 2003, and investors got relief. It was a great year for the stock market. You would have made about 28.5 percent in stock mutual funds alone. If you wanted to be safer by holdings stocks and bonds in a balanced fund instead, you wouldn't have made as much money. Rather than making 28.5 percent in stocks alone, your stock-and-bond mixture gave you about 19.5 percent. Of course, that's an excellent return—nothing to complain about.

Best of all, however, is the relatively quick recovery you would have enjoyed in a balanced fund. If you had put $10,000 into the average U.S.

balanced fund in early 2000—just before the market plunged 49 percent—you would have recovered relatively fast, according to Lipper.. Six years after depositing your money, you would have had about $12,320. A person who had invested only in the average U.S. stock fund in 2000 would have still been in the hole six years later—with only $8,530 left from the original $10,000.

This makes a balanced fund a very attractive choice for cautious people who realize that they can't get along without some stocks.

What to Do

Although I told you previously not to rely on one mutual fund alone, a balanced fund is the exception. You cannot rely on a stock fund alone, because it provides too much risk. You cannot rely on a bond fund alone, because it won't grow your money enough for retirement.

A balanced fund could be held alone, however, because it is designed to be fairly well diversified. It gives you stocks and bonds, so the stocks help your money grow and the bonds insulate you from risks.

If you want a simple one-stop solution as an investor, a balanced fund could be your easy choice, although I'd prefer a little more diversification if you are willing to do it. A balanced fund typically doesn't give you many—if any—international stocks or small cap stocks. A greater variety of investments usually gives you more opportunity. So if your only easy choice for a combination of stocks and bonds is a balanced fund, by all means don't hesitate about using it.

But you may have access to a new invention that has the entire panoply of investments in it: stocks of all sizes and from many countries, plus bonds. These are ideal easy investments, and I've devoted all of Chapter 14, "Simple Does It: No-Brainer Investing with Target-Date Funds," to them.

Some Balanced or Asset Allocation Fund Ideas

Consider Fidelity Balanced (FBALX), Dodge & Cox Balanced (DODBX), T. Rowe Price Spectrum (RPSIX), Mairs & Power Balanced (MAPOX), or Fidelity Four-in-One (FFNOX) .

REITs (Real Estate Investment Trusts)

These are funds that invest in real estate—shopping centers, warehouses, apartment buildings, office buildings, and so forth.

A study by Ibbotson shows that it makes sense to put a little money into REITs because they tend to act differently from stocks and bonds—maybe rising while the others are falling, or vice versa. In other words, they diversify your holdings.

Still, the ordinary person has a huge investment in real estate through a home. So some financial planners would argue that you already are diversified, without also buying a mutual fund that invests in real estate. Others insist that clients put about 5 percent of their portfolio into a REIT fund.

What to Do

If your 401(k) plan doesn't have a REIT in it, don't worry about it. If you do have one, you can diversify your stock and bond investments by putting no more than 5 percent of your total portfolio into that fund.

Sector or Specialty Funds

You probably won't find these funds in a 401(k) plan. But you may make the mistake of following the herd into these in your IRA.

My advice: Stay away from them. Sector, or specialty funds, invest in only one type of business—maybe just energy, or maybe just technology, or maybe just consumer products, and so on. The common person gets lured into one of these sectors when they are hot, but they don't have enough inside knowledge to know when to get out. In fact, even professionals lack that knowledge. It's very tough to guess when a cycle for any particular sector will start or end.

So, buyer beware. You are likely to get throttled in these funds.

Instead, choose a diversified mutual fund that invests in all industries, and let your fund manager choose sectors for you. In a diversified stock fund, the fund manager is always looking for hot sectors. When he or she spots one, the manager might buy a few more stocks than usual in that sector to give your fund some extra oomph. But he or she will also be watching closely to try to get you out of the way when the party ends.

When a diversified fund makes a bet, it tends to be with a small amount of money—maybe 2 percent of the fund's total investments. When novices do it, they jump in with both feet—a very dangerous endeavor.

Stable Value Fund

This fund is more like the bond funds or money market funds covered in the preceding chapter.

It is not a substitute for a stock fund. Instead, it can be used as a temporary holding tank for cash at times when you might be nervous about both stocks and bonds—perhaps when interest rates are rising and people are losing money in bond funds.

As its name suggests, it is a stable choice. It is going to pay you a very low interest rate—one you can count on. It may be just 3 or 4 percent.

This is not a place for young investors to stash their money on a long-term basis. It simply won't grow enough. You may see a stable value fund as a "no-risk investment." And it is. But that doesn't mean you aren't taking a risk. Remember, the biggest risk Americans face is not having enough money for retirement. While young, people must take the risk on some down years in more volatile investments like stocks to avoid the larger looming risk of running out of money in retirement.

For a person within five years of retirement, however, a stable value fund can be appealing when both stocks and bonds are falling. But remember, don't withdraw from stocks completely. If you do, you won't be positioned to grow your money when the cycle suddenly turns up.

What to Do

To provide stability in your 401(k), you might have 5 percent of your money in what's called "cash"—in other words, in an investment that's almost as safe as cash. You could consider either a "stable value fund" or a "money market fund."

If you work for an employer that automatically puts matching money into a 401(k) for you, the employer might deposit your money into either a stable value fund or a money market fund. If that occurs, it doesn't mean the fund is your best choice. Employers deposit money in stable value and money market funds because they are afraid to invest any of your money in stocks and risk a suit if you lose money and panic.

But you cannot count on this fund to grow your money enough for retirement. If your employer has put your money there, contact your benefits office and make a change—sign up for some stock funds, too. The next chapter will help you with quantities.

Company Stock

You may have one choice in a 401(k) that is not a mutual fund. Your employer may give you the opportunity to buy stock in the company where you work. If so, make sure you don't overdose on it.

One of the most frequent mistakes people make with 401(k)s is assuming that they will be safe if they invest in the company that employs them. People tend to feel more comfortable with what they think they know. So they see people going to work every day and assume that the stock in their company must be just fine.

Looks, however, can be deceiving with stocks. Even companies with thousands of employees around the world can end up in bankruptcy or get pummeled by a new competitor. When companies go into bankruptcy court, stocks usually become worthless.

Don't get burned the way people did at Enron—believing that their retirement was safe with stock Wall Street loved before fraud was discovered.

What to Do

Take a lesson from the professionals who run pension funds: Because single stocks are too unpredictable, pension funds never put more than about 5 percent of their money into one stock—no matter how stupendous it looks.

If you have more than that in your 401(k), sell some of the shares and transfer the money to diversified mutual funds instead. If it's painful to do all at once, do it in stages.

Bond Funds

Bond funds invest in bonds, which tend to be safer than stocks. For a detailed explanation, see the preceding chapter.

What to Do

Investors should hold some bonds to buffer the blows of the stock market. A classic combination of stocks and bonds puts 40 percent of the portfolio in bonds and 60 percent in stocks. Young investors don't need to keep 40 percent in bonds unless the stock market scares them. For a brave 20- or 30-year-old, 10 percent in bonds might suffice.

Consider a well-diversified bond fund that invests in a combination of U.S. government bonds and corporate bonds. Generally, an intermediate-term bond fund is a good selection. Often, there are three different diversified bond fund choices: "intermediate," "long-term," and "short-term."

"Intermediate" means that the bonds in the fund will tend to mature in about 5 to 10 years. That makes them safer than "long-term bonds," or those that might not mature for about 20 or 30 years. Bonds are considered riskier when investors must wait a long time to get their money returned to them— so 20 years is riskier than 10 years, 10 years riskier than 5 years, and 5 years riskier than 2 years. "Short-term bond funds" typically choose bonds that mature in about 2 years. Although that makes them less risky than intermediate bonds, they usually provide a lower return.

Ideas for Bond Funds

Consider Harbor Bond Fund (HABDX), PIMCO Total Return (PTTAX), Loomis Sayles Bond (LSBRX), or Vanguard Total Bond Market Index (VBMFX). You can also buy individual bonds for an IRA from a broker. High-quality bonds include U.S. Treasury bonds or corporate bonds that are rated A, AA, or AAA.

10

THE ONLY WAY THAT
WORKS: ASSET ALLOCATION

Stay calm.

I threw a lot of information at you in the preceding chapter, and you might be in the mood now to toss it aside and simply try to pick the one *right* mutual fund.

Please don't.

You will certainly find plenty of temptation in the marketplace. Potential investors are bombarded with ads beckoning to them to trust a winner, and TV shows and publications make stars out of a handful of investing pros. So, when faced with more than 8,000 different mutual fund choices for an IRA or a dozen in a 401(k), busy people often want to find a shortcut. They spot a fund manager being lauded in the news media and then think their problems will be solved: They will hand their money over to that one remarkable genius and be done with it, trusting someone who clearly knows his or her way around the stock market.

Usually, they are disappointed. They end up face to face with the unpleasant truth in investing: There is no single magic fund or investment savior you can count on to always grow your money, keep you out of harm's way, and outsmart the other pros who are trying to be outstanding.

In fact, college finance professors have studied at length whether stars truly exist in the investment world. And the academic research is discouraging. It comes down to this: Fund managers shine for a while, bask in public attention, and attract a lot of headlines and millions of dollars in new money to manage as investors glom onto a winner. Then, often after only a year, the fund ends up fairly mediocre, or even worse.

There's actually a joke about this among investment professionals. It revolves around a coveted award that is handed out every year to an exceptional mutual fund manager. The award comes from a firm named Morningstar, which is well respected for analyzing mutual funds. At the end of each year, Morningstar anoints someone "The Manager of the Year"—the equivalent of the Academy Award in the fund business.

If a fund manager is named "Manager of the Year," it's a tremendous tribute. Firms that receive the honor make a fortune on new money coming through the door as investors seek out the Midas touch. But the joke among fund managers is that it's a dubious honor—an ominous sign—you don't want to win. Often, the next year the "Manager of the Year" falls from stardom.

A few have held on or returned to stardom a few years later, but more often than not all the excitement ends in mediocrity.

Academic studies come to this bitter conclusion: Winners only appear to be winners for a while, but they rarely keep it up. Luck, or being in the right place at the right time during a cycle in the stock market, seems to be why fund managers stand out temporarily. That's very different from possessing unusual investing prowess that lasts. One or two years of amazing returns simply creates an illusion of outstanding skill.

Why Star Funds Fade

When you think about it, there is good reason why an apparently great fund can fizzle into a so-so fund. If a fund manager has only a little money to handle, it can be a lot easier to invest than when he has millions or billions to deploy. If you doubt this, think about what it's like to make a meal for a couple of friends compared to 100, or consider how well you handle one project at work versus many dumped on you simultaneously by multiple bosses.

In investing, it's even more complicated. If a fund manager is famous, he gets flooded with money. Also, other investors try to copy him. There's a rumor mill that circulates in the investing business, and if someone gets wind of a star manager buying or selling a stock, news travels fast. You might think having copycats would be considered flattering. But it messes up a fund manager's life and ultimately the money you will make in the fund.

If traders—who buy and sell stocks for investors—spot the renowned manager buying a stock, they tell clients and their bosses. Those people will want to make money too, so they rush to buy the same stock. The result: The stock price goes up because of the volume of buying. So while the fund manager is in the process of buying the stock, he has to pay a higher price for the stock than intended. Likewise, if the manager starts to sell a stock and is noticed, others will copy—bailing out, too. So the stock will plummet before the manager can sneak away from it. Consequently, if you own the fund that is being copied, you might make less money than you would if your manager was inconspicuous and could buy and sell stocks at the very best prices for you.

More importantly, each manager has a certain style acquired over time in selecting stocks or bonds. Perhaps a fund manager understands how small company stocks generally act during cycles, so she can maneuver through good cycles with skill—buying the promising stocks and avoiding blowups—making mutual fund clients adore her. But she might not be as adept with large caps and might not even be allowed to buy them when they are the beneficiaries of a specific cycle. Or perhaps for years she's been assigned to invest in healthcare stocks, and she looks brilliant while they are the popular stocks. But then along comes a cycle when investors hate healthcare stocks and are grabbing up energy stocks. In that environment, her intuition and knowledge fail her, so she doesn't shine in that particular cycle.

If you owned a Janus fund in 2000, you know what I mean. The funds seemed to be tremendous masters during the growth stock mania in the 1990s. But they became ugly losers in the early 2000s when investors ran away from technology stocks and other growth stocks and wanted safer value stocks—or companies that made widgets and drilled for oil. Janus managers lacked background in value stocks then. Growth stocks of all sizes outperformed value stocks from December 1997 to June 2000, with growth up 164% and value up only 41%. After 2000, the trend was the opposite. Growth stocks dropped 44%, and value stocks climbed 60%. That, of course, left even the savviest growth fund managers licking their wounds. Table 10.1 shows the fluctuations in the cycles of large cap growth stocks and large cap value stocks.

This may bring you to the conclusion that all you need to do is find the all-around pro. But the academic studies suggest the odds of finding the Warren Buffets of the investing world are against you.

Table 10.1

*Good and Bad Investment Cycles in Large Cap Growth Stocks
and Large Cap Value Stocks
(Annual Total Returns through August 2006)*

Year	Large Cap Value	Large Cap Growth
1993	15.48	−1.96
1994	−1.94	3.82
1995	45.22	39.68
1996	20.02	20.11
1997	37.63	32.87
1998	19.87	57.52
1999	14.65	50.59
2000	14.02	−19.03
2001	−1.26	−27.73
2002	−12.76	−28.83
2003	29.35	38.06
2004	12.42	3.29
2005	5.98	8.25
2006	8.48	−3.15

Table based on data from The Leuthold Group.

The One Proven Way to Success:
Asset Allocation

Instead, the studies point to another investment approach that truly does work. And I'm going to teach you how to use it step-by-step so that you can make money over a lifetime without devoting more than a few minutes a year to the effort.

To get ready for it, I want you to start thinking the way you would when selecting doctors. When you need a doctor, you don't pick one brilliant doctor and expect him or her to care for your every need. You pick one with the specialty you need. In other words, you wouldn't go to an eye doctor when you needed heart surgery. And when you needed to have your eyes checked, you wouldn't want the heart surgeon.

Both types of doctors are skilled; both are trained in the basics of the body. But one cannot step in for the other. As you go through life, you need a variety of doctors, with various specialties for all the needs of your body.

The same holds for mutual funds.

That's why, if you went to a qualified financial planner with your list of mutual funds from a 401(k) plan and asked for help, the adviser wouldn't focus on finding you the one *right* fund or the most brilliant fund manager. Your planner would check for well-managed mutual funds, but his primary focus would be on mixing and matching the funds on your list—holding a little of this and a little of that for you so that you would have all the specialties you needed: large cap stocks, small cap stocks, international stocks, bonds.

The mixing process is called "asset allocation." And although asset allocation is not nearly as glitzy as finding an investing whiz kid, it's the one approach that studies have shown works over time.

A crucial study on the matter was done by money manager Gary Brinson in 1986. He analyzed pension funds and found that the key influence on 94 percent of an investor's return comes from how the money is divided up among stocks, bonds, and cash—or "asset allocation."

Only 4 percent depends on how well a manager selects stocks. Only 2 percent comes down to how the manager "times the market"—or figuring out when to buy stocks and when to bail out.

Forget Heroes—Just Match

In other words, novice investors have the entire process backward when they focus on trying to find one brilliant stock-picker with the Midas touch. And if you think you can't be a good investor because you don't know how to pick stocks, this should give you great confidence: Asset allocation is fairly easy, much easier than analyzing a stock. You don't have to scrutinize company operations, follow the economy, or do any complex math.

It's as easy as playing a matching game or following a recipe. Think of the matching games you played as a child. You would have a workbook, and on one page you would see a picture of a two-story brick home. Then, you would have to match that picture to one of four words in an adjacent list: car, house, girl, and dog. You'd draw a line from the brick home to the word "house."

You don't need much more than the ability to match in order to do a fairly good job investing your retirement savings. Really!

That's why I taught you the terms in the preceding chapter: large cap stocks, small cap stocks, international stocks, and bonds. Those are the words you match to the names of funds on a 401(k) list, or the words you use to make a recipe fit for an IRA or any other investment fund.

You combine the various types of funds into a mixture, because each fund acts differently in cycles. When you jumble them together, one or two tend to buffer the blows from the fund that inevitably will be getting hurt or lagging.

It could be the large cap fund or the small cap fund that saves you from harm. It could be the international fund or the bond fund. The point is that right now neither you nor anyone else knows which it will be. So when you buy the entire mixture and continue to hold onto the fund you adore and the fund you despise, you should be ready for the unpredictable changing seasons of the stock market. You will always have a fund that helps you relax while you wait for a rebirth of a laggard.

Start the Sorting—It's Asset Allocation Time

Say that your employer gives you a list of funds for your 401(k) plan, or your broker gives you a list for an IRA. You have no idea which to choose. You see the "Best Ever Large Cap Fund," the "Go Anywhere Small Cap Fund," the "Better Than Best International Fund," and the "Wonderful Bond Fund."

They all sound outstanding. Which do you select?

Maybe, in the past, you would have looked for one fund with a stock-picker who had been touted in the news, but now you know that finding a hero, alone, is unreliable. So, next, maybe you would look at the returns for all of the funds in your 401(k), hoping that one fund will stand out. You see that the Go Anywhere Small Cap Fund was up 20 percent last year, while the Best Ever Large Cap Fund gave investors only a 5 percent return. And the Wonderful Bond Fund was up only 1 percent.

So maybe you think the choice is easy. You will go with the winner, the one that gained way more than any of the others last year—the Go Anywhere Small Cap Fund. That's what many novice investors do.

But you know now that's the wrong decision—the road to destroying hard-earned money.

Instead, the right answer is to pick all four funds—large caps, small caps, international stocks, and bonds. The Best Ever Large Cap fund might just look like a dud at the moment because the cycle at that particular time is not being kind to large caps and is bestowing wealth on small caps. But history shows that with time, fortunes will reverse, and large company stocks will be the winners while investors temporarily shun the small company stocks.

You need all four types of funds to be ready for whatever the market cycles throw your way. That's what the investment world calls "asset allocation," or dividing your money into a variety of specific types of funds.

And that's why you play the matching game—looking for the words you need on your fund list. There are always extra words in the fund names that get in the way. So as you play the matching game, you hunt for the key words I taught you in the preceding chapter. You'll find them within either the fund name or the fund's description that accompanies the fund.

Within the name "Best Ever Large Cap Fund," for example, you would merely focus in on two words, "large cap," and you'll match that fund to the amount of "large caps" that I will give you in Chapter 11, "Do This." You are going to start pouring fund types—or ingredients—into a recipe that will make your retirement savings grow.

After you have matched the large cap fund to your recipe, you are going to go back to your 401(k) list and then hunt for your small cap choice. And there you find it. Buried within the name "Go Anywhere Small Cap Fund," you find the two most important words, "small cap." You are going to match a certain amount of that fund to the small cap proportion of your recipe.

So let's say that you've thrown an approximately correct amount of small caps into your 401(k) retirement success recipe. Then you move to the "international fund" and the "bond fund"—dropping the right quantities into your retirement fund.

That's the process.

But what if you see a fund that doesn't have the key words like "large cap" or "small cap" in the name? That happens sometimes. Funds have names like Fairholme or PIMCO Total Return. In that case, you have to probe a little deeper into the fund's description in your 401(k) materials, maybe using the prospectus (the pamphlet that comes with the fund) or going to www.morningstar.com. At the Morningstar website, you can enter the name "Fairholme" in the white "Quotes" box at the top left of the page and find a page with a lot of information about the fund. You can see under "Key Stats" on the right that Fairholme is a "mid cap blend fund" and has a top-quality rating of five stars.

So, if you wanted a mid cap fund, that could be your choice. You would match it to your recipe.

Getting the Proportions Right

But now you might be wondering how to get the proportions right when you do the matching. That's not difficult either, given all the asset allocation models—or recipes—that are available to you. If you have a 401(k) plan, your employer might have a Web site or printed material with pie charts. A broker or financial planner might show you these, too. The charts might be identified in a brochure or on a Web site under the heading "asset allocation."

These are the recipes to follow, and the slices on the pie charts show you how much of each type of fund to use.

You might have seen these charts in the past and found them meaningless. They won't be confusing anymore, because now you can recognize the mutual fund names and will know how to match names on your mutual fund list to the corresponding slice on the chart.

Still, you might get somewhat overwhelmed because there are many different pie charts. There is a reason you see a variety: How you divide your money depends on when you are going to need it and how nervous you get when the stock market goes through nasty cycles. I will help you identify the pie chart—or recipe—that might be appropriate for you.

First, I want you to be aware of one important point: If you went to various financial planners, each would have a slightly different recipe—or asset allocation plan—for you. That might be unsettling; perhaps all the variations would make you worry about making a mistake. Maybe one says to put 35 percent of your money into large cap funds and another says 38 percent. Instead of being nervous about imprecision, let it comfort you and empower you.

Asset allocation—or mixing and matching types of mutual funds—is essential. You must do it to be a successful investor. But the theory behind it is not so refined that professionals agree on precise portions of the various types of mutual funds. In other words, professionals generally agree you need large caps, small caps, international stocks, and bonds, but they might deviate on the amounts by a couple of percentage points.

Think of it like using a recipe that calls for a rounded teaspoon of sugar. Just what is "rounded"? It's more than a teaspoon, yet whether you rounded the amount of sugar a lot or just a little, the recipe would probably turn out OK.

The critical point, however, is that you use sugar. You don't just leave sugar out of the recipe, and you don't use a cup when the recipe calls for a teaspoon. So as an investor, what's vital to you is this: You use the full mixture—the sugar, or small caps; the flour, or large caps; international stocks for variety; and, of course, bonds. It's the blending of the ingredients that will make your money grow effectively over time.

It's called "diversifying." All it means is this: You aren't going to overdose on a single type of investment but are going to hold a blend of investments so that you are ready for any cycle.

The Logic Behind "Diversification"

If you handed your money over to most financial planners, they would not try to predict when the cycles would come and go or when a certain mutual fund would win or lose. Studies convince investment professionals that guessing tends to be folly. Instead, they simply decide on an appropriate "diversified" mixture of mutual funds for clients based on research showing that small caps, large caps, international stocks, and bonds take turns at soaring and plummeting during cycles.

They figure that if they buy the right mixture for an IRA or 401(k), their client will get the advantage of the 29 percent upturn in large cap funds in years like 1998, when the good times just happen to hit without warning. Likewise, the small cap funds will have their day when a delightful change in the market sneaks up, shaking the tiny stocks out of dormancy.

There's one piece to this approach that may shock you. As cycles occur, and as any one of the mutual funds in an investor's retirement fund takes a thrashing in a day, a month, or a year, most financial planners will not fixate on the moment or let it deter them from a well-conceived plan.

Planners just hold tight to the mixture of funds they created. They focus on historical studies that show that after many, many years, the large stocks in the mixture should climb about 8 to 10 percent on average annually—even if at the moment they are being brutalized. The small stocks should average around 12 percent—even if they are soaring much more than that at that point in time. And the bonds should smooth out the worst bumps, climbing at about 5 percent.

The professionals concoct the mixture based on historical studies that demonstrate how blending all the different categories together provides a decent retirement after 20, 30, or 40 years of letting the mixture sit intact through ups and downs.

Proportions, however, are the key for the long-term outcome. Financial advisers determine which proportions are best for certain types of clients, by using historical data. It shows them what various concoctions of stocks and bonds are likely to do.

They know that a person who relies only on stock funds during a five-year period could lose as much as 12 percent of their money a year or make as much as 28 percent, because there already has been a point in history when this happened.

They know they can soften the impact of a cruel stock market by putting 30 percent of a client's money into bond funds and 70 percent into stock funds. With such a mixture, history tells them the worst loss during five years could be 6.3 percent a year, and the upside could still reach a delightful 22.7 percent.

To be even safer, planners know they could put half a client's money in bonds and half in stocks. Then, the worst anticipated loss would be 2.7 percent a year during five years, if history repeats. And there still would be an upside of potentially 21 percent.

Could the future be somewhat different than the past?

Absolutely. But the past is the best tool available to provide a guide to the future.

With this type of historical data, investment professionals pinpoint the combinations that would best fit people at different points in their life. A 25-year-old would need a lot of stock to harness the power of compounding early and build a fortune. A 60-year-old would need close to half her money in bonds to make sure she doesn't lose a fortune in a stock market disaster on the verge of retirement.

This Isn't about Math

This may sound like a complex endeavor, but it isn't what you might think. Financial advisers don't have to do elaborate calculations to incorporate history into plans for these various age groups. The numbers have been crunched by brilliant professors and math geniuses who have fed years and years of stock market data into computers and turned out some simple models. Those models show up in colorful charts with 401(k) and IRA materials, and they are all over the Internet.

Professionals and people like you have access to these so-called asset allocation models and can follow them without any more math than you learn in elementary school.

Although most people think they can't handle any of this because it must require a math brain, what's actually involved is quite different. If you went to a financial planner, he or she probably wouldn't be doing equations. Instead, that planner would be trying to figure out your psyche.

Planners want to know whether you are going to panic in a market downturn and run away from the combination of mutual funds that they assembled for you based on a simple model. They know that if you panic, you could lock in a tremendous loss and perhaps need a decade or more to recover. That's too costly for you, and they don't want it to happen.

Consequently, if planners think you might flee your stock funds, they will tweak one of the typical models for your age group a little—maybe reducing your exposure to stock funds by 5 or 10 percent.

This is critically important. Novice investors usually get this wrong. They tend to go for all or nothing—either all small caps or no small caps; all stocks or no stocks. In contrast, the professional tweaks: Maybe up 2 to 5 percent or down 2 to 5 percent in a category of stock funds.

The same goes for scary periods in the market. The professional might move 5 to 10 percent of a person's money out of stocks and into a money market fund to soothe a nervous client. But the professional will try to talk clients out of moving every cent to safety, because the pros know that the cycle will change when you least expect it. And being there—ready for the change of seasons—is the sure way to make money.

11

DO THIS

Now you know how professionals think and what they try to do with your money. It's time for you to do the same—to master the finishing touches.

Asset allocation—or mixing and matching a variety of funds—is the most important move you will make as an investor. And you now have all the tools you need to do it well.

You already know what's inside various mutual funds, what makes them soar and plummet in cycles, and how to match the key terms like "large cap" and "small cap" to your list of mutual funds. Now, I'm going to show you how to select the appropriate proportions, and you will be done. You will be a skilled investor.

We'll start with a classic mixture of funds. Among investment professionals, there is agreement that a moderate "asset allocation model" would divide retirement savings up like this: 60 percent into stocks and 40 percent into bonds.

This investment blend would be comparable to the porridge that's "not too hot, and not too cold" in "Goldilocks and the Three Bears."

From now on, think of the 60 percent stock and 40 percent bond combination as a reliable "asset allocation" model that is just right if you aren't adventurous. Then, venture off from that point, if you'd like, into a model that might be even better for you. As you read further, you will become competent at adapting the model to your particular age, years to retirement, and temperament.

The 60:40 mix is a good starting point in learning asset allocation. Over the years, knowing this classic allocation model will give you your guidepost for investing decisions. It can always be your fall-back position if you are ever confused.

If you used it continually, you would be on a better track than most people.

The math whizzes have shown that you can lose money with a 60:40 mix in a single year. But losing money for even two years in a row is unusual.

Asset Allocation Is Simply Matching

Let's say that you have decided to sign up for a 401(k), or you want to overhaul a retirement account you have neglected.

Your employer hasn't given you a recipe, or model, to follow. But it doesn't matter. You now have the classic 60:40 stock and bond asset allocation model in your head, and you are going to use it as your recipe. You have your list of mutual funds on your desk, and you have a form to fill out. It asks you how much of your paycheck to invest in the retirement plan. It also asks you how you want to divide that money among the various mutual fund choices. You will need to state your preferences in percentage terms.

Let's say that you decide to put $100 from each paycheck into your 401(k) plan. So as you fill out your 401(k) form, you think of your $100 as 100 percent of your recipe's mixture and start from there.

The next step is to hunt through the mutual funds on your 401(k) list—to start the mixing-and-matching process. Your 60:40 recipe calls for bonds. So you peruse your list of mutual funds and find only one diversified bond fund. It's called the "Wonderful Bond Fund."

"Wonderful!" you exclaim. "I've found it." The only question is how much. So you simply match that fund to the quantity you need in your recipe. Your decision is easy, because the recipe tells you exactly what to do. You already decided you were going to use a classic 60:40 mixture for your recipe.

So you write on your 401(k) form that you will put 40 percent of your 401(k) contribution into the Wonderful Bond Fund. That's $40 on every payday.

You now have assembled 40 percent of your recipe. The bond portion is done. Next, you return to your list of 401(k) mutual funds to complete the second part of your recipe—pouring in the right amount of stocks. You know the quantity from your recipe. It's 60 percent. You also know from the preceding chapter that a well-diversified large cap stock fund is a key ingredient—a core investment to hold year after year.

You find one large cap stock fund on your list of funds—the "Best Ever Large Cap Fund." So you select it, and you follow your recipe by putting 60 percent of your 401(k) contribution into that fund—or $60 a payday.

You now have a classic 60:40 asset allocation—60 percent of your money is in stocks, and 40 percent is in bonds.

Your recipe is complete, and your 401(k) form now looks like this:

Wonderful Bond Fund—40 percent

Best Ever Large Cap Fund—60 percent

As you go through life, you will have different actual funds in 401(k) plans or IRAs, but whatever they are, you can put 40 percent into a diversified bond fund and 60 percent into a diversified large cap fund. If you kept this approach intact—keeping 60 percent of retirement savings in stocks and 40 percent in bonds—you would be more successful than most 401(k) investors.

But let's say that you feel comfortable taking this a little further, and you should. We are going to fine-tune that 60 percent piece you put into stocks, making a slight change in your recipe, so that you are ready for more cycles in the market. The basic recipe of 60 percent stocks and 40 percent bonds is going to stay intact. But you realize that sometimes small cap stocks do well and large caps are disappointing, and other times large caps win and small caps are scary. So you want to be prepared for both cycles.

I'm going to assume now that your 401(k) plan gives you a choice of one large cap fund and one small cap fund. Not all do. But say that you have those two choices.

Then, go through your list of stock mutual funds and find those that match the two basic U.S. stock categories: large caps and small caps. You will choose both based on a common practice in the investment profession: Typically, a financial adviser would want you to put about 70 to 75 percent of all your U.S. stock money into large caps because they are less volatile and make up a larger portion of the overall stock market than small caps. In fact, large caps make up roughly 70 to 75 percent of all the stocks in the stock market, so that's where the recipe originates. You can simply copy it. When you have tucked large caps neatly away, you dump the remainder into small caps, which make up roughly 30 to 25 percent of the stock market.

Here's how you would follow the recipe and sign up for 401(k) mutual funds—again starting with the original $100 for your 401(k) plan contribution.

First, remember that the basic recipe is 60 percent stocks and 40 percent bonds. Begin by selecting bonds—filling 40 percent of your recipe with a bond fund. That would be $40 on every payday.

Then you would move to stock funds in the 401(k) list and decide how to allocate the remaining $60, or the 60 percent, that your recipe says should go into stocks. You would state on your 401(k) form that you will put 45 percent of each 401(k) contribution—or $45—into a large cap fund, and 15 percent—or $15—into a small cap stock fund. (This might not look like 75 percent large caps and 25 small caps, but it is. Remember, you are simply dividing up your stock money—or $60—into the 75 percent large cap and 25 percent small cap concoction.)

That takes care of 100 percent of your contribution into your 401(k) plan. With the combination of large stocks, small stocks, and bonds, you will be well diversified—ready for most cycles in the U.S. stock market.

For that 60 stock and 40 bond asset allocation, your 401(k) selection form would now read like this:

>   *Whatever Bond Fund—40 percent*
>
>   *Whatever Large Cap Fund—45 percent*
>
>   *Whatever Small Cap Fund—15 percent*

All right, but let's say that your 401(k) also includes an international fund; and you know that sometimes foreign stocks do best, and in other cycles U.S. stocks do best. So you want to be ready for anything worldwide and partake in the global economy—smart!

In this case, let's start fresh with your $100 contribution. First put 40 percent, or $40, into a bond fund. But now you are going to think of your $60 stock portion with a fresh approach. You will think of dividing your total stock money—or 60 percent of your full 401(k) contribution—into two major categories: U.S. stocks and international stocks. And I suggest that you put roughly a third of all the stock money into international stocks.

With many countries going through a growth spurt recently, financial advisers have become increasingly interested in foreign markets. But they are debating how much money to channel there. Some say 50 percent because foreign markets make up about 53 percent of the global economy. A few say no foreign investment is necessary because large U.S. companies sell products everywhere.

So feel free to tweak your foreign allocation a bit, if you'd like. But let's say you decide to put a third of your stock money into a solid, well-diversified international fund—one that insulates you from regional shocks by investing in many countries throughout the world. Then, given your $100 contribution to your 401(k), you would put $40 into a bond fund, then $20 into an international fund, and the remaining $40 would go to the large cap and small cap U.S. stock mixture I previously described.

In other words, you'd put about a quarter of your U.S. stock money in small caps, and the rest in large caps. Now your 401(k) form looks like this:

Whatever Bond Fund—40 percent

Whatever Large Cap Stock Fund—30 percent

Whatever Small Cap Stock Fund—10 percent

Whatever International Stock Fund—20 percent

You are nicely diversified—ready for cycles. With every paycheck, you will put $40 into bonds, $30 into large cap stocks, $10 into small cap stocks, and $20 into stocks throughout the world.

If you are offered a mid cap fund, you can use that to diversify even a little more. In that case, leave everything intact on your recipe except your small cap allocation. Divide the small caps in half—putting a 5 percent allocation of small caps into the mixture. The remaining 5 percent goes to mid caps.

You have a complex, well-diversified portfolio. Your 401(k) form would look like this:

Whatever Bond Fund—40 percent

Whatever Large Cap Fund—30 percent

Whatever Small Cap Stock Fund—5 percent

Whatever Mid Cap Stock Fund—5 percent

Whatever International Fund—20 percent

That's it. You've got the basics. You write down those percents on your 401(k) form provided by your benefits office at work, and you can be done with the task. With every paycheck, your orders will be followed, and you will be ready for the various cycles of the market. You will stay with the plan regardless of market conditions, forging ahead even if one or more of the funds happens to be bleeding cash during an awful cycle.

Picking within Categories

But what if you have more than one large cap fund on your 401(k) list? How do you choose between them? If you find one fund that is described as a "core" fund, that makes your choice easy. It means your fund manager will blend various types of large stocks for you so that you will be ready for a variety of cycles and won't be overly risky. You will have some risky, fast-growing stocks but also more dependable, slower-growing value stocks.

To find such a fund, look for words such as "core" or "blend" in the fund's name or description. But you might not be lucky enough to see that simple language. The fund description for a core fund might, instead, tell you that the fund looks for "capital appreciation," and selects both "growth" and "value" stocks.

If you are lucky, you will find a fund called a "Standard & Poor's 500 Index fund" or a "total stock market index fund" on your fund list. If you do, either of these will serve you well as a core fund. In the next chapter, I'll explain more about why these two particular funds are usually excellent choices.

But if you don't have a "core" fund, you will probably have to choose between a large cap "value" fund and a large cap "growth" fund. The growth fund will be more daring. In certain years you will make more money, and in others lose more money, than you would in a value fund. The value fund will give you a more stable ride—with less shocking losses than in growth.

As I said in the preceding chapter, the value fund—or tortoise in the "Tortoise and the Hare" race—wins over many years of investing. But even if you can't figure out whether you are looking at a tortoise or a hare, don't get hung up on this decision and fail to act. Get started with a well-diversified large cap fund, and you will be headed in the right direction.

Still, if you are up to the task and willing to fine-tune your choices more completely, start trying to identify which of your choices is "large cap growth" and which is "large cap value." Let the matching game begin. Look in the fund name or description for these words to find a growth fund: "growth," or maybe "maximum growth," or "aggressive growth." Typically, a maximum growth or aggressive growth fund would be riskier than a growth fund.

"Value funds" often have words like "income" or "low cost" in the name or description. The description might also tell you that the fund selects stocks that pay "dividends." Typically, when stocks pay dividends, that gives you a certain level of stability—insurance against wild ups and downs. (Think of dividends a little like the interest you get on a savings account, except that dividends are never guaranteed. The company can increase a dividend, leave it the same, or take it away.)

OK, let's get back to the matching game. You will find the same "growth" and "value" labels on both small cap funds and large cap funds.

So what do you do now that you can spot them? If your head is spinning with growth and value and you are asking what's best for you, take a deep breath again and be assured that there is a simple way to handle all of this. In fact, if you went to a financial planner for help, he or she would likely take the simple route. The planners don't know any better than you do whether the cycle in a single year will favor a growth or a value fund. So they don't try to figure it out. Instead, they get the stock portion of portfolios ready for any cycle. They simply divide it up half-and-half—half growth and half value—so that the investor will be ready for the ups and insulated somewhat from the downs.

So let's say that your 401(k) plan doesn't have any core funds in it. Instead, you are given two large cap fund choices—a large cap growth fund and a large cap value fund. And you are given two small cap fund choices— a small cap growth fund and a small cap value fund. What do you do? You can just divide your large cap money half-and-half—50 percent into growth and 50 percent into value. Do the same with small caps.

Here's what it looks like in money: If you are putting $45 into large caps, $22.50 will go into a large cap growth fund and another $22.50 will go into a large cap value fund. If $15 is going into small caps, you will put $7.50 in the small cap growth fund and another $7.50 in the small cap value fund.

That's the process. That's as elaborate as you have to get.

You Don't Need to Use Every 401(k) Fund

Your 401(k) may give you more choices than I have described here. You don't have to use them all. The key is to match the necessary categories—not to use all the funds. Just to reiterate: The necessary categories are bonds and stocks. And for stocks you want international, large cap, small cap, and maybe mid cap. Fill each of the categories with one core fund that blends growth and value stocks, and you will be on the right track. So that's four or five funds. But if your plan doesn't offer a core fund, you can pick one fund for large cap growth, one for large cap value, one for small cap growth, and one for small cap value.

If you do this, you are far beyond the average person. You are assembling your retirement savings the way a financial planner would if you went to one for help.

What's Your Age: 20, 30, 40, or 50?

Depending on your age and how you will feel when conditions get really ugly in the stock market, you may want to alter the quantities in your recipe somewhat. Think again about the rounded teaspoon for your recipe—a close but inexact measurement. Again, there are no absolutely exact measurements with investments because only you can figure out just how much nerve you will have during scary cycles.

But again, here are some rules of thumb.

If you are in your 20s and 30s, and if history makes you comfortable that you will recover from the scariest of stock market downturns, deviate from the classic 60 percent stocks and 40 percent bonds portfolio I have described. Go right ahead with a more aggressive approach to stocks—cutting back on bonds or even eliminating them altogether.

In fact, as a beginning investor in your 20s, you should be more worried about running out of money in your old age than incurring maybe a 20 or 30 percent loss in the stock market now. Financial advisers increasingly are pushing young investors to put 90 to 100 percent of their retirement savings in stocks.

Again, that doesn't mean investing in just one specific stock or one type of stock fund. That's asking for trouble—leaving you way too vulnerable to a corporate mishap or bad cycle in the market.

It does mean taking steps to cushion the impact of cycles—in other words, dividing your money into large caps, small caps, and international stocks. It also means keeping a mixture of growth and value—not the hot mutual fund of the day. You can get growth and value blended into core funds, or select growth and value individually.

So, if you are 22 and signing up for a 401(k) plan for the first time, the combination could look like this:

> *Large Cap Core Stock Fund (maybe a Standard & Poor's 500 Index Fund)—50 percent*
>
> *Mid Cap Core Stock Fund—8 percent; or Mid Cap Growth 4 percent, Mid Cap Value 4 percent*
>
> *Small Cap Core Stock Fund—8 percent; or Small Cap Growth 4 percent, Small Cap Value 4 percent*
>
> *Diversified International Stock Fund—34 percent*

Sometimes, with gutsy 20-something-year-olds who have seriously contemplated the effects of an awful stock market, financial advisers will lean toward more small caps. Instead of putting about 75 percent of the U.S. stock portfolio into large caps and 25 percent in small caps, the advisers might go to 30 percent in small caps or even somewhat higher. But then they might try to cool off some risk by leaning toward small cap value rather than small cap growth to cut the risks.

The closer you get to your retirement years, however, the more conservative you should become. The idea is to cushion your savings so that a stock market tsunami doesn't do so much damage that you will have trouble recovering in time for retirement. So as you go into your 30s, you can slowly add some bonds to your investment portfolio.

By age 40, your 401(k) mutual fund selections and IRA would look about like this:

Large Cap Stock (maybe a Standard & Poor's 500 Index Fund)—40 percent

Mid Cap Stock—7 percent

Small Cap Stock—7 percent

International Stock—26 percent

Bonds—20 percent

During each of the next ten years, consider moving another 1 percent into bonds and taking it out of stock funds. The process of slowly moving money away from stocks continues into retirement. Remember as you do this to stay diversified, following roughly the portions of large, small, and international stocks I have provided.

At about age 60, a classic combination of 60 percent stocks and 40 percent bonds is considered prudent, although some financial advisers accept 70 percent in stocks. Others want to be more conservative, suggesting a 50:50 mixture as you go into retirement. Still, with people likely to live into their 90s, some advisers are afraid 50:50 is too conservative and won't give investors the growth they need for a lengthy retirement.

When people find themselves within five to ten years of retirement, it's a good idea to have a financial planner go over your savings and help you determine how to position yourself for retirement.

I suggest going to a "fee-only" financial planner, and I provide tips on selecting one in the last chapter, Chapter 15, "Do You Need a Financial Adviser?"

Doing Your Gut Check

As you look at asset allocation models that are appropriate for your age and the number of years you have remaining until retirement, don't delude yourself about your personality.

Try to force yourself to consider how you would actually act under certain stock market scenarios.

People have difficulty forcing themselves to do this when they are making money in the stock market. Yet every time the market falls sharply, my phone mail system fills up with calls from anxious people.

In June of 2006, for example, Carol, a 50-year-old Chicago psychiatrist, was among the terrified callers. She had just looked at her international fund, and she had lost about $5,000 in a few days. She wanted to know whether she should flee.

It was only natural that her fund would be down. The international markets had gone through a sharp downturn. In just two weeks, stocks in emerging markets of the world—like Pakistan, Malaysia, and Venezuela—had crashed about 20 percent. It was troubling to investors, but it should have been expected. For two years, emerging market stocks were the sweethearts—bestowing great gains on investment accounts. The herd had piled in and then awoke in May 2006, concluding that the world was growing, but not enough to support the stock prices people had paid. So the stocks fell for a while as investors became more realistic.

Carol didn't know about cycles and didn't understand that she had been a part of an international stock craze during the previous couple of years. All she knew was that she had put almost half of all her retirement money into an international fund, and it was quickly performing a disappearing act.

I told her about cycles and explained that the economies of the world would keep growing. Then I also explained that she had overdosed on international funds during the best of times. She needed to make a change—but not because of the loss she had just taken. She simply did not have the gut for the thrashing investors take whenever they've concentrated heavily on a certain investment.

Typically, about a 20 percent allocation in international funds would have been about right for a person like Carol—about 15 years from retirement. Yet the market had just forced her to do a gut check, and it demonstrated that perhaps even 20 percent in international stocks might be too much for her.

I told Carol not to flee her diversified international stock fund entirely, but to tweak the usual 20 percent model so that she would feel better—maybe using a 15 percent allocation in a foreign stock fund. With that approach, she would still diversify her stocks—tapping the world and the U.S.—but she would be less susceptible to the shocks she could not stomach.

When you do your gut check, use market history to quiz yourself about how you might respond.

Go back to Chapter 9 and look at the best- and worst-case scenarios for the different types of mutual funds and look at Table 11-1. Ask yourself how you would deal with the worst shock, such as losing an average of 12.4 percent every year for five years in an all-stock portfolio, or 10.3 percent with almost all stocks. Realize that when it's happening you don't know when it will end.

Also consider the mixtures I have advocated. Say that you put 70 percent of your money into stocks and 30 percent into bonds. The worst year for that model has been a 32 percent drop. If there is about a 30 percent drop in the future, your $1,000 will turn into $700. I hope you now know enough about cycles and history to hold onto diversified portfolios of mutual funds, knowing that with time you will recover.

Table 11.1 should help you focus on the long run, so you can get through tough times and make your money grow. But be honest with yourself now, rather than amid the carnage. If you tweak your 70 percent stock allocation— maybe down to 65 percent—that could take the edge off of downturns, allowing you to stomach them and come out better in the long run.

Table 11.1

How Stocks and Bonds Work Together
Compound Annual Rates of Return in Percents, 1926–2005

Portfolio Makeup	Historical Average Annual Return	Average Year during Worst 5 Years	Average Year during Best 5 Years
100% Large Company Stocks	10.4%	–12.4 %	28.5%
90% Stocks/ 10% Bonds	10.1%	–10.3%	26.6%
70% Stocks/ 30% Bonds	9.3%	–6.3 %	22.7%
50% Stocks/ 50% Bonds	8.4%	–2.7	21 %
30% Stocks/ 70% Bonds	7.3%	0.12%	21.3%
100% Long Term Government Bonds	5.5%	–2.14%	21.6 %

Source: Ibbotson Associates, a Morningstar, Inc., company

The Easy Rule of Thumb

As the years go by, there may be times when you don't have an asset allocation model to follow.

You may see articles that refer to an old-style, easy rule of thumb that people use as a guide. The approach is to subtract your age from the number 100. That tells you what percentage you should invest in stocks, while placing the rest in bonds.

So say that you are 60. That would mean only 40 percent in stocks and 60 percent in bonds. Currently, with people living into their 90s, the old rule of thumb is considered out-dated and too conservative. So a better approach might be to subtract from 120.

But you could follow another rule of thumb: Tweak your typical asset allocations up 5 percentage points if you think you are braver, or down 5 percentage points if you feel more scared than the ordinary person. Again, there's not an exact answer. There's only an answer that's close to appropriate, one that will make you comfortable.

Just avoid these common mistakes: waiting to invest because you can't decide, being overly conservative when you have years to go before retirement, or swinging for the fences at any age—especially when retirement is just five or ten years away. In other words, depend on diversifying your investments rather than counting on one stock or type of fund. Remember to tweak the proportions by a few percentage points, rather than betting all or nothing.

Starting an IRA

Choosing mutual funds for your IRA isn't as easy as for a 401(k), because your choices are vast.

In a 401(k), your employer gives you maybe up to a dozen choices, so your selection is relatively easy if you play the matching game I just described. It's as easy as looking at your list of maybe a dozen funds, spotting words, and slotting five to ten of your funds into the pieces of an asset allocation model.

With IRAs, if you look at all the mutual funds available, you may indeed be overwhelmed. There are, after all, more than 8,000 different funds. But you don't have to bother with most of them. I'll give you some shortcuts in the next chapter, and you may want to go back to Chapter 9 for some mutual fund suggestions.

For now, I just want you to understand that the same step-by-step approach I laid out for mixing and matching funds in a 401(k) also applies to an IRA. So if you don't have a 401(k) and skipped the previous explanation, go back and read it. The principle of asset allocation and mixing and matching types of stocks applies to all your retirement savings. It's easy, and academic research proves it's the one approach to investing that works.

You play the matching game with large caps, mid caps, small caps, international funds, and bond funds, whether they are in your 401(k), your IRA, or any other account that is aimed at retirement saving.

The key isn't the label on the account. The key is the purpose it's destined to accomplish. In other words, you are saving for retirement. So use the models I've provided for any IRA.

If you are in your 20s and starting your first IRA, however, you are not going to be able to follow the model I have provided you from the outset. With time, you will position your savings in line with the beginning model.

Say that you are starting with just a $1,000 contribution. There's no need to divide that into four different mutual funds. In fact, many mutual fund companies wouldn't let you, because most don't accept $250 contributions.

Begin the first year by investing in a fund that will serve as your core investment for your lifetime—a mutual fund you will buy and hold year after year. In other words, start with a diversified large cap U.S. stock fund—preferably a low-cost Standard & Poor's 500 index fund or a Total Stock Market Index fund described in Chapter 13, "Index Funds: Get What You Pay For."

Then, the next year, you might put another $1,000 into that same large cap core fund in your IRA. You could do this again the third year. But after that, take another $1,000 and buy your next fund—a diversified international fund. Then, the next year, you can take another $1,000 and buy your next fund—a diversified small cap fund. If you originally bought a Total Stock Market Index, you won't need a small cap fund because you already will have large stocks and small stocks in your single fund. (Learn more about this topic in Chapter 13.)

Over time, you will be working toward having a portfolio made up approximately like this:

Large cap (perhaps a Standard & Poor's 500 Index fund)—50 percent

Mid cap fund—8 percent

Small Cap fund—8 percent

International fund—34 percent

You don't have to get any more elaborate than this if you just buy diversified funds. But if you want to fine-tune even further, as the years go by, take each of the pieces and divide them in half—putting one half into a fund with a growth approach and one half into a fund with a value approach.

And then remember, although you may start out in your 20s or 30s with just stock funds, begin buying individual bonds or a bond fund as time goes on. So in your 50s, having 60 percent of your retirement savings in diversified stock funds and 40 percent in bonds would be a solid approach.

If all of this mixing and matching is driving you nuts, you will find a shortcut in Chapter 14, "Simple Does It: No-Brainer Investing with Target-Date Funds." What's important before you head to that shortcut, however, is that you understand the keys to investing that I am laying out first so that they always steer you away from an explosive investment and guide you into an appropriate mixture of funds.

Avoid Market Timing

When investors discover that the market goes through cycles, they come to a fairly logical conclusion: They vow to keep their eyes open and then plan to bail out of stocks as soon as they see hints of danger emerging.

Avoiding trouble works well in many aspects of life. But it's virtually impossible in investing—even for the savviest of professional investors. If you doubt this, consider September 11, 2001. Who would have predicted that terrorists would attack the World Trade Center and that the stock market (Dow Jones Industrial Average) would fall 14.2 percent in just five days? Or consider March 2000, when the stock market was shooting straight up. Investors thought investing was a no-brainer—that they would make money in the stock market forever. People were taking equity out of their homes to put it into the stock market just before it crashed. Little did they know that the stock market was about to fall 49 percent.

Perhaps you feel that you were the only fool in this debacle and that the pros know better. But it's not true. Professional investors, who manage people's money, may be skilled at asset allocation or picking stocks and mutual funds. Yet even the best of them are lousy market timers—in other words, they don't know when to get into stocks or when to flee.

College finance professors have done numerous studies to see whether market timing works. And they have come up with little evidence that it can be done successfully. In one study, a researcher examined the track record of 32 market-timing newsletters over a ten-year period. Not one beat the broad stock market. The reason is easy to understand. Even if you are astute enough to get out of the way of trouble initially by withdrawing from stocks, you probably will miss the next surge up. And that's no small matter. Typically, investors make most of their money over a very few days. If they have put their money into safekeeping outside of the stock market, they may miss those very few days.

If you think a couple of days might not matter, consider research done by respected investor and author Peter L. Bernstein. In *The Portable MBA of Investment,* he notes that if the average investor missed just 10 of the very best days in the stock market over a 9-year period in the 1980s, his or her return would have been reduced by a third. Removing just 30 of the best days would have cut returns by 70 percent.

Most people make a terrible mess out of their own money by practicing market timing—or trying to catch what's hot, or moving away from a falling stock market. They think the market is safe when it isn't. They think they should stash money away in safekeeping when it's time to invest again, or they move from one fund to another trying to find the elusive best one.

The Impact of Market Timing

Fear of having a mishap as an investor sometimes keeps people from doing what's prudent. They wait for the right time to invest and end up waiting forever because they can always spot a potential threat. If you are among them, you might be reassured by some research done by Charles Schwab. Analyst Mark Riepe looked at four different hypothetical investors who took different approaches to market timing during 20 years from 1976 to 1996.

First, he looked at the person who ignored market timing and just put $2,000 into the stock market every year on December 31. At the end of 20 years, that person had accumulated $265,308. Then he looked at the person who had perfect timing and just happened to hit the best time to invest during each of the past 20 years. The results were good: $283,445. But the person who tried to buy stocks only during periods that looked promising and then accidentally blew it by investing just before a crash each year did the worst: $242,182 after 20 years of investing.

The lesson is this: If you knew you could time the market right, it would be worthwhile. But since you can't, automatically investing money each month or each year should provide you comfort. Having $265,308 after 20 years isn't bad when you are simply investing $2,000 a year. Most important, keep one more of Riepe's findings in mind: The person who was afraid he'd make a mess of his money in the stock market and just put his $2,000 a year into safe U.S. Treasury bills ended up with only $85,708 at the end of 20 years.

So instead of trying to time the market, do what financial planners do for their clients: Decide on the asset allocation that seems right to you, keeping in mind that if you use a teaspoon rather than a heaping teaspoon you will still be fine. If you get nervous during a downturn and can't take it, make small changes—maybe shifting 5 or 10 percent out of stocks and into a safe money market fund, instead of yanking all your funds and cowering in a money market fund.

I can't emphasize this enough. As novice investors have called me over the years, they have repeatedly made one common mistake—betting too much money on either ups or downs in the market. If they think times are great, they put everything in hot stocks. If they think times are scary, they naively move everything to safety. Instead, think of tweaking—using what professionals sometimes call "tactical" changes, with 5 percent or 10 percent of your money. Do it if it makes you feel better, but realize that your timing will probably be off.

Also be aware: The stock market does fall. In fact, it falls at least 10 percent or more every nine months, according to Riepe. And it can get very ugly, as with the 2000–2002 drop of close to 49 percent. But throughout the past 80 years, the market has been climbing—not dropping—70 percent of the time. And that's turned $1 into close to $3,000.

Dollar-Cost Averaging

Because investors get nervous during the periods when the market falls just after they have invested money, financial advisers often tell people to follow a process that is less nerve-wracking than simply dumping a large sum of money into the market at one time. The approach is called dollar-cost averaging.

This is the process that's ingrained in the 401(k) system. All dollar-cost averaging means is that with every paycheck, you put a little money into your investments.

Because you do this over and over again with each paycheck over 20, 30, or 40 years, sometimes you will get great deals during low points in the stock market. And sometimes you will be putting money into the stock market at times when you will lose.

It's a sound approach, and it is done more for emotional reasons than any other purpose. It forces investors to keep investing money when their gut says no. And in the long run that pays off.

Rebalance

There's a discipline professionals use instead of market timing that increases the chances you will benefit from highs in the market and not suffer severely in lows.

It's called rebalancing. To do it, you look over your retirement accounts once a year to see which funds have surged in value and which have lagged. Then you remove some of the money from the hottest funds and move it into the slowest funds.

You go back to your original recipe—or asset allocation—to see whether you need to do this.

Let's say that you were working off a very simple model—the classic 60 percent in stocks and 40 percent in bonds. And say that during the past year, bonds have been the place to be and stocks have been lousy. You have lost so much money in your stock funds that your stock allocation is now down to 50 percent, and your bond allocation has grown to 50 percent of your overall portfolio.

You rebalance by taking your bond allocation down to about 40 percent again by removing some money. You move that money into your stock funds so that you have 60 percent of your money in stocks—matching your original model.

At that point in time, making a move like this is going to be hard to stomach. You will think stocks are going to be scary because they have been scary. But if you think of cycles, you will appreciate the concept behind rebalancing. Eventually the cycle is going to turn, and when it does, you will get the benefit of having 60 percent of your money in stocks. Best of all, you moved some money into stocks when they were cheap and neglected. In other words, you bought the stocks "low" and will get a chance to sell when they are "high" during the upturn in the cycle. It's a bargain-hunter's delight.

What You Can Control

Ironically, a common practice that makes novice investors feel cozy is, in fact, one of the riskiest mistakes they can take.

When they look over their list of 401(k) choices, they see one unfamiliar fund after another, so they go with what they think they know best—the stock of the company that employs them. They load up their retirement fund with it.

It's like playing Russian roulette with retirement savings. Academic studies show that choosing a single stock frequently sets you up for disaster. Typically, the person looks around his surroundings—seeing machinery, offices, thousands of people hard at work all over the country, or even around the world—and says to himself: *What could go wrong?*

Need I say it? United Airlines once looked like a corporate titan to its employees and to investors. Yet it had to file for bankruptcy, making its stock worthless. Kmart once looked like the most powerful retail chain in the country, but it went into bankruptcy a few years ago—leaving investors with worthless stock.

Enron was one of the hottest stocks of the 1990s. The press wrote glowing stories about the company, and employees at Enron filled their retirement funds with the stock—figuring they could retire at 50. Corporate executives encouraged them to do it—singing the company's praises even when it wasn't true. Then reality caught up with the company. Much of the glowing news was based on fake numbers, and the company collapsed. People who once thought they'd retire at 50 were wiped out—their dandy nest eggs had turned to zero.

So if your employer lets you buy the company's stock in your 401(k), follow the lead of experts who know more than you: Pension fund managers don't put more than 10 percent of their portfolios into any single stock—no matter how impressive its prospects look. Mutual fund managers often won't exceed 5 percent—even with the stocks they most adore.

If you have a 401(k) and have loaded it up with your company stock, see whether you can sell some of the shares and move your money into diversified mutual funds, using the asset allocation models I have provided. If you can't sell the stock, stop buying it. And put all new money into diversified stock funds.

As a novice investor, you should also avoid buying individual stocks in your IRA—that is, unless you will devote the hundreds of hours it takes to study them and make sure that they remain growing businesses. Only about 30 percent of professional stock pickers do well enough to beat the stock market. So why do you think that—acting on a hot tip—you are going to do any better?

If you think you have the presence to do it, try analyzing a stock with the MSN "research wizard" tool. Find it at www.moneycentral.com. Click on "Investing" and find the research wizard on the left side of the page. (You might have to click More under Investing to find it.) If the research wizard is more than you can handle, or too time-consuming, leave the stock picking up to mutual funds.

12

HOW TO PICK MUTUAL FUNDS: BARGAIN SHOP

It's enough to drive a control freak crazy.

You can't control the stock market as it goes through unpredictable cycles. There's no way to know which mutual funds will be outstanding or disappointing in the years ahead. The most acclaimed investing stars in the mutual fund business tend to fizzle with time.

Those realities may be making you feel a little out of control at this point—perhaps wondering just what power you have over your money.

You actually have quite a bit—just not the type people imagine when they think their future depends upon picking a hot stock or a top mutual fund. Remember, "asset allocation"—or mixing and matching categories of mutual funds—sets you up to grow your money well if you've matched the ingredients in your recipe diligently.

But beyond that, there is one other factor you can control as an investor. And you should, because it's the one "sure thing" you can count on to make a huge difference in the money you will accumulate over a lifetime.

I'm talking about fees—or the expenses you pay when you invest. You may not know that you are paying anything. Most people don't realize it. But whenever you buy a stock, a bond, or a mutual fund, you pay fees, and costs vary greatly. If you don't pay attention to them, they will rob you of the easy money you could make—not just nickels and dimes, but thousands and thousands of dollars.

Suppose that you are 22 and invest $1,000 for 40 years in a mutual fund that keeps your expenses low. If your fund averages 8 percent annually after you've paid all the expenses, in 40 years your $1,000 will have become about $21,700. Contrast that with a high-priced fund, charging you only 2 percent extra in expenses over the low-cost fund. In 40 years you will have only about $10,300—or just half as much as you could have if you were attentive to fees.

To most people, the costs they pay for their mutual funds are invisible. If you have money in a mutual fund now, the fund company is removing fees automatically from the money you have invested. When you pay the fund company, the money goes toward everything from the fund manager's salary to advertising costs. That's right: You pay the fund company to lure potential new investors. You pay fees whether the fund makes you rich or loses your money.

It's all part of the deal—the way the fund industry operates. But fees also differ significantly between funds, so you can save yourself a bundle if you just notice two simple numbers: the "expense ratio" and "loads." Don't get nervous over the math-sounding word "ratio." You don't have to do any math, and being aware of these two numbers will take less than a minute of attention—saving you thousands of dollars over a lifetime of investing.

I'll explain more about how to do it later. For now, I just want you to understand the control you have over the fees you pay. When you see a fund charging you 0.18 percent, you have found a good deal. When you see another charging 2 percent, you need to be on guard.

Tiny Percents Have a Huge Impact

Although 0.18 percent and 2 percent sound like tiny, insignificant numbers, the difference between them ends up being gigantic over time. That's because of the power of compounding, which you can review again in Chapter 2, "Know What You'll Need." Compounding helps your money grow, and the more money you have invested, the more it can grow. When you give up money by paying unnecessary fees day after day, it sets you back for life. Every year that you pay an extra percent, you reduce the money you earn that year and every other year afterward—robbing your nest egg forever.

Let me illustrate this using some research done by Edward O'Neal, a professor at Wake Forest University. O'Neal examined 5,000 mutual funds in 2004 and determined that the average fund charges investors 1.41 percent a year on their money.

In other words, if you have $10,000 in the average mutual fund, you are paying $141 a year in fees. That doesn't sound so bad. But consider the alternative. You can get funds that charge just 0.10 percent, or about $10. You tell me: If you went into a store and saw two identical shirts—one for $141 or one for $10—which would you buy?

O'Neal, in his study, took a modest approach—focusing on the low-cost funds charging an average of 0.314 percent, or about $31.

If you chose one of those low-cost funds, invested $10,000, and the investment earned 10 percent annually, you would have about $63,200 in 20 years. If you instead held onto the fund charging 1.4 percent and earned the same 10 percent return on the investments, fees would shortchange your future by over $12,000. You would have only about $51,000.

It has always shocked me that people will drive for miles across town to save $50 on some household item but will literally throw away thousands on their mutual funds without giving it a second thought.

I think they do this because numbers like 1 percent sound so small and because mutual funds are so confusing that people just want to get the job done.

Mind Your Money: Your Broker Might Not

Also, there is no incentive among brokers or many of the mutual fund companies to tell clients that they are paying more than they need to pay for their mutual funds. The higher your fees and commissions, the more money the fund companies make, and the more the brokers make.

Talk about a conflict of interest: If the broker sells you what's best for you, it very well might hurt him by reducing his compensation.

It's easy to control costs. And here's what may shock you: Cheaper funds generally do better than those that charge you more.

You may find that surprising because, as consumers, we generally are taught that "you get what you pay for." Some financial advisers use that line to justify the exorbitant fees they charge clients. But the assertion simply is not true when it comes to investing in mutual funds.

Cheap Funds Work

Morningstar, which is known for its mutual fund research, has studied fees in depth. The firm's director of research, Russel Kinnel, says that "each move up in price greatly lowers the likelihood that a given fund will be able to beat a corresponding low-cost index fund."

Index funds generally are the cheapest funds, and I will explain more about why you should use them in the next chapter. For now, I just want you to understand why you should not be led astray by sales pitches for expensive funds.

According to the Morningstar study, if you have money in a fund that charges you more than 1 percent, you probably won't even keep up with the cheapest funds you could have bought. So you are throwing money away. Your expensive fund has only a one-in-seven chance of doing as well as the cheap fund.

Why does this happen? Because investing money—even for the top fund managers—is difficult. I've talked with many of the nation's pros, and they are thrilled if they can generate a return for you that's even 1 percent higher than the stock market as a whole. Because it's so tough to do, fund managers who do beat the competition—even by a little—get paid bonuses.

So realize when you buy a fund that a half of a percent—or 0.50 percent—is a big number in the fund industry. If a fund manager excels by even that much, he or she might earn a bonus for outstanding performance. It's also enough to take thousands from your nest egg, and paying it doesn't necessarily get you anywhere.

Let's say you have a mutual fund that has an excellent year—with a return of 11 percent on the stocks in the fund. During the same year, let's say there is another mutual fund with a return of only 10.5 percent on its stocks. Your fund manager is superior—at least that year. But the fund is only outstanding before your fees come out. Let's say your fund charges you 1.5 percent of your assets. In other words, your return is going to dip from the 11 percent you would have earned on the stocks in the portfolio to just 9.5 percent after paying your fees. And if the fund that earned 10.5 percent on the stocks only charges investors 0.50 percent, that fund turns out to be a better deal after the fees are paid. The fund's return—or the money the investor gets after fees—is 10 percent.

The bottom line: A clever fund manager who picks stocks and bonds skillfully may end up doing you little good if a fund is gouging you on fees.

It gets worse. Morningstar has found that funds that charge high fees also take exceptional risks with your money—apparently to try to boost returns to overcome the effects of the fees. It doesn't work, and it puts you in danger of losing more money than other funds do on average, according to the research.

So here's a no-brainer strategy: To stretch each dollar you invest as far as possible, try to select low-cost mutual funds.

Watch Out for Loads

First, try to avoid paying what are called "loads," which are nothing more than a fee you pay a broker or financial adviser to select funds for you. Instead, select what are called "no-load" funds. In other words, they don't charge you for advice.

If you pay a load, it works like this: Say that you are putting $10,000 into a mutual fund with a 5.75 percent load. That means that you give your broker $10,000, and she keeps $575 of the money as her commission and puts the remaining $9,425 of your money into a mutual fund for you.

Instead of earning a return on your hard-earned $10,000, you earn it on only $9,425. The result: Compounding works on $575 less than what you intended to invest. So over 35 years, if you average a 10 percent annual return, you end up with about $265,000—not bad. But it could have been about $16,000 more if that $575 had gone into the fund originally.

Try the calculation yourself on your own loads using a cost comparison calculator at www.sec.gov/investor/tools/mfcc/holding-period.htm. Perhaps an easier calculator is www.dinkytown.net/java/FundExpense.html. To look at loads at the dinkytown site, insert the "sales charge"—or load—and add no "operating expenses" to the calculation. It's easy and takes literally half a minute. You will probably be shocked by the impact.

Most mutual funds sold by brokers and many financial planners include either conspicuous or inconspicuous loads. Be aware of this so that if a broker assures you that you aren't paying anything up front in fees, you also realize what you will pay later—perhaps what's called a "back-end load." Many funds that don't charge you up front—or "front-end loads"—end up costing you more because they charge you a lot for operating your fund year after year.

To protect yourself, you can ask a broker to show you all "fees, loads, and mutual fund expenses" you will pay, and ask him or her to do the math for you—showing you what you will pay and what that will do to your earnings over a lifetime of investing. This calculation should include both loads and what's called the expense ratio. After you have the figures, you can also plug them into the calculators I mentioned previously.

Your broker won't be anxious to talk about fees and commissions because they are the bread and butter of the profession. But you are entitled to know the information, and you can ask to receive it in writing.

Also, to avoid loads, you can skip a broker and take your money directly to a mutual fund company and buy what are called "no-load funds." These funds do not charge you for a broker's advice. To buy funds directly, you call a mutual fund's toll-free telephone number and tell them you want to put money in a certain fund.

Even if you buy no-load funds directly from a mutual fund company, you still have expenses and must pay attention to them.

It's easy to examine them without doing any math. Aside from loads, everything you pay is blended into one number called the expense ratio. It sounds like a complicated term, but it isn't. You will spot it in the materials—or the "prospectus"—you are given when you buy a fund, get it from the telephone staff at your fund's toll-free telephone number, or ask a financial adviser to point it out to you.

Every fund will charge you to pay for the manager of your fund, the paperwork for running your fund, and even the fund's advertising. All of those various expenses are bundled together and reported in the expense ratio.

Examining that one number, alone, shows you what percent of your money goes to pay all your various costs.

Whenever you buy a fund, you need to take a quick look at that one number. If the expense ratio is 1.41 percent, you have average costs. With $10,000 in the fund, it means you will pay $141 a year for the privilege of being an investor.

Although that's the industry average, most investors are paying less because many of the largest mutual fund companies have reduced fees. The ordinary investor pays about 0.93 percent for U.S. stock funds, according to Morningstar's Kinnel. For international funds, the average is 1.1 percent, or $110. For bond funds, expenses average 0.85 percent—$85.

There is generally no reason to pay more than those numbers, he says. And there are fine U.S. stock funds—called "index funds"—that charge only 0.18 percent, or $18. Contrast that with some of the higher-priced funds at 2.5 percent—or $250.

To see the impact, go back to the mutual fund expense calculator at www.dinkytown.com that I mentioned previously. Let's assume that you put $10,000 into a fund with no "sales charge" or "load," and an expense ratio of 0.18 percent. (The website uses the word "operating expenses" for the "expense ratio.") Over 35 years, your investments average a 10 percent annual return. You end up with about $264,000. But along the way you had to pay about $5,000 in total fees. It was your cost of doing business with the mutual fund. If you hadn't had to pay anything, you would have ended up with about $281,000 because each penny would have been earning a return for you.

Still, $264,000 isn't bad at all. Now let's assume that you paid 2.5 percent every year after making your original $10,000 investment. You would end up with only about $116,000 after paying $40,000 in fees. But you would have lost a lot more than the $40,000 in fees. By paying the fees, you slashed the opportunity to have compounding work on more of your money. Losing that opportunity cost you $125,000.

With 2 percent in fees, you would have ended up with about $138,500 after 35 years and given up the opportunity to make another $106,200.

So there you have it. As an investor, you should know that there is nothing you can do to foresee cycles in the market. A bet on even the best fund can go terribly off course. But you do have control—a lot of it. It's the easiest thing to do. Just examine two numbers: the "expense ratio"—or "operating expenses"—and the "load"—or "sales charge"—and you will probably make more money than people who think that finding a phenomenal fund manager will make them rich.

I offer you two warnings, however: First, if you are going to procrastinate about investing unless you go to a financial consultant for some hand-holding, then go and get the help and pay the fees. If brokers are conscientious, they might offer American funds, a group of relatively attractive funds that charge loads but keep costs fairly low. Just stay in the game by asking your broker about fees. And make sure you understand the conflicts of interest that the broker might have, as he makes trade-offs between your need to build a nest egg and his need to boost his pay. Refer to the final chapter of this book so that you get good advice instead of wasting money on high-priced funds.

13

INDEX FUNDS: GET WHAT YOU PAY FOR

You may find this shocking. But when you invest, simplicity works best.

So now that you know the general rules of investing, I am going to make life very easy on you. I am going to lead you to the sweetest deal the mutual fund world offers.

It is your foolproof way to amass a fortune. Tuck it into your retirement fund, and you should be more successful than many Wall Street stock-pickers with years of experience and elaborate strategies.

I'm talking about what are known as "index funds."

If you have a 401(k) and are overwhelmed with the stock fund choices in it, simply look through the list and try to find the word "index" on one of the funds. It probably will say something like "Standard & Poor's 500 Index," or maybe "total stock market index."

If you spot those words, buy one of those funds. You have found a special kind of mutual fund that has "success" written all over it. That single fund can be your core investment for life—a no-frills, uncomplicated, cheap mutual fund that invests in 500 of the nation's largest companies, or what is roughly referred to as "the stock market." With an index fund, you can be a stock investor the easy way.

You can put money from every paycheck into one of these index funds and turn your back without giving it a second thought. Because you will have 500 or more stocks, you will be well diversified. Because the fees in index funds usually are very low, you are likely to make more money with it than other funds that invest in large companies.

Likewise, if you are starting an IRA and are overwhelmed with the thousands of choices out there, you can go to a mutual fund company known for its low-cost index funds. Then, simply plop your money into what is called a a "total stock market index fund"; hold it forever; feed new money into it every week, every month, or every year; and stop worrying about how to discriminate between all the funds with the wacky names.

If you do this, you will have to pay attention to just one thing: getting the proportion right in your portfolio. A total stock market index fund invests exclusively in U.S. stocks—no bonds, no foreign stocks. So if you are in your 20s and feel comfortable with the ups and downs of the stock market, you could simply begin your investing years with 100 percent of your money in this fund. If you are somewhat older, the index fund will be fine for your stock money, but you will need a bond fund too. I'll help you with quantities later in this chapter.

Now, I want you to be aware that index funds come in different varieties. The most common two—the ones most often in 401(k) plans—invest in either the "Standard & Poor's 500" or "the total stock market." When you see those terms, they mean roughly one thing: *the stock market.* These are the mutual funds that make sense to buy and hold for life.

If you put your money in either, you will be a stockholder. On the days you turn on the news and hear that the stock market has gone up, you will be able to assume you made money. On the days you hear that the stock market has gone down, you will assume you lost money.

If history repeats the way it has for the past 80 years, you will average about 10 percent annually on your money in that index fund over a lifetime of investing. Remember, I said average. Some years you will lose—maybe 20 percent or more. Some years you will win—maybe 20 percent or more. Over the past 80 years, all the wins and losses in the stock market have blended into a decent gain.

For example, if you'd had a Standard & Poor's 500 index fund, you would have lost 22 percent of your money in 2002 and gained 28.5 percent the following year. After blending together all the gains and losses over the last decade, you would have averaged about an 8.8 percent return annually for each year of the past 10 years.

You might think, "Earning about 9 percent a year is not so good. Those index funds didn't even grow at 10 percent—the historical average in the stock market." But the slightly lower return didn't happen because the fund was a dud. It happened because the stock market itself went through some tough years between 2000 and 2002. And if you had decided to try to out-smart the market by seeking a fund manager who would excel, you would have likely done worse.

The simple total stock market index fund beat 75 percent of all the other funds that have hired savvy investing professionals to pick the best large company stocks, according to Morningstar research. In other words, if you had bought an index fund, you would have skipped all the expensive strate-gies that Wall Street peddles, and you still would have been the winner—a do-it-yourselfer beating the best and the brightest. That's how you become an extraordinary investor without effort.

The past 10 years have not been an aberration. Year after year, the sim-ple index fund has proven its stuff. It has triumphed over the majority of stock-pickers who get paid handsomely to try to do better.

What's an Index Fund?

To understand index funds, you have to first know what other mutual funds do. As I explained in previous chapters, most funds in a 401(k), and almost all the funds sold by brokers, employ an investing pro to pick stocks for you. He or she gets paid a lot for helping you make money—about $500,000 on average, and often over $1 million.

The pro's goal is to cherry-pick through the stock market for the very best stocks—those that will become very valuable and make you money in your mutual fund. When the investing professional—or "fund manager"—thinks she sees a winner, she buys it. If the fund manager spots a loser, she avoids it. If the fund manager has already bought a stock that's become a dud, she sells it.

All of this sounds very attractive to the ordinary person. None of us wants a loser. We all want winners. As I explained in the preceding chapter, the investment industry is built around the concept that investors should be willing to pay a pretty penny for the opportunity to have a pro navigate through the stock market for them.

The trouble is that selecting stocks is very difficult. Even the very best investment pros let investors down. All the cherry-picking usually leaves investors with less money than they'd have if they simply said they'd be willing to accept all the losers, along with the winners, in the stock market. They'd simply close their eyes and buy the entire stock market, including its shining stars and warts—great stocks, awful stocks, and mediocre stocks.

This is what index funds do. They don't hire expensive fund managers to navigate through the stock market for you. They just buy everything in the stock market. When you buy a Standard & Poor's 500 index fund, or a total stock market index fund, you are buying the full array of stocks that make up what's known as "the stock market." The secret to their success: They don't charge you much—perhaps only 0.18 percent. So you keep more of your money than you would if your fund used a stock-picker.

Since this very simple, low-cost approach enables investors to repeatedly beat the pros, I think the conclusion is easy: Just invest in the full stock market through an index fund.

A broker may tell you that you can only get mediocre returns that way. They've said to me, "A person doesn't want to be an ordinary student, a mediocre athlete, or an average worker, so why would they want to settle for average as an investor?"

The answer is simple: Mediocre just happens to be better than the most highly paid, highly respected fund managers tend to do. People who know a lot more than the novice investor see it this way. Pension funds, which have investment experts at the helm, often use index funds as a core investment in the stock market.

Typically, pension funds use a simple index—like the Standard & Poor's 500 index—for close to 50 percent of the money they invest in the stock market. These people have a tremendous responsibility: They must amass enough money to pay retirees' pensions in the future. That should tell you something: Byron Wien, who was a Morgan Stanley strategist in 2004, said then that using an index fund once would have been considered "heresy" in his profession—which makes money by selling investors on the value of stock-picking. During the past few years, it is simply considered smart. In 2002, 93 percent of all money that flowed into stock funds went into index funds—just a no-frills investment in the stock market.

What's the Stock Market, and What's a Stock Market Index?

We all have a sense of what the stock market is. Each day TV and radio news tells us, "The stock market was up today," or "The stock market was down today."

What most people don't know is that the stock market isn't just one thing. There are different stock markets—or, more precisely, different pieces of the full stock market. Each has a name you might recognize. Knowing the names is necessary for picking an index fund, because there are various index funds—some that make that perfect all-around investment I mentioned, and some that add spice to the core investment you can buy and hold for life.

The Dow

Most people have heard of the Dow Jones Industrial Average. That's usually what TV and radio reports are referring to when they say the stock market is up or down that day. The Dow is simply an index—a collection of stocks used to easily report on the stock market. It is not really the entire stock market. There are actually more than 5,000 stocks that people buy and sell every day. The full stock market would actually include all 5,000 stocks, and then some. The Dow just includes 30 stocks.

Why is there so much attention every day to the Dow? Because that index contains an array of 30 powerful companies from every industry. The 30 stocks are looked at as a group—through the Dow index—as a means to take the economy's temperature or get a glimpse of how corporate America's health is perceived.

If investors think companies will be delivering strong profits in the near future, they will buy stocks, the prices on the stocks will rise, and then the Dow will be up that day. If investors are worried about the health of all or part of the economy, investors will sell stocks, the prices on stocks will fall, and the Dow will be down.

If you invested in a Dow index fund, the fund manager wouldn't try to pick the winners from 30 stocks and avoid the losers. The fund would buy all 30 stocks so that your fund mimicked the Dow index. Consequently, you would own a tiny piece of all 30 industrial giants—everything from ExxonMobil to General Electric. You would have the winning stocks that would become more valuable investments and the losing stocks that might become less valuable, or even ghastly investments. But the individual stocks wouldn't matter to you. You would make money based on the average value of the full array of 30 stocks in the Dow index.

The Standard & Poor's 500

If you buy an index fund in your 401(k), it's likely to be a different index from the Dow, but the concept is the same as I just described. The most common index fund in 401(k)s is what's called a "Standard & Poor's 500 index fund."

Instead of containing just 30 stocks, the Standard & Poor's 500 includes 500 stocks from the largest American companies. So a fund manager for a Standard & Poor's 500 index fund would buy all 500 stocks—paying no attention to winners and losers. If you owned a share of a Standard & Poor's 500 index fund, you would own a tiny piece of everything from Exxon and Johnson & Johnson to Wal-Mart and Microsoft. When you'd hear that the stock market was up one day, you could assume you made money.

Generally, when you hear Wall Street experts talking about "the stock market," they are not talking about the Dow. They are usually referring to the Standard & Poor's 500. When you hear that the stock market has averaged a 10.4 percent return a year over the past 80 years, people are referring to the Standard & Poor's 500. It is sometimes called the "S&P" for short. It is Wall Street's favorite shorthand way of taking the temperature of all the stocks bought and sold day in and day out.

Because the stocks in the Standard & Poor's 500 index are so large, the index represents about 70 percent of the value of all stocks that are available. But even though Wall Street repeatedly calls the Standard & Poor's 500 "the stock market," it is not really the full market. It's missing the smaller stocks that make up approximately 30 percent of the stock market.

The Total Stock Market

There are a handful of other indexes that represent roughly the full stock market. One is called the Wilshire 5000. And it includes more than 5,000 different stocks—very large ones like General Electric and Johnson & Johnson, but also smaller ones like Linens & Things, Zale, Brookstone, Coach, Denny's, Continental Airlines, and many small companies you've probably never heard of.

It's the smaller companies, and the huge quantity of companies, that make this index different from the Standard & Poor's 500 index.

If your 401(k) plan has a fund that contains words such as "total stock market index," the fund is about the most diverse one you can find. It is probably designed to mimic the Wilshire 5000, or perhaps a somewhat smaller index known as the MSCI Broad Market Index.

A total stock market index fund is an easy one-stop pick. If you select it, you will have large stocks and small stocks. You will be a long way toward doing what every investor should do—having a diverse mixture of stocks. Your fund will always contain some winners and some losers. The average annual return—despite the losers—over the past decade has been about 9 percent.

Again, the beauty of an index fund—the reason it beats many other funds—is that it's cheap. For the privilege of investing in the entire stock market, the investor in the Vanguard Total Stock Market Index (VTSMX) pays only 0.18 percent of his or her assets—a lot less than the 1.4 percent on a fund employing a professional stock-picker to find winners and avoid losers.

If you had two funds that had the same return before you were charged fees—a traditional one with a professional stock-picker and average fees, plus an index fund—you would end up with a lot more money in the index fund. That's because you give up only 0.18 percent of your money to have the index fund. You give up 1.4 percent to have the stock-picker.

So the decision is easy: For your core large cap stock fund, simply buy an index fund full of large company stocks. Two of the lowest cost funds are the Vanguard Total Stock Market Index and the Fidelity Spartan Total Market Index.

Using Index Funds in a 401(k)

When you have a 401(k), your choices are limited. Your employer gives you only a few mutual fund options. You might not have an index fund among them, but the chances are that you do have one. About 60 percent of 401(k) plans offer an index fund, and if you work for a large company, an index fund is probably embedded somewhere in the midst of your fund list.

Usually, the choice would be a "Standard & Poor's 500" index fund. If you find this index fund, select it for your exposure to large cap stocks. You won't need any additional large cap stock funds.

Then, of course, return to your 401(k) list to complete your selections for all the other categories you need. You should sign up for a small cap stock fund, an international fund, and a bond fund to complete the mixture of investments you need. If you are confused about the right proportions of all of these, go back to Chapter 11, "Do This."

If your 401(k) plan also includes a "total stock market index fund," you can make life even easier on yourself. Instead of choosing a large cap and small cap fund, you can simply choose that one total stock market index fund. With that one fund, roughly 75 percent of your money will be invested in large company stocks and 25 percent in small ones. This gives you your complete U.S. stock portfolio. It's an all-in-one choice. So if you select it, do not also choose a Standard & Poor's 500 index fund, because you'd be doubling up—your total stock market index fund includes virtually the same large stocks as the Standard & Poor's.

If you are debating between the Standard & Poor's Index or the Total Stock Market Index, the total stock market would make investing easiest for you. After picking it, all you would need to do for a very simple portfolio would be to select an international fund and a bond fund, and you would be set.

Your portfolio might look like this if you were in your 30s:

60 percent in the total stock market index

30 percent in an international stock fund

10 percent in an intermediate term bond fund

In your late 50s, it might look like this:

40 percent in the total stock market index

20 percent in an international stock fund

40 percent in an intermediate term bond fund

If your 401(k) gives you the choice of a "total stock market fund" and a "total bond market fund," you have hit the busy person's jackpot.

Simply divide your money between those two index funds, hold the appropriate proportions throughout your lifetime, and don't worry about sorting through the hodgepodge of other funds.

Let's say that you are in your 40s, and you want 70 percent of your money in stocks and 30 percent in bonds. You would put 70 percent from each paycheck into the "total stock market index" and 30 percent in the "total bond market index." You'd be done.

Over time, your stock index fund would help your money grow, and your bond index fund would insulate you from sharp downturns in the market. You'd be missing just one extra piece—international stocks—which probably isn't the best move. If you are willing to tweak a little more, put about a third of your stock money into a diversified international stock fund that invests throughout the world.

You might even be lucky enough to find an index fund that invests in international stocks. It would likely have a name like the "total international stock index," and the description would say that it mimics the MSCI EAFE index. That's the index of stocks from throughout developed countries— everything from Europe to Japan. If you are offered this type of index fund, you can again save yourself money by buying a broad range of stocks cheaply.

As with the other index funds, there would be no professional at the helm, trying to buy winning stocks or winning countries. No one would be avoiding losers. The goal would be simple: Just provide stock exposure worldwide.

Now, look at what this complete portfolio would look like for a person in his or her 30s. This is similar to the previous portfolio for a 30-year-old but includes the names of the indexes. Also notice the ranges for fund quantities. The idea is to adjust portions based on your stomach for risk.

> *10 to 20 percent in a total bond market index fund (identified as the Lehman Aggregate Bond Index)*
>
> *25 to 30 percent in a total international stock market index (identified as the MSCI EAFE index)*
>
> *55 to 60 percent in the total U.S. stock market index (identified as maybe the Wilshire 5000 or MSCI Broad Market Index)*

Some Index Fund Ideas

Here are some fine low-cost index funds: Vanguard 500 (VFINX), Vanguard Total Stock Market Index (VTSMX), Vanguard Total International Index (VGTSX), Vanguard Small Cap Index (NAESX), Vanguard Total Bond Market Index (VBMFX), Fidelity Spartan 500 Index (FSMKX), Fidelity Spartan Total Market Index (FSTMX), Fidelity Spartan International Index (FSIIX), and T. Rowe Price Equity Index 500 (PREIX). There are also many low-cost index funds for mid- and small-size companies. Among them: Vanguard Small Cap Index (NAESX) and Fidelity Extended Market (FSEMX).

Tweak Your Portfolio Once a Year: "Rebalance"

Just one word of warning: After a while the proportions that you are supposed to keep constant in your portfolio—or your recipe for investment success—get skewed without your noticing it.

So remember to revisit your 401(k) or IRA at the end of each year, look over the portions in each fund, and make sure they still fit the model you chose in Chapter 11, "Do This." You will recall that this year-end process is called "rebalancing."

If, for example, you are 35 and want 20 percent of your money in the bond index fund, 25 percent in the international stock fund, and 55 percent in the total stock market fund, your intent should be to keep those proportions roughly intact until you purposefully change them as you age. Yet, if international markets have been soaring, and the U.S. has languished, you could find 35 percent invested in your international fund and only 45 percent in the U.S. This, of course, is not your intent. Your model has been distorted. So you would move some money out of the international fund and into the U.S. fund following the model you preselected. That way, you will be prepared for the next cycle.

Using Index Funds in an IRA

Remember the reason for using index funds: They give you broad exposure to stocks, and they are cheap. Because they are cheap, you tend to get a better return from them than you would with a traditional mutual fund that employs an investing pro.

Index funds are perfect for an IRA, as well as a 401(k). With an IRA, you are in the driver's seat because you are not constrained by funds someone else selects for you.

My advice: Make life easy on yourself. Go to a firm like Vanguard, known for its low-cost index funds, and start building your nest egg with the simple funds.

Say you're in your 20s and have $3,000 to invest in your first IRA. You could start the first year by putting your full IRA contribution into the "Vanguard Total Stock Market Index." Eventually, you will add some extra funds to your IRA over the years so that you will be exposed to all the investments you need. (If you are confused about this, go back and review asset allocation in Chapter 10.)

But you don't have to move into two or three funds immediately. Just focus on that first index fund for a while. Maybe the second year you contribute to your IRA again. Simply put some more money into the Vanguard Total Stock Market Index. After that, start filling in the slot for another type of investment. If you are young and aren't squeamish about losing money in stocks, you can make your next IRA contribution to the Vanguard Total International Stock Market Index.

As the years go by and you continue to invest in your IRA, you would eventually put some money into a bond market index fund. Let's say that you have reached your mid to late 30s; your IRA might look approximately like this:

> *20 percent in the Vanguard Total Bond Market Index (VBMFX), which mimics the Lehman bond index*
>
> *26 percent in the Vanguard Total International Market Index (VGTSX), which mimics the MSCI EAFE Index)*
>
> *54 percent in the Vanguard Total Stock Market Index (VTSMX), which mimics the MSCI Broad Market Index*

You can continue to keep investing money in those three index funds throughout your retirement saving years, simply changing the proportions a little year after year to be safer as you approached retirement.

Let's say that you are in your mid 40s. At this point, your portfolio might look about like this:

30 percent in the Vanguard Total Bond Market Index

23 percent in the Vanguard Total International Market Index

47 percent in the Vanguard Total Stock Market Index

When you are on the verge of retirement, it looks more like this:

40 percent in the bond index

20 percent in the international index

40 percent in the total stock market index

Indexes Come in Many Varieties: The Advanced Lesson

You now know the layman's language for the four basic of indexes: the Standard & Poor's 500 for large companies, the total stock market index for the full market of large and small companies, the total international index for foreign stocks mostly in well-developed nations, and the total bond market index.

There are actually dozens of other indexes, so keep your eye on the four basic indexes to simplify your investing decisions. The basic four will serve you well.

On the other hand, if you are an investor who likes to tinker with your investments, a growing array of index funds will allow you to do it. New index funds let you fine-tune investments—slicing the market into tiny pieces like microcaps (extremely small companies), emerging markets (developing foreign country stocks), just value small stocks, or real estate companies.

Let's say you are interested in fine-tuning your portfolio more than I described with the very broad index funds, and you know that over decades small company stocks have provided greater returns over long periods than large companies. Let's say you are willing to take on the short-term risk that small companies can crash hard. Let's also say you want some real estate exposure, besides your home, to diversify your investments. In that case, maybe you would reduce your holdings in the Standard & Poor's 500 somewhat and increase your small company investments.

Here's one mixture that shows you how you could tinker. Notice that, even when the investor believes in small caps outperforming, she doesn't use all or nothing. She still keeps a diversified portfolio intact.

30 percent in the Lehman Aggregate Total Bond Index (AGG)

20 percent in the Standard & Poor's 500 (IVV)

10 percent in the Standard & Poor's MidCap 400 (IJH)

10 percent in the Standard Poor's SmallCap 600 for growth companies (IJR)

10 percent in the Russell 2000 Value for small value companies (IWN)

15 percent in MSCI EAFE for foreign stocks (EFA)

5 percent in the Dow Jones Diversified Real Estate Index (IYR)

You could do this through a fund company like Vanguard or Fidelity, matching the names of indexes listed previously to the appropriate index fund. For mid caps, for example, you see that you would choose an index fund that mimics the Standard & Poor's MidCap 400 Index. Knowing the exact name of the fund isn't critical. Knowing the name of the index you want to mimic is the essential piece of information. Just ask for an index fund that mimics the index you want.

Exchange Traded Funds

There is another way to use indexes. You can also go to a broker's office or find a broker on the Internet, such as Scottrade (800-619-7283), TD Ameritrade (800-934-4443), or Charles Schwab (866-232-9890. Through the brokers, you could buy another form of index fund called "exchange traded funds," or ETFs for short.

Don't be concerned about the new vocabulary word I've thrown at you. Many ETFs are just like index funds, except you buy them in a different way. You go to a broker and buy an ETF like you would a stock, instead of just sending your money to a mutual fund company.

How do you decide between going to a firm like Vanguard or Fidelity for traditional index funds and going to a broker for ETF index funds?

Base it on this: If you want to make contributions from every paycheck or several times a year, it's going to be cheaper to feed that money month after month into a traditional index mutual fund at a company like Vanguard,

Fidelity, or T. Rowe Price. You can set up an account so that your money flows into a fund from every paycheck, automatically—a smart move.

If, instead, you want to make only a single $4,000 contribution once a year into one fund in an IRA, the ETF can be a good, simple approach. Look at the portfolio I described previously for the investor who likes to tinker. After each type of investment, I have put letters in parentheses. These letters are the "ticker" or "symbol" you will use to identify an ETF when you buy it.

In other words, if you want to buy the Standard & Poor's 500 exchange traded fund, instead of a typical index mutual fund, you would visit or call your broker or reach him or her on the Internet. You say, "I'd like to buy the IVV exchange traded fund," or maybe you prefer another one called Spiders (SPY). There are many different ETFs, mimicking the same indexes. You give your broker the money, and he or she buys shares of ETF for you. With time, you would save money if you bought the ETF over the Internet through the broker's Web site. The broker will tell you how to do it.

When buying ETFs, however, make sure to keep your costs down. If you go to a full-service broker such as Merrill Lynch, you will probably face high commissions—compared to those charged at so-called "discount brokers" like Scottrade. Whether you pay $7 at a discount broker or $50 at a full-service broker, an ETF is the same. So there is no reason to pay $50.

If you are just starting out and need some help, consider a discount broker like Charles Schwab. It has offices around the country and brokers who will help you at a lower cost than full-service brokers. But after you know what you want and don't need help, go with the cheapest broker—one such as Scottrade.

For more information on exchange traded funds, go to www.etfzone.com, www.morningstar.com, and www.amex.com.

Opening an IRA with Nickels and Dimes

Unfortunately, some of the cheapest index funds that are sold directly by mutual fund companies aren't available to people who don't have much cash.

Vanguard, for example, requires that you have $3,000 to deposit immediately up front. Don't let that deter you.

You can use the SSgA S & P 500 index (SVSPX) in an IRA if you deposit $250.

T. Rowe Price is a fine firm and lets you get started in mutual funds or index funds with very little money. For example, T. Rowe Price offers the T. Rowe Price Equity Index 500 (PREIX). The price of entry is only $50, as long as you commit to adding another $50 each month. That's a great way to build up retirement money without feeling like you are depriving yourself. If you could provide $50 from every paycheck, or $100 a month, that would be even better.

Warning: Not All Index Funds Are Good

About a year ago, I was on a radio show and a man named Don called me to ask whether I thought he had a good index fund. He told me the fund's name, but like a lot of investors, Don was focused on the wrong thing. It wasn't the name that was important, because his index fund was pretty much like any other. Remember: Index funds offered by one company or another should be almost identical in content. That's the idea: One Standard & Poor's 500 index should be the same as another because both funds have only one job: to mimic that index.

Consequently, the key factor to scrutinize in Don's index fund—or any index fund—is fees. Always keep that in mind. The cheapest one will be the winner.

I looked up Don's fund at www.morningstar.com, and I ached for all the people who had purchased it.

Don bought his index fund from a financial consultant who charged clients commissions. That was costing Don a bundle. The fund had a 1.25 percent load—which you will recall is the sales charge you pay a broker or financial planner to sell the fund to you. In addition, the fund was charging Don 1 percent in fees—which you recall is noted as the "expense ratio."

I ran the numbers through the SEC mutual fund cost calculator I mentioned in Chapter 12, and here's what I found: If Don invested $10,000 in his index fund for ten years and averaged a 10 percent return, he would end up with about $23,100. If he instead chose a low-cost fund like Vanguard's, he would pay no load and only 0.18 percent in expenses. The result: He'd have about $25,400 after ten years and save himself more than $2,000 on expenses.

Everyone would like to earn $2,000 more if they could over 10 years. That's not the half of it. Look at what the power of compounding did to Don. If he kept averaging a 10 percent return and kept the money invested for 40 years, he'd accumulate only about $299,000 in his expensive index fund. The cheap fund would have provided him a whopping $421,000—simply because expenses weren't eating away his return.

Keep in mind that if you go to a broker or any financial adviser who works on commissions, you will likely have to pay excessive costs for index funds. That really doesn't make sense because index funds are the easy funds—those that most people should be able to select on their own without an adviser's help. In other words, a broker cannot add value selecting a basic index fund like the Standard & Poor's 500 or Total Stock Market Index, so why pay him or her to do it?

Instead, if you want to find affordable index funds easily, simply think Vanguard, Fidelity, or T. Rowe Price.

Is Your Fund Good or Bad?

Although you can intentionally select index funds for IRAs, you may not get that choice in a 401(k). Your employer might not give you the opportunity.

Also, whether you have an IRA or a 401(k), you might want to venture off from index funds for some funds—perhaps wanting a stock-picking pro for small caps and international stocks.

There is some research that suggests that very skilled stock-pickers can be worthwhile in the small cap and international arenas. The reason is simple: Among large caps, it is difficult for any fund manager to stand out, because all managers can find an abundance of information on large stocks.

Small caps and international stocks, on the other hand, are more difficult to examine because information isn't as plentiful. So a great sleuth may earn his keep.

Still, it's up to you to make sure that when you spend money on a stock-picker, it is worthwhile. And if you have a mutual fund that's acting like a loser, you will want to know whether you should keep it or dump it and buy another.

To compare funds, you must analyze performance of funds in two ways. First, you must compare only similar funds, and second, you must compare each fund to an appropriate index.

So if, for example, you have a small cap fund and think it's rotten, compare it only to another small cap fund, not a large cap fund, an international fund, a mid cap fund, or a bond fund.

Remember, cycles will affect each category differently. So if your small cap fund is down 5 percent, but the average small cap fund is down 10 percent, your fund is actually outstanding. If your small cap fund is down 5 percent, and your large cap fund is up 10 percent, it doesn't mean your small cap fund is bad. It probably means the cycle—at that moment—is friendly to large caps and not small caps.

Advanced Comparison Lesson

If you are debating between two funds in the same category, that is a valid comparison. Say that you have two large cap growth funds in your 401(k). How do you know which to pick?

Your employer may offer you a Web site with what's called "Morningstar" information on it. Morningstar is a company known for its research on mutual funds. That research, available at www.morningstar.com, will make your decisions easier.

To find out whether your fund is a good one, follow this process at the Morningstar site.

Type in the name of your fund, and when you come to a report on your fund, look for the words "Performance, More" on a black strip. Click on it.

I want to draw your attention to what will be marked "performance history." It will tell you whether your fund did better (+) or worse (–) than others like it. The performance information will also tell you whether your fund was better of worse than the index—in other words, whether you would have done better with an index fund.

The easiest thing to do, however, is to focus on "% rank in category." This will show you how your fund compared to other funds like it. If your fund ranks close to 1, it is outstanding. If it ranks close to 50, it's average, and that's fine. If it's below 50 percent, that's not a good sign. It means that the fund you are considering did worse than half the other funds like it.

Keep in mind, however, that one year is insignificant. You want a fund that consistently is in the top half of funds like it, or one that performs as well if not better than an index fund…but not just for one year. You want to base your decision on several years, because one year might have been a fluke, being in the right place at the right time during a cycle.

Notice performance for five years and ten years. Then, check to make sure that the same fund manager who was there five years ago is still running the fund.

If the fund has been outstanding, but the fund manager recently left, all the performance figures from the past are probably irrelevant—unless a co-manager who was working alongside the old manager simply takes over where the old manager left off.

But if there is a brand new manager who hasn't worked with your fund in the past, he or she is starting fresh. You really don't know what that new manager will do with your money. He may or may not handle your fund like the previous manager did. If this concept seems difficult to understand, think of the teachers you have had over the years. Fifth-grade math is fifth-grade math, but if a new teacher comes into the course mid-year, the new teacher may offer a class very different from the teacher you first had.

Then, focus on one more piece of information about the fund. You should be able to guess. It's the expense ratio—the one number that tells you more about how you are likely to do with that fund in the future than using any other measurement. If your expense ratio is below 1 percent, if your fund has consistently been in the top half of its peers, and if your fund is performing better than an appropriate index, and if the manager is still there, you probably have found a keeper.

Remember, what doesn't matter is whether your fund made a lot of money or lost a lot of money. What matters is how it compares to the index. If you have a large cap fund that's up 13 percent, but the Standard & Poor's 500 is up 15 percent, your 13 percent is stinky. You've been wasting your money on high expenses to do worse than an index. That's foolish—maybe not in just one year, but if it happens year after year it certainly is.

On the other hand, if the Standard & Poor's is down 5 percent for the year, and your fund is down only 1 percent, your fund manager earned his keep. You have an outstanding fund if it keeps outpacing the Standard & Poor's 500 year after year.

The indexes are the key to measuring and evaluating your mutual funds. Savvy investors, like pension funds, use indexes to tell them whether they have been employing a worthwhile investment manager. They are what the mutual fund industry uses to determine whether they should give a fund manager a juicy bonus.

Here's a simple process to use to compare your funds. For any fund you own or are considering buying, simply see whether its returns measure up to the appropriate index:

For an international stock fund, use the MSCI EAFE.

For a large cap fund, use the Standard & Poor's 500.

For a large cap growth fund, use the Russell 1000 Growth.

For a large cap value fund, use the Russell 1000 Value.

For a small cap fund, use the Standard & Poor's SmallCap 600.

For a small cap growth fund, use the Russell 2000 Growth.

For a small cap value fund, use the Russell 2000 Value.

For mid cap funds, use the Standard & Poor's MidCap 400.

For bonds, use the Lehman Aggregate bond index.

If your fund performed better than the index for at least three years and hopefully five or more, you have an outstanding fund if the manager is still there. If it performed much worse, ask yourself why you have spent more on fees to get less. Consider dropping your fund and buying an index fund instead.

You can find the indexes and their performance on the Internet. Many of the indexes can be found all at once at https://new.morningstar.com/index/ IndexReturn.html. To analyze any single fund, go to www.morningstar.com, type in the name of your fund in the white Quotes box, and compare its performance to the index that Morningstar provides.

How to Analyze a Fund

Let me walk you through an example. Say you have been putting money into the Fidelity Contrafund in your 401(k) for years. You want to know if it's a good fund or a bad fund.

You go to www.morningstar.com, type in Fidelity Contrafund, and click on FCNTX—that's the ticker investors use to get information on that fund. After you click on FCNTX, you come to a report on the Contrafund. Immediately, you see on the top of the right side of the page that the fund is a "large growth fund." So you know that the matching words you need to focus on are "large growth fund." In other words, this fund invests in large company stocks, and it would not be meaningful to compare that fund to any other fund except another large cap growth fund.

You can also see on the upper right that when Morningstar compared the fund to similar large cap funds, it was outstanding. See the five stars? That's Morningstar's top rating—five stars, on a scale of 1 to 5.

That's a very good sign. But you aren't done. Beneath the stars, you see .91 percent expense ratio. That falls within the 1 percent threshold that's acceptable for fees. So expenses are OK if the fund performs well.

Now, you are going to examine the fund's performance—or how investors do when they put money in the fund. Under the fund's name, you see "Performance, More," and a graph that shows how the fund has done for the past few years. Look at the words under the graph: "Trailing Returns." You will see that for 5 years, the fund has given investors an average annual return of 12.7 percent. But you think, "Is that good or bad?"

The answer comes in the information you see just below 12.7 percent. You see a critical piece of information about that return. The Contrafund's return is being compared to an index—the Standard & Poor's 500 (large cap stock) index—and the results are very good.

You see that the return has been about 4.5 percent above the index (the Standard & Poor's 500 index) for five years. That's extremely important. It means the investors are ending up with more money than they would in an index fund, and that's very unusual—especially for five years or more. If, instead, Morningstar had shown that the fund's return was worse than the index—or –4.5 percent—that would be a bad sign. It would suggest that an index fund would be a better deal.

There's one more check to run before deciding the fund is for you. Check on the manager by clicking on "Management" in the blue block on the left. You see that the outstanding manager is still at the fund and has been there since 1986.

Looks like the fund is a keeper!

You can do more research by clicking on all the choices in that blue block where I had you click on "Management." But you have the basics. You have found that the fund has continually beat its index, the expenses aren't out of line, and the savvy manager is still there.

Doing this analysis took about five minutes.

If analyzing funds still seems like too much work, you can avoid the headache by simply using low-cost index funds—those with an expense ratio of 0.35 percent or less. On the other hand, I have one more shortcut for you— the simplest of anything the mutual fund industry offers.

Now that you understand how to analyze fees and to evaluate asset allocation models, you have the background necessary to use this shortcut wisely. It's a couch potato's delight. And you will find it in the next chapter.

14

SIMPLE DOES IT: NO-BRAINER INVESTING WITH TARGET-DATE FUNDS

Now, for the easiest choice of all. I mean easy…as easy as putting money into a typical savings account at a bank, only with a much better chance that you will be able to travel and go out to dinner once in a while when you retire.

The mutual fund industry has caught on that people are busy and overwhelmed with the strange words that are thrown at them. So the industry has created a new type of fund that could have been named "mutual funds for dummies" or "mutual funds for couch potatoes" or "mutual funds for nervous Nellies."

In fact, the funds actually are called "target-date funds," or sometimes "life-cycle" or "retirement-date funds." I know I've just thrown another set of vocabulary words at you. But these are easy to spot, and well worth it. If you peruse 401(k) choices and see a number embedded in the name of a mutual fund, you can sigh in relief. Your quest for the simple way out has been solved. Perhaps you will see a fund with a name like "Target Retirement 2045" or "Retirement 2010," or maybe your employer is holding meetings to tell you about these popular new additions to 401(k) plans. If you consider retirement investing a hassle, you will never curse the process again.

You can buy one of these "couch potato mutual funds" for your 401(k), and, away from work, you can do the same in your IRA. With these funds, you can put all your retirement savings onto autopilot for the rest of your life.

If you select a target-date fund, you won't have to worry about sorting through mutual fund names and categories like large caps and small caps. Nor will you have to do any mixing and matching or move money around between risky investments and safer investments. The fund itself will do all of this for you—and not just for tomorrow, but for your entire life.

You will need to know only one thing: when you'd like to retire. That's it. Simple. Just give the fees a once-over to make sure you aren't paying too much, and you can be done. You won't need any more funds beyond that one.

You might be confused now because I told you previously that you cannot rely on a single fund, and you must combine many in your portfolio. A target-date fund, however, is the exception because it is designed for one-stop shopping. A single target-date fund gives you large caps, small caps, and international stocks and bonds, and as you age it tweaks the proportions so you have what's appropriate for your age.

So if you are procrastinating because you are afraid of making a mistake, fear no more. This is a no-brainer.

Look for a Date

Half of 401(k) plans now offer these delightful investing shortcuts. If yours does, look for one detail: the number that matches the year you will retire. Let's say you are 39 years old now and plan to retire at 67. That's simple. You will retire in 2035. So you want investments geared toward that target—the year 2035. Now all you have to do is find a target-date fund with the date 2035 on it.

Every target-date fund has a year in its name. So if you are looking through a 401(k) list and wonder how to find one, look for a name of a fund with a number somewhere in the 2000s on it. You might see several. Some might have names like "freedom" or "life path" or "milestone" or "strategy," and an array of different dates on them.

Don't let the variety worry you. The different dates on them exist merely because each person needs to find the fund aimed at his or her particular retirement year. And the words like "life path" or "freedom" are simply supposed to clue you in on the intent—to get your money ready for your retirement date.

If you are 40, you wouldn't pick a fund that said 2020 on it unless you intended to retire early.

If you are 40 and are planning to retire at 67, an appropriate fund would be one with 2035 in the name—getting you ready to retire in 2034. The fund dates put you close, but not exactly on your actual retirement date.

Most likely the 2020 fund would be right for someone who is 54. For someone 30, the 2045 fund would be smart—preparing the person for retirement at about age 67, or the year 2045.

If you are 25 and are nervous about investing but have a 401(k) with a fund that says "2050" on it, you can use it and relax from that point forward. You can also do the same with an IRA. You simply contact a firm like Vanguard (800-997-2798), T. Rowe Price (800-638-5660), or Fidelity (800-544-8544); select a target-date fund with the number 2050 in its name; and barely give it a second thought for the rest of your working years. Tell the mutual fund firm to take money automatically out of every paycheck and put it in that one mutual fund over and over again throughout your life. At age 67 you should be set, even though you devoted almost no attention to your investments during three decades.

Tweaking as You Age

Target-date funds are designed for one purpose—to grow your money in the most effective way, so you have as much as possible, for a set date. You simply clue the fund manager in to what he or she needs to do for you, by giving the manager your "target." So you tell the fund manager the date you plan to retire by buying the appropriate fund—the one carrying your retirement date. Then the manager knows what combo of stocks and bonds will work best for you at every stage of your life. As you age, the manager adapts the mixture each year for the rest of your working years so it's always appropriate for your age. You will never need to buy another fund.

Your fund manager will be acquainted with all the academic studies that show how types of stocks and bonds work over time through different cycles. So the fund manager will buy a well-reasoned mixture—with market-cycle shock absorbers built into the mix—always tweaking the recipe for your age and the number of years to retirement. When you are young, you will have mostly stocks in your target-date mutual fund, and maybe somewhat riskier stocks. As you age, the manager will slowly, year-by-year, cut back on stocks, adjust the types of stocks for less risk, and keep more money in bonds and cash.

I don't want you to think that these are magical devices that won't lose money at times. There are stocks in these funds, so when the stock market goes down, you should expect to see your fund drop somewhat. As with any portfolio you put together, the key is to have the money grow effectively for a future point in time.

Instead of focusing on the day-to-day ups and downs in the market, target-date fund managers will let academic studies be their guide. The studies direct them to combinations of stocks and bonds best geared—based on historical returns—to get people where they need to be maybe 10, 20, or 30 years down the road.

Although a novice might respond to market shocks by yanking money from stocks, academic studies show that keeping a portfolio steady—basing it on a person's target retirement date—tends to give the best results.

Of course, you don't need a target-date fund to get these results. In fact, you could keep your fees lower and likely make more money over time simply by investing in a mixture of low-cost index funds. I have given you all the tools to do this planning yourself, because getting the recipe—or asset allocation—close to right is your most important job as an investor. But if you are reluctant to give your money the attention I've described in the preceding chapters, a target-date fund will do it for you.

Say that you are 50 and buy the T. Rowe Price Retirement 2025. In that single fund, you will have the mixture that's appropriate for a person your age on the way to retirement. In mid 2006, you would have had about 64 percent of your money in U.S. stocks, about 18.5 percent in international stocks, 13.5 percent in bonds, and 4 percent in cash. But this is not a static mixture. It's designed only for a 50-year-old who wouldn't panic if the stock market acts scary at any particular time. Each year, the fund manager makes changes based on your age—keeping your money safer as time goes on.

A look at another T. Rowe Price Retirement fund illustrates what happens. Consider the T. Rowe Price Retirement 2010, aimed at a 62-year-old retiring in about three years. A person on the verge of retiring can't afford to lose money. So that portfolio is a lot safer than one for a younger person. It looked like this: 52 percent in U.S. stocks, 13 percent foreign, 24.5 percent in bonds, and 10.4 percent in cash.

One last comparison will help you understand the shifts. Let's now go to the 29-year-old who would buy the T. Rowe Price Retirement 2045. That person is trying to grow his or her money as much as possible and can take risks because there is plenty of time to regain ground if the stock market swoons for a while. So here's the portfolio: 69 percent U.S. stocks, about 21 percent foreign, 6.5 percent in bonds, and 3.4 percent in cash.

What to Do When 401(k) Funds Lack Target-Date Funds

If you have a 401(k) and your employer doesn't offer one of these no-brainer funds, get your coworkers together and ask the person in charge of benefits to add one. Encourage the benefits staffer to select a low-cost target-date fund such as those offered by T. Rowe Price, Fidelity, or Vanguard.

Even if you can't nudge your employer or don't have a 401(k) at work, don't worry. Target-date funds can help you even if you never invest in one. They can serve as your models for asset allocation. If you ever wonder whether you have the right mixture of stocks, bonds, and cash, simply peek quickly at a target-date fund's portfolio and copy it.

Just go to an Internet site for a firm like Vanguard, Fidelity, or T. Rowe Price; look up their target-date retirement funds for your retirement age; and mimic their portfolio. In other words, if you are 25 and don't know what to do with the small selection of funds an employer has given you in a 401(k) plan, just piece together the puzzle by matching your fund categories to those in a target-date fund. You will then have your "asset allocation"— or percentages of various funds—about right: a tried-and-true recipe.

But if you ask your employer to add a target-date fund, you are likely to have a receptive ear. About 38 percent of companies were offering them in 2005, according to research by benefits consultants Hewitt Associates. And a pension law change in 2006 is encouraging employers to add them. Also, to operate efficiently and stay within government rules, employers need to get as many employees as possible to participate in 401(k) plans, so there's an incentive to listen to employees' desires.

How to Select a Target-Date Fund

If you get your benefits staff to listen or if you select a target-date fund on your own for an IRA, there are two major issues that need attention: the riskiness of the stock and bond mixtures in each fund, and the fees you will have to pay for each fund.

There has been a debate among managers of target-date funds the past few years. When the funds were first created about five years ago, they held fewer stocks than many do now, because the managers were afraid investors would see a loss in a bad cycle and bolt. Many have come to the conclusion lately, however, that investors need to be focused on the risk of running out of money because they are likely to live into their 90s. So the fund managers have been adding more stocks to portfolios and limiting bonds until savers are very close to retirement.

In your 401(k), this probably won't be an issue because you will likely be given one target-date fund for your particular retirement date, and that will have to be your choice.

Yet if you go shopping for a target-date fund for an IRA, you will have to decide whether you are more worried about the shorter-term risk of losing money in a bad stock cycle or the longer-term risk of running out of money in retirement because you were too cautious with investments.

Here's an example of the differences. In the Fidelity Freedom 2015, fund managers keep only 50 percent of your money in stocks when you are about ten years from retiring, and the rest goes into bonds. The T. Rowe Price Retirement 2015, however, is much more aggressive and could consequently lose more of your money in a down cycle occurring rather close to your retirement. Within about ten years of retiring, about 70 percent of your money would be in stocks.

For younger investors, T. Rowe Price target-date funds also tend to have more mid and small cap stocks than Fidelity and Vanguard. That makes the T. Rowe Price funds riskier. Still, investors opening an IRA should think about how daring they want to be about the short run and the long run. For a quick peek at your risks in each target-date fund you consider, look up the fund at www.morningstar.com, click on "Portfolio," and you will see the percents of stocks and bonds in the funds. Then you can decide whether one feels more comfortable to you than another, perhaps rereading Chapter 9, "Know Your Mutual Fund Manager's Job."

As you consider the fees that each target-date fund will charge you, it might also help to review Chapter 12, "How to Pick Mutual Funds: Bargain Shop." But here it is in a nutshell: The fees you pay for funds can strangle your returns, even if they look like small numbers. And target-date funds can layer on relatively huge expenses that can reduce your nest egg years into the future. So look at what can happen.

Assume that you are going to retire in 2035 and you have $25,000 to invest in a target-date fund. You consider two of them: The Hartford Target Retirement 2030 fund and Vanguard Target Retirement 2035. The fees don't look so bad at first glance. Hartford will charge 1.4 percent of your assets (or money in the fund) and Vanguard 0.21 percent. But assume that the investments in both funds do equally well—climbing 8 percent on average a year. With the cheap Vanguard fund, you will have about $236,190 after 30 years. With the more expensive Hartford fund, you will have only $164,800. Why? Simply because of fees. In the Vanguard fund, you paid only about $6,160 over 30 years. For the Hartford fund, you paid $32,580.

So with life-cycle funds, as with any other type of mutual fund, pay attention to fees in addition to the track record—or returns—over at least the past three years. Morningstar analysts suggest keeping the expense ratio under 1 percent, because there are quality funds within that realm. If you buy one on your own, I'd steer toward funds charging no more than Fidelity at 0.94 percent, or T. Rowe Price at 0.82 percent. Vanguard would be even more attractive at 0.21 percent.

There is no reason to buy a target-date fund with a load, or a sales charge. As you probably recall from Chapter 12, loads are supposed to compensate brokers for the advice they give you. But target-date funds are no-brainer funds, so you shouldn't need to pay a broker for assistance.

As you evaluate funds offered by Fidelity, Vanguard, and T. Rowe Price, think of Vanguard as the low-cost standout and T. Rowe Price as the greatest risk-taker, because its target-date funds tend to hold more stocks than others.

T. Rowe Price is the best choice for investors opening an IRA with very little cash. While most funds won't let you through the door unless you have $1,000 or more, T. Rowe Price accepts investors with as little as $50. With that sum, however, you must be willing to add $50 a month to the fund.

If this detail makes you nuts about the choices in front of you, don't hesitate. You can't go wrong with any of these funds. All are set up to give you a blend of investments—exposing you to the levels of risks that are roughly appropriate for your age, and giving you a chance to make a solid return. Procrastinating, however, will do you in. Skipping stock market risks altogether will do you in. Swinging for the fences with a single stock or one hot fund will almost certainly do you in.

Getting started is much more important than picking the perfect fund.

Just keep in mind, if you pick a target retirement fund, you don't need any other funds. This might be confusing for you because I told you in previous chapters that you needed to diversify and couldn't rely on a single fund. I'm not contradicting that now, however. A target-date fund is a different animal from a simple large cap stock fund or a small cap stock fund. It puts everything you need into one fund. So it's a complete diversified portfolio— one with an appropriate mixture of stocks and bonds. If you choose a target-date fund and even one more fund in a 401(k), you will throw off the formula—taking on either too much risk or not enough.

The same goes for your IRA. If you pick a target-date fund for it, you are done. You don't need other funds. That's the beauty of it.

Other Similar Choices

The easiest fund of all is the target-date fund. For the person who doesn't want to bother with asset allocation, it would be my choice. But your 401(k) might not offer a fund with a date in the name.

Instead, you might see other so-called "life-cycle" funds. These funds do not manage your money specifically for a certain retirement date, so they aren't quite as simple to use. But the concept is close. They require you to do a little more thinking. They ask you how much risk you are willing to take. And then they decide on a mixture of stocks and bonds based on that.

So you might see funds with names like "life strategy" or "spectrum" or "asset manager." When you choose one of them, you might have to decide between one that takes the most risks ("aggressive" or "growth"), one that takes fewer but still significant risks ("moderate growth"), and one that is low risk ("conservative").

The beauty of these funds is that they take some of the asset allocation concern off your hands. But, unlike target-date funds, they don't remove the entire burden. They all buy a blend of stocks and bonds, but since they base it on risks—rather than the time frame to retirement—you can't stick with the same fund for life.

You need to sell one fund and move into another less-risky fund as you age. For example, you might start in your 20s with an "aggressive" approach, move to "moderate growth" in middle age, and become "conservative" during retirement.

Just don't fall asleep at the switch with one of these funds. You'd be making a mistake to have all your money in one aggressive life-cycle fund on the eve of your retirement.

Old-Style Life-Cycle Funds

Your 401(k) may not give you a choice of a target-date or life-cycle fund because they are relatively new. Small employers might simply have a few choices—ones that have been around for years.

But do not fear. You still may have a very easy choice.

Look down the list. If you see the word "balanced," that fund will also make life easy on you. It won't tweak your mixture of stocks and bonds on the basis of your age. But it will blend stocks and bonds for you at all times— roughly 60 percent in stocks and 40 percent in bonds.

So it might not be as aggressive as you want to be at age 25. But if you find the entire selection process overwhelming and don't know where to start, you won't go wrong with a balanced fund.

You can always start your 401(k) putting all money into that one fund. It's a classic. Then get comfortable with investing. Learn more, and then maybe get more aggressive—taking more risks with stock funds—a few months later. Keep the balanced fund as a core fund. And add a little more stock to your investments with one or two more stock funds later.

15

Do You Need a Financial Adviser?

Want to escape from all of this, turn your money over to an expert, and be done with it?

Go for it, if you really think you need help. But before you do, I have some bad news for you. Finding a reliable financial planner who will be right for you could be harder than following the investing steps I have laid out for you in this book.

Some financial advisers are superb, but a lot of them are not. If you blindly turn your money over to those who are ill-trained or unscrupulous, it could cost you dearly.

Over the years, I have seen the remnants of awful advice. As a columnist, I get calls from people when they aren't sure who else to consult. I have had widows call, crying, because the brokers their husbands turned their life's savings over to decimated the nest eggs after their husbands died. The brokers put the money in inappropriate volatile stocks and churned from one investment to another—sometimes out of ignorance, often to wrack up commissions for themselves.

I have had a 22-year-old parking lot attendant ask me to explain the life insurance policy he had just been sold. This was a young man, who was scraping by, intent on doing what would be right for his future. He relied on "a great guy" who parked his car at the lot and offered the parking attendant help on his finances. Shame on that life insurance salesman! The young parking attendant had no wife, or kids, or anyone counting on him. He didn't need life insurance. He needed an IRA. But if the insurance salesman had helped him open an IRA and invest it in a low-cost mutual fund that would truly help this young man, the salesman would have foregone his own hefty commissions.

I could go on and on with these stories—including doctors who trusted brokers with hot tips on dubious medical company investments, or people who met financial advisers at church and so concluded they had to be trustworthy.

"The con men can do it because they appear more honest than the honest person," retired Minneapolis financial planner Henry Montgomery once told me, as he urged me to tell people to investigate even highly recommended advisers.

Perhaps some of the wayward advisers never intended to hurt people. They may simply have been foolish, rather than unethical. Typically, they are indoctrinated by companies that want them to sell their high-priced annuities, insurance, and mutual funds.

Here's what you need to know before charging into a financial adviser's office, proclaiming your ignorance and dumping your finances blindly into someone else's lap: The person you are turning to for expertise may be virtually as ignorant as you about financial matters.

This is shocking to people. But anyone can call himself or herself a financial planner. The person needs no education and is not required to take a competency test. In fact, in many states, hair cutters need to jump through more regulatory hoops than financial planners.

So if the phrase "buyer beware" ever applied to anything, it applies to financial advisers.

The federal government's approach to regulating the financial services business has been to require the people who serve you to "disclose"—or tell you about—their background and what they plan to do for you. You are then supposed to know how to make an informed decision about them. The trouble is that the disclosures are full of lingo and legalese—more wacky words to understand. Also, some financial advisers think they will seem more valuable if they make investing complicated to you. Even those who have your best interests at heart sometimes forget to speak plain English.

When most people hear disclosures or investment explanations, they aren't sure what they've heard. They have gone to a financial adviser in the first place because they feel insecure about their knowledge and consequently don't want to ask what they fear might be "dumb" questions. Also, they are there with one objective: to make life easier on themselves. The last thing they want to do is devote time to checking out the person who will take their money headaches off their hands.

It's ironic when you think about it. If that adviser ultimately is going to be responsible for turning your hard-earned pennies into a retirement fund of $500,000 or more, you'd think you would take a lot of care. We are talking about thousands of dollars—not a few hundred. But, in fact, people spend more time scrutinizing the fabric in the clothing they buy or reading *Consumer Reports* about an electronic device, appliance, or car, which cost a lot less.

Here's what you have to do if you are going to work with financial advisers—whether they call themselves brokers, financial planners, financial specialists, financial consultants, wealth managers, investment managers, investment advisers, "certified" whatever, or something else: Start out by interviewing at least three people, perhaps getting recommendations from a trusted lawyer, accountant, or friend. You can also get referrals from three respected financial planning organizations. Contact www.fpanet.org (888-237-6275), www.garrettplanning.com, (866-260-8400) or www.napfa.com (847-366-2732).

But don't stop with the recommendation—even if it comes from a person you trust.

As you consider financial planners, be cautious of the titles they attach to their names. This industry has become competitive, and people who aren't well versed in planning have attached flimsy certifications to their titles to make it look as though they are better trained than they are. Look for a "certified financial planner." (The common shorthand designation is CFP.)

Unlike people who call themselves "financial consultants," the "certified financial planner" designation actually means something. The person has had training and passed a test.

Even the CFP designation doesn't guarantee skill or ethics. You will need to dig deeper as you interview three potential financial planners. That first consultation should be free.

Don't work with anyone before checking to see whether that person has been in trouble for ethical violations or even illegal practices. Your state has an office that oversees the securities industry. You can check there. But nationally, go to the National Association of Securities Dealers, or NASD (800-289-9999, or www.nasd.com), to check out any adviser's regulatory background.

Then, when you interview planners or money managers, ask to see their full "ADV" forms. You are entitled to see them. Part I explains any legal or regulatory problems the adviser or firm has had. Part II covers fees and strategies. Also consider the following questions.

Does the Financial Adviser Focus on People Like You?

There's a natural inclination among people to try to search for a professional who has the reputation of being the "best" in the field. Unfortunately, in the financial advice arena, the very best often aren't focused on people with a few thousand dollars to invest in a 401(k) plan or an IRA.

Many highly respected financial advisers desire clients with $250,000 or more to invest. And that means $250,000 outside a 401(k) plan. Often, they make their money by charging the client a percentage of the money they manage. About 1 percent of assets is common. But think about it. If you want advice on your 401(k) plan, you have no money to turn over to the financial adviser. How can the adviser make money?

Here's where the mischief too often begins. The adviser needs to put food on his or her own table. So, to make money, the adviser needs to sell you investments outside your 401(k) that charge high commissions. That could include unnecessary insurance and annuities or high-priced mutual funds.

Although there would be nothing wrong with this person encouraging you to open an IRA, too often the funds he or she might sell will be mediocre and expensive. Of course, if you read Chapter 12, "How to Pick Mutual Funds: Bargain Shop," you know what that means. Over a lifetime of saving, you could end up with a third less—or possibly even worse—in your retirement nest egg. Remember my $10,000 example, earning $264,000 in a low-cost fund and $116,000 in an expensive one. Variable annuities—a favorite product for advisers seeking high commissions—can give you even uglier results.

It's tricky for people of modest means to find competent advice during their savings years. Often, if they go to a well-regarded financial adviser, the top adviser will hand off the small account to an underling. If you select a financial planner, ask who will be dealing with your account, check the person's credentials, and make sure you will be valued as much as a client with millions.

Also, if you are getting attention from someone who works with retired millionaires, your needs may be very different as you struggle paycheck to paycheck and raise children. Find out whether the financial adviser works with other clients like you so that you can be assured that the adviser is cued in to the needs of people of your economic background. For example, financial advisers who work with wealthy people typically help them avoid estate taxes. Applying the same approaches to a middle-income family could destroy their opportunity to one day send their children to college with some financial aid help.

If the adviser is going to do a financial plan for you, ask to see three plans the adviser has done for other clients—including one for a person like you. If all the plans look alike, with similar investments, they are of dubious value.

You should know that many firms that promote themselves as financial planners aren't really focused on planning at all. They are glorified salesmen who turn out mass-produced financial plans from their computers with brilliantly colored pie charts and graphs.

"The dirty little secret in my profession is that most planners don't do financial planning," Laura Tarbox once told me. She's a California financial planner who has taught other financial planners at the University of California–Irvine.

Instead, the mass-produced plans—which typically cost you around $500 or less—too often are used as a marketing mechanism, she said. The planners turn out a plan that appears to be custom-made for an individual, but in fact it becomes the device used to sell high-commission mutual funds, annuities, life insurance, and other products.

A financial plan, truly designed for you, is an elaborate work and often costs about $3,000 or more.

Does the Financial Adviser Have a Conflict of Interest?

Whenever a financial planner gets paid on commissions, there is the potential for an inherent conflict of interest because he or she won't make as much money by selling you less-expensive funds—even when they might be better.

The U.S. Securities and Exchange Commission has been concerned about this and has provided warnings for consumers about widespread abuses in brokerage firms. Too often brokers, who may call themselves "financial consultants," work for firms that induce them to sell mediocre expensive mutual funds by offering them bonuses, prizes, or even trips for a lot of sales. Those who don't meet certain quotas can be punished and may lose their job.

To protect yourself, refer to the ADV form I mentioned. It will explain how the adviser is paid. If the adviser is getting paid by commissions, you must be on guard—realizing that the salesman might be trying to generate the highest commission for himself rather than the best results for you.

Also, the Securities and Exchange Commission suggests asking your broker or financial adviser whether he or his employer has a so-called "preferred list"—or a list of mutual funds from which he chooses. If he does, those funds may not be there because they are top quality. Instead, they may just pay him and his firm top price, and he may consequently neglect to tell you about a better mutual fund that will cost you less.

Ask the adviser the following questions:

How does a fund get on the preferred list, and how often do you recommend funds that aren't on the list?

Are you and other brokers in your firm involved in contests or rewards programs for selling certain funds, annuities, or other products? Do you or your firm get any type of payment for selling funds or other products on your preferred list?

What percent of funds on your preferred list don't make any payments to you or your firm?

How do you scrutinize the funds you will sell me?

A good answer will focus on keeping your expenses below the 0.93 percent average paid by investors, and selecting only funds that consistently perform as well, or better, than an index like the Standard & Poor's 500. Of course, you also should hear that the adviser never ties mutual fund choices to a prescribed recommended list.

If the adviser gets commissions, don't expect a recommendation for a low-priced index fund. There will be loads, which will erode your performance. There is no reason to pay a load on an index fund. It defies the idea of buying a low-priced fund.

Instead of suggesting index funds, an adviser who depends on commissions is likely to tell you that the more expensive fund will be better. Ask to see a Morningstar report on the fund so that you can determine whether that's true. Morningstar studies mutual funds, and you will want to see whether the recommended fund is at least in the top half of similar funds for five- and ten-year periods and still employs the manager who had excellent performance.

If the adviser won't show you this information, or if the fund has been in the bottom half of its fund category for three years or more, I would have doubts about the quality of advice.

If you are overwhelmed with evaluating fees and commissions, you can also ask your broker to tally all of them and show you in dollars and cents what that will do to your investment over 20 years. Don't expect the broker to be eager to do this. But you deserve the information. Make sure you ask for all "fees, front-end loads, back-end loads, operating costs," and any other fees that make up the "expense ratio" so that nothing is glossed over. You can also take the fee information and calculate it yourself using the calculator I mentioned in Chapter 12. Find one at www.sec.gov, or another at www.dinkytown.com.

After you see this information, you may want to reevaluate what you need.

Get Limited Advice

I have always respected the advice of Paula Kennedy, a New York financial planner, who no longer works with individuals. She realizes that sometimes people want some hand-holding, instead of handling their 401(k) and IRAs alone. They need the extra confidence of working with a financial adviser to get the job done.

Rather than procrastinating, and putting your future on hold by not getting started, Kennedy suggests going to a certified financial planner once a year for advice. That may mean one or two hours—at a fee of perhaps $150 to $250 an hour, depending on where you live. Clarify the time involved and the fee upfront so that fees don't get out of hand later.

Then bring your 401(k), IRA, and any other investments to the planner and ask whether you have the right mixture of funds.

With that information, you should then have the confidence to go another year—simply feeding new money, paycheck after paycheck, into your 401(k), IRA, or other accounts.

Finding an Adviser

To make sure you get solid advice, work with a certified financial planner who will work for you only on an hourly fee basis, not by charging you commissions. When you assure yourself that there are no commissions, you can be confident that the planner will evaluate your funds on their merits.

To find a financial planner, contact www.fpanet.org, www.napfa.com or www.garrettplanning.com, and specifically request one who will accept an hourly fee.

When you reach the point in life when your decisions are more complex than simply saving and investing money in a 401(k) or IRA, then you might want to engage a planner. It's a good idea when you are about five to ten years from retirement, or when something unique, like a major inheritance, falls in your lap.

If you select what's called a certified financial planner, you will assure yourself that the person has training in a broad range of planning disciplines. However, this still does not assure you of the person's ethics, so make the call to the NASD. Also, although training prepares a planner to select mutual funds, significantly more education would be desirable for selecting individual stocks.

When finding financial advice, be aware that there are many people competing for your business by creating titles that sound impressive. Many titles mean nothing. For example, brokers increasingly are calling themselves "financial consultants" but are paid to be salesmen. You will also see many designations that start with the word "certified." Yet they may mean little more than a person having received a few hours of training.

Finally, keep in mind that talented and honorable people in one discipline are not necessarily equipped for another. For example, all doctors are highly trained, but you wouldn't go to a knee surgeon for a hearing problem. The same applies to financial advice. This list will help you select the right person for your needs.

Certified Financial Planners, or CFPs, are trained in overall financial planning ranging from asset allocation to taxes and estate planning. They have passed a two-day test and have a college education—not necessarily a business or finance degree. They are qualified to select an appropriate mixture of mutual funds for you and help you aim at fulfilling financial goals—like saving enough for retirement. They will be familiar with some tax issues but are not generally trained as well as a certified public accountant in taxes. And they should refer clients to lawyers for help with legal matters like wills and trusts. Their typical training does not equip them to pick stocks.

Chartered Financial Analysts, or CFAs, are the elite, highly trained stock- and bond-pickers of the financial professionals. They have had extensive education in analyzing investments—ranging from futures and options to stocks and bonds—and have passed a three-day test that is so rigorous that many fail. Having this background would be important for a money manager who will be selecting individual stocks and bonds for you. They also have familiarity with some tax issues, but that's not their primary focus. Nor would they be experts on debt management or know some financial planning matters, such as how to pick college savings plans.

Certified Public Accountants, or CPAs, are experienced and trained with accounting and taxes. They typically have at least a bachelors degree in accounting, have passed a demanding test in that area of expertise, and are licensed by a state. They are equipped to scrutinize (or audit) corporate financial records and would be most skilled at advising individuals about strategies to keep tax bills low. But they may not be well prepared to do financial planning or pick stocks, bonds, or mutual funds.

Chartered Financial Consultant (ChFC) or Chartered Life Underwriter (CLU) designations primarily focus on insurance—everything from health insurance to life insurance, but not investing. If you sought investment advice from these consultants, they might be inclined to suggest insurance products such as variable annuities when low-cost mutual funds might be a better choice.

Financial consultants, or stock brokers, sell stocks, bonds, and mutual funds. They are hired to be salespeople, and most don't have financial planning training. Most also haven't been educated about analyzing stocks. They might have sales quotas to meet.

Credit counselors focus on people with excessive debt. They may have little training, and some firms enhance financial troubles rather than helping clients escape them. To find a reputable firm, call the National Foundation for Consumer Credit (800-388-2227). Avoid firms that advertise.

Advice at Your Workplace

Increasingly, employers are bringing financial advisers into the workplace to help employees handle 401(k)s. I encourage you to go to any one-on-one session you are offered and to listen to any presentations on selecting 401(k) funds. Also, call any telephone adviser your employer offers you. This help will be particularly valuable if you feel paralyzed or merely want to double-check your own investment decisions.

Also, once a year it's important to make sure that the previous year's strongest fund hasn't started to dominate your mixture—throwing off your asset allocation plan. An adviser can help you with the process called "rebalancing"—or moving a little money from your strongest funds into areas that the latest cycle has not favored.

Still, although I encourage you to avail yourself of the help offered at work, I also must provide a warning. Skill levels and ethics vary greatly among the advisers who are providing 401(k) help in workplaces.

So take in the help, but also be cautious. Over the years, I have seen consultants who use 401(k) presentations to build their credibility. Then, when an individual seeks their advice, the adviser suggests that they plan a meeting outside the workplace. And the adviser then tries to sell expensive high-commission mutual funds, insurance, or annuities that the individual shouldn't have.

To guard against this, evaluate the adviser in your workplace based on the criteria I have outlined in this chapter. The adviser might simply be a glorified salesman. Don't forget to examine fees. And be skeptical if the adviser tries to talk you into taking your money out of the company 401(k) and investing it instead in an IRA or another product outside the workplace fund. I've heard horror stories about this from individuals who had perfectly good 401(k) plans and no need to "roll over" their money into an IRA.

The Bottom Line

Go to the right adviser with the right types of questions. To get the most from the adviser's help, be somewhat well informed yourself.

People do need financial advisers at certain points in their life—especially for a little advice just before retirement. You also might need a financial planner if you are too afraid of making a mistake and consequently are procrastinating, squandering away the years that will make a difference to your future.

Yet I want you to know that following the step-by-step actions in this book will make you successful. No matter what your age, you will make yourself wealthier than you ever imagined if you start now, open a Roth IRA every year, feed your 401(k) to the max if you have one, and mix and match mutual funds using the easy investing strategies and models in this book.

If you are lucky enough to be in your 20s, just investing $20 to $25 a week will put you on course to being a millionaire. If you are older, you can still accumulate plenty without living like a pauper. If you vow now to correct the investing mistakes that have destroyed your hard-earned savings in the past, your money will be kind to you in the future.

You now have all the tools you need to invest with skill. Just start. Procrastination is your worst enemy. And if you have any questions, you can find me at www.gailmarksjarvis.com.

INDEX

W–Z

LIZ PULLIAM WESTON

Your Credit Score

Second Edition

How to Fix, Improve, and Protect the 3-Digit Number that Shapes Your Financial Future

Fast fixes for your credit score • Save money
Lower your interest rate • Understand your
FICO score • Fix and error on your report
Lighten your debt load • Cut your credit
card rates • Review your credit history

Your Credit Score
How to Fix, Improve, and Protect the 3-Digit Number that Shapes Your Financial Future, 2nd Edition
Liz Pulliam Weston

In the past five years, a simple three-digit number has become critical to your financial life: your credit score. It not only dictates whether you get credit: it can dictate how much you'll pay for it. What's more, it's being used by insurers, employers, and others who can determine your financial future. A bad score can cost you tens of thousands of dollars in higher interest costs, bigger insurance premiums, and missed employment opportunities. Now, MSNBC/L.A. Times personal finance journalist Liz Pulliam Weston rips away the mystery surrounding credit scoring and tells you exactly what you need to do to build, rebuild, and maintain your good credit in the second edition of *Your Credit Score*. In this updated edition, you'll learn how many credit cards you should have, whether carrying a balance helps or hurts you, and when you should or shouldn't close a credit account. Weston explains how to bounce back from bad credit and bankruptcy and tells you exactly how credit counseling, debt negotiation, and other credit "solutions" can affect your score. Above all, this book offers an action plan for discovering and improving your credit score and reaping the benefits.

ISBN 0132254581 ■ ©2007 ■ 240 pp. ■ $18.99 USA ■ $23.99 CAN

For Turning Silver into Gold
How to Profit in the New Boomer Marketplace
Mary Furlong

As they age, America's 78 million baby boomers will live more active, creative, inventive lives than any generation before them. This represents enormous business opportunities. In this book, one of the world's leading authorities on marketing to "post-50" baby boomers offers a complete blueprint for profiting from that opportunity. Dr. Mary Furlong reveals breakthrough product and service opportunities and gives you the tools, resources, techniques, and data you need to build a profitable business around them. Furlong draws on her experience leading SeniorNet and ThirdAge Media, as well as the Boomer Business Summit and $10,000 Business Plan Competition, where she has reviewed hundreds of new business plans targeting these emerging markets. Turning Silver into Gold offers powerful insight into baby boomers' new lifestyle transitions in housing, health, fitness, finances, family, fashion, romance, travel, and work, and the new brand choices they're about to make. Furlong shows how to segment baby boomer markets and find opportunities to innovate entirely new categories of products and services. You'll discover which sales and marketing strategies really work and even uncover opportunities in the surprising worldwide boomer market. Throughout, Furlong combines extensive, authoritative market research with inspirational case studies from passionate, tenacious entrepreneurs and brand leaders who are blazing new trails in these fast-growing markets.

ISBN 0131856987 ■ ©2770 ■ 272 pp ■ $24.99 USA ■ $29.99 CAN

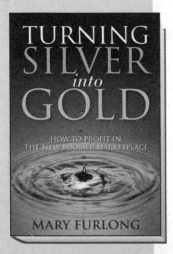

TURNING SILVER into GOLD

HOW TO PROFIT IN THE NEW BOOMER MARKETPLACE

MARY FURLONG